To Ge
Best wishes

GOT TO DO
THE 42

A TOUR OF EVERY SCOTTISH LEAGUE GROUND

MARTIN McNELIS

First published in 2014

EMPIRE PUBLICATIONS
1 Newton Street, Manchester M1 1HW
© Martin McNelis 2014

Front cover: Tynecastle as the Edinburgh derby kicks-off.
Back cvver: Top - Arbroath's Gayfield. Middle: Forfar Athletic club shop; (right) Cappielow Park and (left) Stairs at Dens Park.
All pictures copyright of the author.

ISBN: 978-1-909360-21-1

In Memory of Neil
31st July 1978 – 1st August 2012

CONTENTS

ABOUT THE AUTHOR

MARTIN McNELIS lives in Renfrewshire and has worked in Local Government for twenty years. He is married with three children and has been obsessed with football since an early age. His priorities revolve around the family and out with contributing to various fanzines and fan websites over the years. This is his first formal written publication.

ACKNOWLEDGEMENTS

With thanks to:
Tour members: Kenny Hudson, Billy Cameron, Paul Lucas, Conor & Ryan.

A sincere thanks to Alister Rutherford for his time, effort and guidance with the proof reading.

My understanding football widow wife, Donna and my daughter Bethany. Also to my parents, Martin and Jacquie.

Ronnie Kirk, Danny Goff, Les Gaff, David Hilley, Jim (Barrhead) McLaughlin, Jim (Crookston) McLaughlin, Gordon Reid, David James, Jeff McMonagle, Drew McKinney, Kenny Boyle, Elaine Duncan, Paula Kydd, Colin McKelvie, Mark McAdam, Jim Slaven, Stephen Rankin, Colin Slaven, Alastair Davidson, Ian & Lisa Burrett, Andrew Waldon, Peter Rundo, Derek Rae (BT Sport), Alison Robbie (Radio Clyde), Sheelagh McLaren (Radio Clyde), Douglas Beattie (BBC), Eddie Annand (Clyde), Nicky Lowe (Aberdeen), Gerry Dunbar (NTV Fanzine), Karen Brown and Duncan Adams.

The clubs: Robert Wilson (Alloa Athletic), Dennis McCleary (Berwick Rangers), Alastair Donald (Forfar Athletic), Riki Grauer (Dundee United), Stuart Brown (Morton), Dennis Cook (East Fife), Frank Meade (Albion Rovers), Scott Struthers (Hamilton Accies), Ann Marie Ballantyne (Airdrie), Tracy McTrusty (Ayr United).

FOREWORD

WHEN MARTIN FIRST TOLD ME of his plan to 'Do the 42'
I was not surprised. Apart from being a family man the first thing
that struck me about him when we first met was his passion for
all things football. If you are looking for the ultimate definition of
"football supporter" then Martin is it!

We first met about seven years ago as we both stood on the
touchlines watching our boys play for their local football team. We
started chatting and it became apparent that he just simply loves
and cares about the beautiful game.

I was lucky enough to play football at a level for over a number
of years within Scotland, starting with Stirling Albion. I have played
at all the lower league grounds, both old and new. Having endured
tight parks, sometimes questionable pitches and all types of weather
conditions along with a variety of supporter humour and abuse, I
finished my career playing for our great institution's oldest club,
Queens Park and had the pleasure of turning out at the National
Stadium, Hampden Park.

When Martin told me over a pint about his plans to visit every
professional league ground it seemed like a great idea. It never
entered my mind that he planned to complete it in the same season
but I should have known better.

As the tales came back from every ground he and his fellow
travellers visited, it stirred memories for me of the times I had
played at that particular venue, the Aberdeen to Edinburgh train
passing Starks Park, letting you know that it was 4:40 and you only
had a few minutes to hold out until full time. The petrol heads
waiting to get amongst the giant 'polo mint' tyres of Cowdenbeath,
the sight of the crane stood towering over the sugar sheds as you
drive into Greenock.

Many things have changed over the years within Scottish
football and our game is much maligned but one thing you will

take from this book is that these thoughts are often misguided. It provides a great insight into the condition of our national game these days and the dedication of the supporter to follow their team.

I hope you enjoy reading about it as much as Martin enjoyed completing it.

MARK McGEOWN
Former Stirling Albion, Raith Rovers, Stranraer, Airdrie United, Ayr United, Dumbarton, Queen of the South and Queens Park goalkeeper.
677 league appearances, 1 goal (for Stranraer)

INTRODUCTION

ANYONE WHO KNOWS ME will realise that I eat, sleep and breathe football. As a kid, I played football on a public park, literally just over our back fence and could be found there for hours on an almost daily basis. In my teenage years, I played for a few local sides and still play 5 a-sides at least once a week.

Over the years, a lot of sacrifices have been made to ensure that social events do not impinge on my attendance at a game! Even my own wedding day was planned around the close season, to ensure it didn't interfere with the regular Saturday fixture list!

I have amassed a wide range of football memorabilia in the last four decades, from programmes, ticket stubs, to replica shirts, books and autographs. I even have a seat from Manchester City's Maine Road stadium, before it was razed to the ground in early 2004.

One thing I had always wanted to accomplish was to visit the ninety two grounds in England and the forty two in Scotland. Going to all the English league grounds is a dream bordering on fantasy, but I have always thought the latter would be achievable. Like many things in life, saying and doing are two entirely different things. This is usually down to finding the time, juggling work, family and financial commitments and I am certainly no different.

I took along two books on football grounds with me to read during our family holiday last summer, both written by well known authors in this particular area, Duncan Adams and Simon Inglis. The purpose for this, during any occasional moments of boredom, was to test the kids on which club plays at what ground.

During the pre-season, the Scottish Football Association announced that Rangers would be playing football in Scotland's fourth tier at the start of the 2012/13 season. My own workplace, like many others up and down the country, had a number of people keen to express their opinions on the future of the Scottish game.

Proceeding on from this, the subject matter in work changed

to away days, attendances, pricing and value for money. We shared experiences and reminisced about old games, before someone posed the question, "how many grounds have you visited?"

Some of the younger lads had been to more than twenty, which I thought was quite impressive. On totalling up my own figure, I was horrified to find out that it was as low as sixteen. Unfortunately for me, grounds that are no longer with us, such as Love Street, Paisley; Muirton Park, Perth; Douglas Park, Hamilton; Boghead, Dumbarton and Kilbowie, Clydebank, were deemed not to count!

Just as the new season got underway last August, two separate events took place, only weeks apart, that affected my family and changed my outlook on life completely. After an initial spell of illness, my eldest son, Conor, was diagnosed with type 1 diabetes and is now insulin dependent. We were fortunate enough to get away on holiday, having initially been told by the hospital he would not be fit enough to travel. Not long after we had returned home, I was back in work and received a call from my brother, who informed me that a friend of ours, Neil, had been involved in a fatal road accident.

It got me thinking about all the things that bother you in your every day and how irrelevant they actually are in reality. I thought about how I could change and influence certain things in my own life, while acknowledging that life is too short.

It may seem almost unhinged to some people, but I now had the incentive and desire to go on and visit every ground in Scotland. It would be a personal accomplishment if you like and I intended to see it through. I met up with a few close friends and worked on a strategy for going round the country.

It started off with the intention of going to the odd ground that none of us had visited before. The first game chosen took us to Fife, to Central Park and the home of Cowdenbeath. By the end of October, we had been to five grounds and things were ticking along nicely. As we entered November, Dave in my work suggested that, as well as taking photographs of where we have visited, we should write about our experiences. I looked into a couple of blog sites and eventually created one called: www.scottishfootballgroundstour.wordpress.com

As progress was being made and a good fifteen grounds had been visited, it was put to me by a fellow football enthusiast, Stevie, that we should try and get to every ground in Scotland during the one season. I had concerns about achieving this, mainly due to the amount of time, finance and dedication it would require, but eventually I warmed to the idea.

The main objective for us when we started the grounds tour in September 2012, was to visit the actual venue, take pictures, check out the club shop and any other landmarks. We planned and timed each sojourn, with the intention to return to base as soon as possible.

When putting this project together, I wanted it to be slightly different to the others available on the market. It is a lighthearted view of our journeys, the individual clubs, grounds and games. It does not provide travel information on how to get there, or give a history lesson. As we had the kids with us, it was not an old fashioned away day drinking session with a crowd of lads, so we did not focus on the local pub scene!

As the season entered the last quarter, the games came thick and fast. At the end of March 2013, we covered six games in seven days and April was much the same. The first weekend break from football I had was at the start of June!

The Grounds Tour had been like a crusade and pretty much consumed the last ten months of my life! My wife had given me grief at the start, but was very understanding and supportive as the months passed by. Many other people have shown an interest and encouraged us, collectively, across the finishing line at Aberdeen and Peterhead on the last days of the season.

I have missed a few social engagements in this time, which will no doubt have annoyed a few people, but I had to see this through to the end. It was a tremendous journey, most of it enjoyable and it proved to be an education, in so many ways!

MARTIN MCNELIS

Central Park, Fife, Not New York

Cowdenbeath 3, Morton 4
Division 1 - Saturday 15th September 2012

SO AFTER MUCH TALK and deliberation about going to visit grounds we've never been to before, we were on the road to Fife, for hopefully the first of many 'tours', with the first match choice being Cowdenbeath hosting Greenock Morton.

We had a beautiful day for travelling and for watching football. We had planned the route well in advance and borrowed a sat nav, which got us there in ample time! To pass the car journey, we tuned into BBC Scotland's 'Sports Sound' and joked about the potential of meeting this guy "Ken" the people in this part of the world all talk about!

Once in town the ground is well sign posted and we parked in what looked like a local leisure centre car park, which is literally two minutes walk away from the entrance. There appears to be only one way to access the ground, a couple of turnstiles next to a big fence which are used for everyone entering. Once in, you have the option of walking round to the terraced areas or going into the main stands.

As we walked round to the back of the main stand there is the "Blue Brazil Shop" which is a portakabin selling club merchandise, and the main entrance which was for players and officials. Underneath the stand are toilet facilities and a catering area. We eventually took up a position that allowed us as decent a view of the pitch as we could get, having tried a few other areas prior to settling for this one.

Just before the teams finished the warm up, we were drawn to watching this guy in a suit walking about the pitch, quite the thing, hands in his pockets, without a care, just strolling about. It turned out to be the distinctively facial haired QC, Donald Findlay, who is the current Cowdenbeath Chairman!

Hearts and Wolves midfielder Colin Cameron was player/manager of Cowdenbeath at the time (he left by mutual consent in November 2013). Under his guidance the Blue Brazil had won the 2011–12 second division title. They have Thomas Flynn as the first choice goalkeeper, with a defence that included Scott Linton and John Armstrong.

Cameron played the role of midfield anchor man, with Thomas O'Brien and Jamie Stevenson alongside him. In the forward positions, the threat would come from Kyle Miller and the height of Lewis Coult.

The game got under way, with the home side in their distinctive blue kit and Morton in their yellow away colours. Both teams shared the early possession and made some progress in getting forward without any real threat on either goal. The central midfield area proved to be an interesting contest with the experienced Cameron up against the combative figure of Morton's Fouad "Freddy" Bachirou.

After eleven minutes it was the Greenock side who took the lead, when a Taggart cross on the right was headed home from close range by Peter Weatherson. Morton continued to exert themselves on the home team and doubled their lead with twenty-five minutes on the clock. David Graham's cross found Weatherson in the box and he controlled well, before finishing low into the net to double their advantage.

Just after the half hour mark it was nearly three, when a galloping run by full back Scott Taggart ended with a stunning shot from about twenty five yards which thundered off the bar. Had it gone in, it would have given Cowdenbeath a mountain to climb. However, five minutes after that scare the hosts were back in the match, albeit against the run of play.

A Scott Linton corner landed in the middle of the goal and the Morton defence did not cover themselves in glory. The Ton 'keeper Derek Gaston was left exposed, as John Armstrong lurked to head home at the back post and change the complexion of the game.

The second half was just seconds old when Morton extended their lead. A through ball by O'Brien was latched onto by Archie

Campbell, who calmly slotted his shot past Thomas Flynn in the home goal. It certainly delighted his female fan club in the away end, who shouted encouragement to "Erchie" throughout the match!

Cowdenbeath then lost their towering centre forward Lewis Coult to injury before things worsened even further for the hosts, when Morton added a fourth goal. Some nice link up play on the right by Weatherson was rewarded when David O'Brien collected the ball and went through to fire a shot that went in off the under side of the cross bar.

With an attendance of only 611, there were certain points in the match when you could hear players' shouts, instructions from the sidelines and the odd bit of choice language on the park! After one foul too many, Colin Cameron found his name being taken by the referee, Stephen Finnie. As Cameron walked away, it was somewhat amusing to see a seasoned professional being summoned by the official, shouting his full name twice to come over to him like a naughty school boy! At around the same time, the tannoy announcer came on to advise that the winner of the half time draw had not come forward to collect the £178 prize!

The game looked to be over as a contest and it appeared as if Morton boss Allan Moore thought the same as he substituted his two front men and scorers, Weatherson and Campbell, for two fringe players, Wallace and Stirling. With eighty two minutes played, Cowdenbeath's perseverance paid off when a long throw into the box was not cleared and from close range Mark Ramsey scored to make the scoreline a more respectable 4-2.

As some fans began to drift to the exits, Cowdenbeath were still causing problems for the visitors. Derek Gaston had to deal with a good effort from Scott Linton, and Mark Ramsey also saw a shot go over the bar for the hosts.

Morton were under sustained pressure and the full time whistle could not come quick enough. With four minutes of added time played, Cowdenbeath scored a third goal when, from a similar scenario as the last goal, James Stevenson headed in from a few yards out, following an initial throw in from Scott Linton. You would have thought that would be full time, but still referee Finnie played on!

With the time nearly 5pm and in the sixth minute of stoppage time, Morton's players and fans were delighted when it was all over and a hard fought three points went back to Greenock.

As we got outside, the place was a hive of activity with groups of people and their families milling around the back of the stand. There was a queue of traffic trying to park outside, comprising mainly of cars and vans with trailers as they brought their stock cars to race. For a moment, it seemed to be busier outside the ground than inside for the football! Towards the end of the game, we had become conscious of a droning sound outside, I just did not expect the sight that greeted us!

Central Park is quite an intriguing venue. The Main Stand is almost split into two small separate stands, with both combined covering the length of the pitch. Its oval shape design probably has something to do with its dual purpose, which is hosting football and the stock car racing.

The stand nearest the entrance is the newest and is occupied by the home support. The older one, which is where we were sitting, is for the away fans. It is an old fashioned wooden stand with metal benches, some of which were insecure and for the best view it is best to sit in the middle or the front.

If you sit at the very back you will not see the ball if it is played high in the air and there are numerous posts and pillars which obstruct your view, not to mention a perimeter fence. There are also a number of large tyres round the pitch for the car racing. They are painted white and from a distance look like giant polo mints!

Directly opposite the main stands, is terracing which had a mixture of supporters from both clubs and there did not seem to be any animosity when the goals were scored. There is some limited terracing behind both goals with some sections having small grass embankments, which are fenced off and unavailable for use.

With the pitch set back some distance from the stands and terrace due to the track, I would imagine the terrace is probably the best area to watch the game without a restricted view. At least you have the option to sit or stand at Cowdenbeath!

It certainly is not the most modern of football grounds, but there is something homely and traditional about it, so much so that I opted to use one of the pictures taken as you enter Central Park as the main photo on the 'tour' website home page.

Cowdenbeath 3

(Armstrong (40), Ramsey (82), Stephenson (90+5)

Greenock Morton 4

(Weatherson (12), (25), Campbell (46), O'Brien (54)

Referee: S.Finnie

Attendance: 611

No Diamonds For Airdrie

Airdrie 2, Morton 3
Division 1 - Saturday 29th September 2012

WE SET OFF FOR NORTH LANARKSHIRE, to take in Morton's visit to the venue with a multitude of names! The Shyberry Excelsior stadium, The Excelsior or known in some circles even as New Broomfield. Regardless, it is the base of Airdrie, Airdrieonians or Airdrie United FC!

This was the second time we had seen the Greenock side so far this season and questions might be asked in some quarters about where my loyalties lie! I can confirm that my very good friend, and one of the tour companions, is an avid follower of the blue and white hoops, so there!

It was a lovely late summer's day and we got into the town of Airdrie with very little difficulty, before the navigator seated in the passenger seat took us off course! In a generation which offers so many forms of satnav technology, I thought the days of pulling up to the kerb to stop and ask locals for directions were long gone, today however, proved otherwise.

Despite this episode, we still arrived in good time and opted to park outside the perimeter gates of the stadium, after we saw a guy in a high visible jacket with his hand out collecting money.

With fifteen minutes to spare before kick off, we walked round a bit of the stadium and took a few pictures. It is quite a smart ground and does not merit the somewhat disappointing sight of three of the four stands completely unoccupied, though this maybe highlights the difficulties affecting clubs in the Scottish game right now.

Before heading up to the stand with the others, I went in search for someone selling the match programme, but I would have been better off asking if anyone had seen Lord Lucan! I asked four people at four different locations on the long concourse and was met with weird facial expressions, grunts, a "dunnoe" and a foreign lad, who clearly had no idea what I was on about and who just politely smiled at me!

In fairness, I never saw any fans with a programme, so I am not sure if they were actually on sale and it may well have sold out by the time we got there. Since the game however, I managed to get hold of one thanks to the very helpful Managing Director, Mrs Ballantyne.

Airdrie are managed by a former player and coach, Jimmy Boyle (and still were when this book went to press) and he has been in charge of the first team since the summer of 2010. They had budgeted for a season in Division 2, but like Dundee found themselves catapulted up a tier at the last minute, following events at Ibrox.

Boyle is lucky to have some experienced players in his ranks, like Kenny Arthur in goal, David Lilley, Michael Hart, Paul Di Giacomo and Willie McLaren. They can also boast the young talents of Nathan Blockley, Ryan Donnelly and John Boyle making their mark in the first team.

Once the match got underway, Airdrie probably had the better of the opening exchanges before Morton, in their yellow and blue away kit, took a firm grip of the game and created a number of clear cut chances. David O'Brien on the wing and Archie Campbell through the middle for the Ton, were causing havoc for the Airdrie defence, who had a lot of luck on their side throughout the first half.

I am not sure if it was tactical or forced upon them, but Marc Warren replaced Cameron MacDonald for the hosts after only a quarter of an hour.

The game was played at a very high tempo and the ball zipped up and down the synthetic surface. Campbell saw a shot parried by Arthur, only for Morton to pass up the rebound. Campbell was in amongst it again, when he hit the post from 20 yards out, following a mazy run, but the ball was cleared to safety.

After a decent passing move, Michael Tidser fired a shot at the Airdrie goal from twenty five yards out, Arthur parried it onto his left hand post, before gathering it at the second attempt.

You got the impression that a Morton opener was imminent and some of the fans were showing their frustration at having the bulk of the possession, but not converting their chances. Out of the blue my youngest lad pipes up, "I wish Carlos Tevez was playing". Okay son, not sure where that came from, but away and have a lie down!

As what tends to happen in football, when you fail to take your chances, you will be punished. Five minutes from half time, a Morton free kick was played deep into the Airdrie penalty area, the ball bobbled around, before being cleared to near the half way line. A casual pass across the pitch from Tidser was read by young Boyle up front, before he collected the ball and ran at the two defenders.

With limited options available to him and the two opponents backing off allowing some space, he placed a superb left foot drive into the bottom left hand corner of the net, from about twenty yards out to open the scoring.

Morton hit back straight from the re-start and came close when Arthur saved superbly from a close range effort, but for all their dominance, the visitors went into the break a goal down.

The second half was only three minutes old when Morton equalised. Just prior to that, Airdrie had forced a couple of corners and nearly extended their lead when they hit the post from a close range header. From that move breaking down, a long pass over the Airdrie defence saw Campbell latch onto the ball after the defender mistimed his jump, before expertly lifting it over the on rushing Arthur's head, into the net.

Morton boss Allan Moore made his first change on sixty five minutes, introducing another winger, with David Graham replacing Tidser and within two minutes they took the lead.

Airdrie lost possession on the half way line and the ball was played down the left channel, for Naismith to run onto and cross. It bounced around the penalty box, before ending up on the right hand side with Graham. He played the ball in low across the goal mouth and it found its way to the back post, where the unmarked O'Brien was lurking to tap home from a couple of yards, despite claims for offside from the home fans.

Airdrie introduced the experienced Paul Di Giacomo for McLaren as they went in search of an equaliser but they ended up going further behind. From an attack on the left by the home side, the ball was whipped into the Morton box and headed clear only as far as the unmarked Weatherson on the eighteen-yard line. He controlled the ball and hooked it over his head, for the lightening quick Campbell to run onto. The forward outpaced Evans and managed to finish with a powerful low shot into the net for Morton's third.

Airdrie struck back seconds later through young Boyle again and what a finish. A cross from the left was met by the head of Di Giacomo, 'keeper Derek Gaston made a very good reaction save, but from the rebound Boyle volleyed powerfully into the net to set up a grand finale.

A Nathan Blockley header was then tipped over the bar by Gaston, before Airdrie were reduced to ten men with five minutes left, following the dismissal of David Lilley for a professional foul on Campbell. The Greenock side saw out three minutes of stoppage time to collect the points and continue their good run of form.

This was a very good, entertaining game with five excellent calibre goals and there were chances a plenty for both sides. On those terms alone, we could not complain and again, it proved there is some real talent in the First Division.

Airdrie had previously played at Broomfield from 1892 until 1994. The ground had become quite dated in its latter days and the club decided to sell out to a supermarket chain. After four years sharing Clyde's Broadwood, the club moved into the 10,000, all seater, purpose built Excelsior Stadium in 1998.

It is quite impressive, comprising four similar sized stands, though only the Main one (Jack Dalziel Stand) tends to be open on a match day. The seats are in red, white and black, with diamond logos on them, which of course incorporates the club's nickname.

After a turbulent start to the millennium, which culminated in liquidation in 2002, Airdrie were reborn again, having taken on the licence of Clydebank FC. The club has felt the pinch like many other clubs over recent seasons and have slipped down the divisions, though they have brought through some promising players as a result of their successful youth set up.

There were several moments in the game though that would suggest they have qualities that will help them along this season, not to mention the potential goals from young John Boyle and Ryan Donnelly.

Although it was busy inside and out, I was disappointed to read the official attendance was only 1,054, as the noise generated by the travelling support alone suggested there was more than that present.

The facilities are good and well kept and would be a fitting venue at a higher level in the Scottish game. It was a decent day out and on the way home it was established that we could have got to the stadium by a quicker route, instead of negotiating the town centre!

During the journey home, I got a text from a good friend of mine who had given me a couple of suggestions for the weekend football coupon. The polite version was that I would be collecting £65 from Mr P.Power, to end the day off nicely!

Airdrie 2
(Boyle (37), (80))
Greenock Morton 3
(Campbell (49), (79), O'Brien (68))
Referee: J.McKendrick
Attendance: 1054

PARS GRIND THE FALKIRK WHEEL

Falkirk 2, Dunfermline 2
Division 1 - Saturday 6th October 2012

THE FIRST WEEKEND in October saw us head to Falkirk for their home game with Dunfermline Athletic.

This fixture is something of a derby match, a fact of which I was unaware and a decent crowd was expected. The stadium is situated just off the motorway and although it was busy on the approach, we did eventually find reasonable parking, in space next to an industrial area, five minutes walk away from the Main Stand.

In terms of atmosphere and entertainment it didn't disappoint, it was just a pity that our pre-match experience was soured by events in the ticket office. Having arrived a good twenty minutes before kick off, we were unsure if there was a pay at the gate option, so we asked a steward, who told us to "try the next stand". We asked the same question to the next steward and he said he didn't know!

Going for third time lucky, we eventually got a straight answer from a member of staff with some courtesy, who confirmed that we required a ticket to get in. He said that we would have to go back round to the club shop, which is situated next to the main stand, as the ticket office is also in there.

As we waited in the queue, we heard the staff telling someone it was "sold out" and thought for a minute the game was a sell out. When it was our turn to be served, it transpired that the Family section was allegedly sold out. I explained that we were not locals, that we were just here to see the game and if any discretion could be used. Our only alternative apparently, was to buy individual match tickets at £19 for adults and £9 concessions.

This meant that it would personally set me back £37 to watch a Scottish First Division game! Is it any wonder football crowds in this country are in rapid decline?! It is somewhat ironic for me, that the admission prices of the current top two clubs in this league are less than half of that figure, while Falkirk linger in the lower reaches.

So having bitten the bullet with the admission prices, we then set about finding whereabouts in the Main Stand we would be seated.

Falkirk have been playing at this venue since 2004, having left their former home, Brockville, in 2003. It had been the club's home venue since 1885 and like many other grounds in the last two decades, made way for a supermarket site.

It had latterly been deemed unsafe by the Scottish Football Association and the new stadium criteria prevented Falkirk taking their place in the SPL.

For season 2003/04, the club ground shared locally at Stenhousemuir's Ochilview, until the 9,000 capacity, purpose built, Falkirk Stadium was completed. It was originally known as The Westfield Stadium, but over the last few seasons it seems to be commonly referred to as The Falkirk Stadium.

On the park, both teams have had mixed fortunes, with Dunfermline starting the season in fine winning form, in what was manager Jim Jeffries' first full season in charge. He would be up against his former captain at Hearts, Steven Pressley, who led his young Falkirk side to the League Cup Semi Final and a respectable finish in Division One last season.

The home side have former Celtic reserve keeper, Michael McGovern, as their number one, with the experienced Darren Dods at centre half. Two of Falkirk's promising players have been midfielders Blair Alston and Jay Fulton, while Englishman, Lyle Taylor up front, has grabbed a few headlines with his goals so far this term. Also in the Falkirk line up was the much travelled defender Robbie Neilson, turning out at right back as a Trialist.

For Dunfermline, they had the experienced Paul Gallagher in goal along with former Manchester City and Burnley defender, Stephen Jordan, at left back. They can also count on the goals from Andy Barrowman, not to mention the useful Craig Dargo and Andy Kirk who were on the bench.

It was Falkirk though who dominated the early proceedings and had the 'Pars' defence under pressure from a couple of long throws into the box. The home side had a half chance just before a quarter of an hour was played, when Lyle Taylor nearly took advantage of a poor Andy Dowie header back to his 'keeper, Gallagher, but the situation was cleared up by defender Callum Morris.

The away side did get more of a foot hold in the game and after a nice exchange of play on the half hour mark, Jordan McMillan shot just over from a Joe Cardle cross. A minute later though, it was Falkirk who took the lead. It wasn't quite route one, but a stunning low through ball from Kieran Duffie, midway through his own half, found Lyle Taylor. He took it in his stride and outpaced two Dunfermline defenders, before going on to slip it past Gallagher's left hand post to open the scoring.

The visitors only reply after going behind was a Barrowman header that went over the bar, meaning they went into the half time break a goal down. They did however start the second period better than they had started the first and 'Bairns' goalkeeper McGovern, held firmly, following a dangerous Ryan Wallace cross.

Ten minutes after the restart Falkirk doubled their lead and again it was Lyle Taylor who did the damage. A clearance out of the Dunfermline half by Jordan was immediately headed back and controlled fortuitously by Blair Alston, who back heeled it into the path of Sean Higgins. He then lifted a superb weighted ball over the Dunfermline defence for Taylor to smash a shot low into the net past the helpless Gallagher.

Dunfermline hit back and had a couple of set pieces from Stephen Husband and Joe Cardle that kept the Falkirk defence on their toes. The 'Pars' manager, Jim Jeffries, made his first change in order to salvage something from the game, replacing Josh Falkingham with Ryan Thomson.

The experienced Stephen Jordan then found himself in the referee's book, when he took his protest too far following a penalty claim for handball from a Cardle corner that wasn't given.

Alston nearly made it three for Falkirk when a long distance shot was well held by Gallagher. Dunfermline then threw on Andy

Kirk for Cardle to try and get a goal and his introduction did make a difference with him linking up better with Barrowman.

In the opposite dug out, the bearded and brown brogued Steven Pressley made a couple of changes to try and close the game out and preserve the potential three points. His antics on the sideline were very amusing, as he gestured to his players, with note pad in hand, like he was taking an aerobics class!

The Falkirk coaching staff have an interesting routine for when the player being replaced comes off the pitch. Each one is embraced with a 'man hug' by Pressley before Alex Smith, Stevie Crawford and Neil MacFarlane all follow suit!

With twelve minutes left, Dunfermline were back in the game. A long ball played down the right wing was picked up by Ryan Wallace. He managed to put a low cross into the box, where it looked to have taken a slight deflection off a Falkirk defender. It merely fell to Andy Barrowman who swept a left foot volley high into the net and reduce the deficit. Game on.

Dunfermline were shooting into the end which housed their large travelling support for the second half and they were a source of inspiration to the players. Ryan Wallace was pivotal in everything they created and having got themselves back into the game, three minutes later the scores were level.

A Wallace corner from the left was floated to the front post, nobody tracked the run of substitute Ryan Thomson and his bullet header left McGovern with no chance. Falkirk were on the back foot and were in danger of not even taking a point from this game, as Dunfermline went all out for a winner.

Another Wallace corner had the home side in a panic, as McGovern saved from Thomson and then Barrowman, who maybe should have done better from a header six yards out.

There were no more chances after that and the sides shared the spoils. You could argue that Falkirk threw it away but it was a resilient display from Dunfermline as they remained top of the pile after the weekend's fixtures.

Exiting the stadium is by going down the steps of the main stand and onto the track then out the right hand corner gate. It was busy getting out onto the main routes, but as you are next to the motorway we were on the road home not long after.

The Falkirk Stadium has three impressive stands, though one side, opposite the Main Stand, is currently vacant land. During the recent seasons in the Premier League this area had a temporary enclosure.

Outside, the Main Stand has a similar façade to that of Hampden Park. It is very modern looking and the facilities inside are clean and well maintained. Around the perimeter of the ground it has well kept paths and walkways, with a club shop that caters well for home supporters.

With the exception of one steward, the rest were not very helpful, but the other staff we encountered were certainly pleasant enough. Where we were situated, the fans were vocal and supportive of their team.

On contacting the club the following Monday about the pricing for this game, the response received was unfortunately pompous and arrogant. The whole episode was especially disappointing, as we were a group of strangers going to the Falkirk stadium to experience a home game for the first time. An impressive stadium certainly, but not one we will be back to visit again in a hurry.

Falkirk 2 (Taylor (30), (55))
Dunfermline 2 (Barrowman (79), Thomson (82))
Referee: B. Colvin
Attendance: 4,691

Final Fling For Doonhamers

Queen of the South 2, Arbroath 1 (After Extra Time)
Ramsdens Cup Semi Final - Sunday 14th October 2012

AS IT IS AN INTERNATIONAL WEEKEND, the only domestic games on in Scotland are the Ramsdens Cup Semi Finals on the Sunday afternoon. So we are on the road to Dumfries, for Queen of the South versus Arbroath, much to the annoyance of my other half!

The drive down was very pleasant, in fine autumn conditions, ideal for football. It was achieved in an hour and a half and with only one wrong turn made getting to the ground, which was not bad for me! We found a couple of streets at the back of the away end for parking, which were literally a minute's walk to the turnstiles and this would also be ideal for a quick get away at the end of the game.

As we headed round to the main stand for a look about, I could have been doing with a comfort break. Before I could look for any toilet facilities, I got a call from my old man. It was his birthday and he was down at Heathrow Airport with his partner, awaiting a connecting flight to Las Vegas. I am sure he was exceptionally envious of our location!

We had plenty of time to have a look around, having maybe slightly over estimated the journey time, leaving us with a good half an hour before kick off. Not wanting to sit on potential regulars' seats, we found a decent vantage point to sit, near the front of the main stand on the left hand side. We watched the warm up, read the match programme, familiarised ourselves with the players from both teams, then opted to count the Arbroath fans in the sparsely populated away end!

As we were in the ground really early, it never really dawned on us that a very healthy crowd of just over 2,300 were in attendance. Both teams had already met at Palmerston on league duty this season and the visitors left Dumfries with their tail between their legs following a 6-0 hiding.

Arbroath reached the semi-finals following victory over Stenhousemuir in the last round, with Queen of the South getting there after a penalty shoot out against Rangers in Glasgow.

Queen of the South are one of the promotion favourites in Division 2 and have started the season in excellent form, under the guidance of player/manager Allan Johnston and his number two, Sandy Clark. The side is made up of a few familiar faces, like goalkeeper Lee Robinson and defenders Ryan McGuffie, Kevin Holt and Chris Higgins. In midfield, Queens have former Aberdeen man, Derek Young, in the centre, along with Gavin Reilly and Danny Carmichael. Up top, there are plenty of goals in both Derek Lyle and Nicky Clark, who is the son of the Assistant Manager.

Arbroath have come a fair distance to be here in the borders and their small band of fans were very vocal, mainly about their dislike for Montrose! They too have their own Player/Manager in Paul Sheerin. The 'Red Lichties' have a few key players in their team, from defenders Alex Keddie and Stuart Malcolm, to midfielders Colin Hamilton and Brian Kerr. They also have players who have a good track record in front of goal, through having the services of Steven Doris and Derek Holmes, a former Palmerston player.

Queens started the better of the two sides, having more of the possession and scoring chances. An opening goal seemed inevitable and although scored by Derek Young for the home side, it was with a lot of good fortune, when his shot on nine minutes from the edge of the box, took a big deflection off a defender to wrong foot the keeper and trundle into the net.

For all their pressure Queens should have capitalised on their lead but were unlucky with some of their finishing. Arbroath forced the home keeper, Robinson, into a couple of saves and could have done better with a couple of half chances that they created.

Arbroath had Brian Kerr, formerly of Hibs and Motherwell, in the centre of midfield, along with Colin Hamilton in the number eight shirt, who from a distance looks like Frank Lampard.

Unfortunately for him, that is where the similarities with the Chelsea star ended! They were completely overrun in the middle of the park during the first half, though they picked up in the second following the introduction of David Banjo for Hamilton at half time.

I am unsure if the home side felt that they were as good as in the Ramsdens Cup Final, as they gave away possession and surprisingly started the second half on the back foot.

Arbroath had pinned them back a bit more and probably deserved the equaliser they got just before the hour mark. From a corner on the far side, big defender Alex Keddie was pretty much unchallenged as he rose highest near the front post to head home. This opened the game right up and the play was quicker, with both teams showing an enthusiasm to grab a winning goal.

Queen of the South made their first change of the afternoon bringing on forward Derek Lyle for Dan Orsi. With what seemed like his first touch, Lyle had the ball in the net, only for it to be disallowed, possibly for offside but we were well placed and did not see much wrong with it.

There were a couple of half chances for both teams towards the end and although we would have welcomed a winner for either side, to prevent it going to extra time, it ended one a piece after the ninety minutes. It was then decision time for us, do we stay for the thirty minutes extra time, plus the possibility of penalties, or do we head off up the road? My eldest lad and chief navigator for the day, said that we had achieved our goal by visiting Palmerston and had seen the majority of the game, so we left!

Once we had made a bit of progress on the journey home and were able to get a decent internet connection, we learned that Queen of the South's centre half and captain, Ryan McGuffie, had scored the winner in the 117th minute. They would be joined in the Final, to be played in April, by Partick Thistle, who defeated Cowdenbeath 1-0 at Central Park.

I quite enjoyed this visit and thought the game was decent, with some good players on either side. There were some impressive moments of individual skills, passing and control, although equally, some poor decision making and lack of composure on the ball. The pick of the bunch were maybe Carmichael for the home side and Sibanda for the visitors.

Palmerston itself is quite traditional and an almost homely venue with a mixture of standing and seating areas. The Main (Dumfries and Galloway) Stand is old fashioned in appearance and takes up most of one side but not the full length of the pitch. The tunnel and dug outs are situated here, with some limited terrace behind them.

Opposite this is the relatively new Galloway News East Stand, which houses both home and away fans. To the right of the Main Stand, behind the goal, is the Teregles Street terrace, which is uncovered and currently unused. Across from this, is the Portland Drive Terrace, which is a covered terrace that has a roof that does not cover all the spectators. Similar to the Main Stand, it has a classic look about it and has a clock perched on the apex of the roof, reminiscent of Arsenal's old Highbury stadium.

There is a friendly atmosphere in and around the ground, although we felt very much like outsiders as prior to kick off and especially at half time, everyone round about us seemed to know each other, on a first name basis too! Recently the Scottish National Under 21 side have played a number of fixtures at Palmerston and the locals have embraced the fixture by turning up to support the next generation of the national side.

With regards to the Ramsdens Cup Final, both Queen of the South and Partick Thistle are well supported clubs and are currently top of their respective leagues. The venue for the Final is scheduled for Livingston and I would imagine it will draw sufficient interest to fill it to capacity, making for a great day out and hopefully a positive advert for the Scottish Football League. I wish them both well.

Queen of the South 2
(Young (9), McGuffie (117))
Arbroath 1 (Keddie (58))
Referee: K. Clancy - Attendance: 2,310

Hamilton Not At The Races

Hamilton 1, Livingston 2
Division 1 - Saturday 20th October 2012

THE GOOD WEATHER on the road continued, as we visited South Lanarkshire for the First Division fixture between Hamilton Accies and Livingston, at New Douglas Park.

Getting here had been easy enough, up until the last part of our journey. Although we could see the floodlights, we were going round the town centre in circles, on the one way system for about ten minutes, trying to find decent street parking away from the retail areas that surround the ground!

Before setting off for the game I had given my daughter money to go out with her friends, however on arriving in Hamilton, I realised that in doing so, I had actually left myself short of money to get into the game! I went to the main office to see about buying tickets from there and possibly switching the payment, but they no longer had this facility, so it meant a long and unfortunate walk round to the Morrison's cash machine!

As it goes, the inconvenient detour worked out in our favour. As we went to enter the ground, I had been talking to a steward and the turnstile operator, when a guy behind shouted on me to ask if I was paying my son in. Confused, I said I was intending to and before I could say anything else, he shook his head and said "don't, here, use this and give it back to us once yer in". It was a concession season ticket which wasn't being used for this game and which saved me £8 so I was well chuffed!

I offered to buy him and the young girl with him a programme or something from the food kiosk as a gesture, but he politely declined saying he only wanted to save us some money. It was reassuring to know there are still decent people in society, it is just a pity we did not meet someone like him at Falkirk recently!

Hamilton had been playing at the old Douglas Park since 1888 and left there in 1994. The club then spent seven years ground sharing with Albion Rovers and Partick Thistle, before moving to the new purpose built, 5,500 seated stadium in 2001. I vaguely recall attending a game at the old ground in the mid 1980s and it is ironic that both grounds' locations are merely yards apart.

Following relegation from the top flight in 2011, the Accies have continued to place a lot of emphasis on their youth players breaking into the first team. In the last couple of years, they have taken in close to £2 million for the individual sales of midfielders James McCarthy and James McArthur, both to Wigan Athletic.

Manager Billy Reid had Kevin Cuthbert in goals, with a defence built around the experienced Martin Canning. The midfield contains Alex Neill as the combative midfielder, alongside the likes of Jon Routledge, Louis Longridge and Ali Crawford. Up front, the goals would be expected to come from Stevie May, on a season long loan from St Johnstone. He has a peculiar mane of hair like that of the singer Michael Bolton, but he knows where the goal is!

The visitors are managed by former Falkirk, Celtic and Hibernian defender, John Hughes. Big "Yogi" has been in charge at Livingston for eight months and has raided his former club, Hibernian, for half of his team! From 'keeper Andy McNeill, defenders, Kevin McCann and Callum Booth and another key playmaker from the Easter Road Academy, Stefan Scougall. In the forward positions they have youngsters Jordan Morton and Marc McNulty, supported by the much travelled Iain Russell.

We sat in the right hand corner of the Main Stand and got a section of seating pretty much to ourselves. If you were not in early enough for this one, you risked missing one or all of the goals, as they were all scored in the first ten minutes of the game!

Both sides had enjoyed a mixed start to the season. Both clubs predominantly depend on youth and are giving promising young players an opportunity in the first team. The down side is the team can tend to lack consistency, due to not having enough experience or leaders on the pitch. Still, each side did have a couple of players who I recognised and who had played in the SPL in recent seasons.

Seconds into the game, Accies' on loan striker, Stevie May, found himself out on the left hand side. With little support around him and with Livi looking like they had adequate defensive cover, May cut inside a couple of players and got to the byline, before squeezing the ball from a very tight angle, under 'keeper McNeill, into the far corner of the net.

Minutes later, Livingston were level and it was completely avoidable. Accies 'keeper, Kevin Cuthbert, rolled the ball out to the edge of the box, full back Grant Gillespie then tried to play a short pass across to Alex Neill. This was intercepted by Stefan Scougall and from 18 yards out, he curled a shot into the bottom right hand corner of the net to equalise.

Merely five minutes after that catastrophic piece of defending, Accies were at it again, when they lost possession near the half way line. A couple of passes later, the ball found its way through to Marc McNulty and from a relatively tight angle, he calmly lifted the ball over Cuthbert, to put the visitors ahead.

The home crowd were beginning to get on the backs of the players and their manager, Billy Reid. Livingston had a couple of good chances to extend their lead, but over passed the ball, when the better option was to get shots away. It was not all one way traffic though, as Accies did force Andy McNeill into a couple of saves before the break.

Whatever was said at the break by the home manager, it seemed to work as Hamilton Accies looked the hungrier side in the early stages of the second half. For all their endeavour though, they just could not break down Livingston's defence. Despite hitting the side netting and making two positive substitutions on the hour mark, with Keatings and Fisher replacing Longridge and Fraser, it just looked like it was not going to be their day.

What they did not need was to lose Alex Neill to a straight red card with twenty minutes left, following a full blooded challenge on the Spaniard, Garcia Tena. From our position it looked like a 50/50 challenge but judging by the reaction of the players, it was clearly more than that!

Livingston lost their extra man advantage only minutes later, when full back Kevin McCann received a second yellow for a cynical tackle on the half way line. The visitors then survived a penalty claim very near the end, when Stevie May appeared to be caught by the defender, but the referee waved play on. Again from our position it looked like a penalty and the home players and fans could rightly feel aggrieved at the decision.

In the dying minutes Keatings linked well with Gillespie for Accies, but the youngster fired his shot past McNeill. In the end, Livingston held on to claim all three points, in what was a very open and attacking game of football.

We left the ground right on the final whistle and headed up the hill to get the car. We got talking about how that was a decent game and venture out, when I ended up in the wrong lane and was forced to go south, heading for Carlisle!

There were not many negative things of note, though I would suggest the club look at considering a parent and child gate. If I had taken both my boys to the game, it would have set me back £32 and I do not think that represents value for money.

Without linking the crowd with the prices, the attendance of just under 1,000 for this game was disappointing, especially so near the start of the season, for what I would consider two of the better sides in this league. Although it has only two stands, New Douglas Park is quite a smart ground both inside and out and the staff we spoke with were helpful and friendly. It comprises the Main Stand, which is for the home fans and the North Stand, behind the goal on the left, which houses the away support.

Behind the other goal is a small fence and an astroturf 5-a-side pitch, with a warm up area which the substitutes can use. Opposite the main stand there is a very small seated enclosure with a television gantry, which is dwarfed by the back of the local Morrison's food store. This area is only used on occasion, though not likely to be used regularly in the First Division.

Hamilton 1 (May (1))
Livingston 2 (Scougall (3), McNulty (9))
Referee: G.Salmond - Attendance: 943

A REPLAY FOR ROVERS

Albion Rovers 1, Morton 1
Scottish Cup 3rd Round - Saturday 3rd November 2012

THE ROMANCE OF THE CUP is probably more prevalent in England than it is in Scotland these days, but as it is Scottish Cup 3rd round weekend we were at Cliftonhill, Coatbridge, for Second Division Albion Rovers, who are hosting First Division high flyers, Greenock Morton.

We took advantage of a free sat nav app on the iphone for the first time and arrived in plenty of time for kick off. The sky was clear blue, but deceptively very cold and we bore the brunt of this a couple of days later when two of the travelling party were overcome with early stage 'man flu'. A condition that gets no sympathy from the female fraternity!

After getting decent street parking, five minutes along from the ground, we got a programme outside, paid and got up the stairs on the right, which is for the away supporters. Before identifying a decent vantage point to stand and watch the game, I thought I would go to the gents, but could not see any signs for the toilets. I noticed a female steward near the pitch side and went to ask her. She wryly smiled and said "that's them behind you". I paused for a minute to see if she was being serious, as what was indeed behind me, was two single portaloos!!

Given that the SFA in recent years were hell bent on clubs having the likes of under soil heating and a minimum 8,000 all seated stadia, I thought there would be certain criteria for sanitation, but hey, the portaloo still served its purpose!

Rovers found themselves in the Division 2 Play Offs last season and defeated Stranraer on penalties in the Final to retain their status in Scotland's third tier. Following Paul Martin's resignation as manager in the summer of 2012, former Rovers player Todd Lumsden took over in a player/Manager role.

The club have no household names, but are a young, part time side, whose aim will be retaining their place in the division again this season. Goalkeeper Matt McGinley has played the last three games and started again for this one. In front of him were the likes of Alan Reid, Tony Stevenson and Mick O'Byrne.

In midfield the main player for the home team was Ciaran Donnelly, who was supported by Simon Marriot, David Crawford and Gary Phillips. In the forward positions Steven Howarth and Chris Boyle would have the task of finding the goals.

Morton boss, Allan Moore, stuck with his attack minded side which contained a mixture of height, width, experience and pace. Their goalkeeper, Derek Gaston, was signed from Albion Rovers in the summer and he is fortunate to have the presence of both Kevin Rutkiewicz and Mark McLaughlin in defence.

Michael Tidser continued to pull the strings in the centre of the midfield, with David O'Brien and David Graham providing the width. Peter Weatherson and Archie Campbell were the men chosen up top.

The pitch looked quite heavy, after a few days of rain earlier in the week and I wondered if this would play a significant part in the outcome of the tie. Morton started the brighter, forcing a few corners and the Rovers 'keeper into a couple of saves, but could not find the net. Morton had played some decent football so far this season, but whether it was down to the pitch, or just an off day, they could not get their passing game going at all.

Right on the stroke of half time and against the run of play, the visitors failed to clear their lines from a cross on the left and Rovers opened the scoring. Their big defender, Tony Stevenson, caught the ball sweetly, volleying low into the corner of the net from twelve yards. Some Morton fans gave their manager, Allan Moore, some stick as the teams were going up the tunnel and he gestured to them to get behind the team.

The second half started pretty much as it had ended. Just before the hour mark from a Tidser free kick, Peter Weatherson turned in the six yard box and hooked a low shot past McGinley into the net to equalise. Either side of the goal Morton replaced Wilkie with

Wallace to provide more width and Rovers introduced Innes for Marriot.

The pitch was cutting up and there was not much football being played on the deck. Morton then lost central defender McLaughlin and 'keeper Gaston to injury, with David Hutton going between the sticks and O'Ware coming on at centre half. You sensed among the support that it could be an interesting end to the game.

McGinley saved from a Wallace shot and at the other end Hutton blocked a Howarth effort. Rovers then made a couple of changes themselves, with Brannon and Crooks replacing Boyle and Howarth respectively.

Hutton then had to make saves from Brannon and Crooks, as the game entered the last ten minutes. Rovers were enjoying more of the possession and forced a couple of corners in quick succession. Morton were on the back foot and did not look likely to get up the other end and score.

After four minutes of stoppage time referee Crawford Allan blew for full time, as the game ended all square. It meant that both sides would have to play it out again at Cappielow to decide the tie.

There is not a great amount to describe about Cliftonhill. When you are outside walking towards it, the Main Stand seems to be perched on a hill. It is also unmissable, due to the large 'Reigart Demolition' sign of its sponsor, printed in blue, on a bold red, yellow and black background. It is small, with open standing space in front of it and at either side.

I found the standing area where we opted for, to the right of the players' tunnel, to be quite a reasonable location to watch the match. There were only a couple of the Main Stand's supporting pillars in the way, though they did not obscure the view of either goal.

There is a covered terrace on the opposite side which runs for a majority of the pitch length, with a bit uncovered on either side and looks like it could be used for a slightly bigger fixture if required. There are grass embankments occupying the ends behind both goals and are therefore out of bounds to fans.

There was a decent travelling support for this game and it did seem as though there were more people in attendance than the official figure given of just under 700.

Cliftonhill is quite a humble venue and I really enjoyed the visit. The staff and stewards we encountered were friendly and helpful. The admission pricing was very reasonable too, even though it was higher due to this fixture being a cup tie.

The official match programme is of a very high standard and at £2 offers great value for money, with interviews, features on both teams, local information and club statistics.

Albion Rovers 1 (Stevenson (45))

Morton 1 (Weatherson (58))

Referee: C.Allan

Attendance: 656

Bhoys Pick-Pocket Points From Barca

Celtic 2, Barcelona 1
Champions League Group G - Wednesday 7th November 2012

IT IS NOT EVERY DAY you get the chance to see some of the finest players in world football, so we are at Celtic Park for the Group G, Champions League tie, as the hosts took on the might of Barcelona.

We parked along the Gallowgate, about a mile from the ground and walked up. With the floodlights visible up ahead, the closer you got to the ground, the noisier the eager and excited gathering of supporters got. After queuing for a programme, we made our way inside and took in the sight and sound of the vociferous crowd.

In the build up to the game there had been some team news that threatened to overshadow the event. Full back Emilio Izaguirre, Celtic captain Scott Brown and top scorer Gary Hooper were all sidelined through injury, leaving manager Neil Lennon to alter his entire game plan. It meant a start at left back for Welshman Adam Matthews. Ledley and Wanyama would be the main focus in the centre of the park, with the on loan Venezuelan, Miku, playing as the lone striker.

Barça, under the stewardship of Tito Vilanova, were in fine domestic form. The Spaniard, who had replaced Pep Guardiola in the summer, has continued where his predecessor left off, although in their home tie versus Celtic last month, they did struggle to claim all three points. They too have had to contend with a couple of injuries to key players, although it had not affected their early season momentum! Most notable of the absentees, is the curly mane of Carles Puyol at the heart of the defence. They could however, still call upon the Brazilian Dani Alves, Jordi Alba and young Marc Bartra who was getting a chance at centre half. The extra cover options would come from Alex Song and Javier Mascherano. Although not fully fit, Gerard Piqué also made the bench for the Catalan giants. In midfield, there were the familiar faces of Iniesta and Xavi, with the width of Alexis Sanchez and Pedro on the flanks, to feed some wee guy called Messi up front!

Prior to kick off there was an incredible colour display of the original club crest, to commemorate Celtic's one hundred and twenty fifth anniversary. The display was arranged by the 'Green Brigade', a fans' group who have a dedicated section they occupy in the ground. It involved every fan in the ground holding up the allocated plastic sheet, which had been left on the seats.

As the Champions League music came over the sound system, the noise within the stadium reached fever pitch and it does almost make the hair on the back of your neck stand up. Celtic started the game purposefully, retaining the ball and closing down the early Barça attacks. The first chance of the match came in the sixth minute, when Forster got down well to deal with Xavi's close range shot, which had deflected off Sanchez. Another sweeping move minutes later ended with a Messi shot that went just over the crossbar.

With barely ten minutes gone Celtic could count themselves fortunate when Lustig looked to have made contact with Sanchez as he burst into the box. I have seen them given, not just at this level but in similar circumstances. However, the Dutch referee, Bjorn Kuipers, waved play on. Barcelona continued to ping the ball around the field and it was fascinating to watch, but for all their possession, Celtic closed down the space and broke up their play. On the limited times Celtic strung a few passes of their own together, they were relatively composed on the ball, though their distribution and use of the ball could maybe have been better.

In these kind of fixtures, always expect the unexpected! With twenty minutes on the clock Celtic forced a throw in near the Barça penalty area and the ball was put deep into the box by Ambrose. It was headed straight back out to the Nigerian, whose attempted cross came off Sanchez for a corner. Mulgrew's subsequent kick went straight to the back post, where the unmarked Victor Wanyama headed firmly past Valdés, to open the scoring. Celtic Park erupted, though it was elation mixed with a bit of surprise!

The reply from the visitors was swift. Another nice passing move ended with Alba cutting the ball back to Messi, which saw the Argentinian superstar fire a superb shot goal wards. It was touched onto the bar by Forster and out of play, although bizarrely, no corner was given.

Just after the half hour mark Jordi Alba, again down the left wing, managed to cut a cross along the six yard box, but once again there were no takers. Ten minutes from half time Barça again came close to an equaliser: a quick free kick on the right wing saw Alves whip a ball into the Celtic penalty box. He picked out Sanchez, whose well-timed downward header came back off Forster's left hand post, before being cleared.

Five minutes from the break, Barça came close again, as Lionel Messi weaved his magic once more. After a patient build up Messi played a defence splitting pass for Alba to collect. The full back timed his cross to perfection which met Messi, who had darted to the front post. However, Forster dived bravely at the striker's feet to save.

Barcelona continued to press but the Celtic defence managed to restrict their shooting abilities and held firm, to take an important psychological lead into the interval. Although it was an opportunity for Neil Lennon to regroup and plan their strategy for the second half, it began as the first had ended, with Barcelona controlling the midfield and retaining possession. The constant threat came from both flanks with Alba and Alves getting forward at every opportunity. Ten minutes in Alves again put a tremendous ball across the six-yard box and again, there was surprisingly nobody on the end of it.

Just after this Alves, once again on the right, picked out Pedro but his header hit the side net, with Forster looking to have it covered in any case. Celtic then enjoyed a short spell of doing what Barça had done to them, retain the ball and let the opposition chase them! It was never going to last and just after the hour mark Forster saved comfortably from a Messi shot some twenty yards from goal. Alexis Sanchez conceded a foul on Lustig, just inside the Barcelona half. Ambrose floated the ball into the box and Valdés saved easily from Lustig's header. With twenty five minutes left, a pivotal moment in the game was orchestrated once again from Messi. He rolled a perfectly weighted pass through for Sanchez, who fired a shot on target from close range. It was well saved by the big English keeper, who was also on hand to block the follow up, as Celtic once again got off the hook.

That proved to be the end of Sanchez' contribution, as he made way for David Villa. There are not many clubs in football who can make substitutions of this magnitude! It was like for like in terms of attacking options, but I was surprised that Vilanova didn't contemplate taking off Alex Song. Having been cautioned early in the first half, he continued to concede foul after foul, without any further punishment and Barça ran the risk of being a man down, as well as a goal down.

Tito must have heard me, as ten minutes later Barça made a double change, with Cesc Fàbregas replacing Song and Piqué coming on for Bartra. Celtic made a change of their own, which went almost unnoticed, when Tony Watt replaced Lustig. It meant a reshuffle, with Ambrose slotting into right back, Mulgrew dropping to centre half, Miku playing deeper in the midfield, with Tony Watt given a free role to play off the last defender.

With fifteen minutes left Iniesta tried his luck from distance, but his shot cleared the bar. As we entered the last ten minutes there was a couple of minutes of extreme fantasy football. Ambrose conceded a cheap foul on Iniesta, some twenty two yards from goal. Messi took charge of the situation and took the kick himself. He got his shot up and over the wall but it was comfortably saved by Forster.

The big 'keeper then launched a kick up the field and Xavi, under no pressure, looked to have the ball under control, but he uncharacteristically swiped at fresh air, leaving Tony Watt to run in on goal. Despite the close attentions of Mascherano, Watt went on to bury his shot low into Valdés' right hand post. Celtic Park erupted; you could feel the stand almost vibrate, as the fans dreamt the impossible, that they could actually win this game!

Five minutes later the home side could have and maybe should have scored a third goal. Kris Commons, from his own penalty box cleared it long down field. With Barça chasing a goal, the only player back was Mascherano, who struggled to match Watt for pace. The young striker could almost see the whites of Valdés' eyes and as he went to pull the trigger, he appeared to be caught by the Argentinian. Referee Kuipers decided there was no infringement and waved play on.

Barça continued to pour forward, but Ambrose and Mulgrew were resolute in their defending. However, they failed to hold on until the end. As we entered the first of four minutes of stoppage time, another Barça move with ten passes in the build up, culminated in a one-two in the box between Fàbregas and Pedro, before the latter fired a low shot into Forster's left hand post. The big 'keeper did well to get down to the initial shot, but from the rebound, Messi buried it high into the net to reduce the deficit.

You began to wonder if Celtic could hold on for all three points, or was there an equaliser to come from the visitors? Commons and Miku did their best to run the clock down by wasting time in the left hand corner. The only other significant action was again at the other end, when Pedro went down theatrically looking for a free kick just outside the box, but the referee played on and the ball ran out for a goal kick. Forster hit it long up the park and seconds later it was all over, as Celtic claimed a result that nobody saw coming!

The fans celebrated like they had won the Champions League itself and why not? It is not often Scottish football can celebrate a momentous result like this. The celebrations continued down the stairs and on the streets, as we made our way back to the car.

Celtic Park has undergone some dramatic changes in the last two decades. From an old terraced ground, which was in dire need of upgrading, it is now an enclosed, 60,000 all-seated stadium, that has gained a reputation for having one of the best atmospheres for big games in the whole of Europe. For normal match days the crowd are a lot more subdued, with the corner, which contains the 'Green Brigade', generating the only atmosphere for domestic home matches. Renovation work to rebuild Celtic Park started in 1994, when new owner, Fergus McCann, laid out details of his five year vision for the club. It meant that the team would have to play their home fixtures at Hampden Park for one season, but on their return for the summer of 1995, the Glasgow skyline now had the impressive North Stand, which could be seen from some distance. It also overhung the graveyard behind it, which caused some consternation with the City Council.

There was temporary seating put in behind the old Celtic end (West Stand) behind the goal during the 1995/96 season, while work began on what would be named The Lisbon Lions Stand opposite (the old East Stand area). By 1998, the West Stand had been built too and would be given the name, The Jock Stein Stand.

This completed the rebuilding work, though left the old South (Main) Stand looking very small in comparison. The only changes made to it were to put in green seats to replace the old discoloured orange ones. It also had a perspex roof fitted to allow sunlight in for the benefit of the pitch.

Celtic Park is an impressive venue which has held a number of high profile matches, past and present. In its current form it has held music concerts, Cup Finals and international football. The facilities are decent and like most football grounds in the top league, they charge inflated prices for food that does not match a standard that offers value for your money.

Outside, there are a number of vendors selling unofficial merchandise, as well as a couple of club fanzines and various musicians busking. The area surrounding the ground has seen massive changes take place over the last couple of years, with new housing and roads built, in what has been a complete overhaul of the East End. The new traffic infrastructure, which is being put in place for Glasgow to host the Commonwealth Games in 2014, will most certainly alleviate dispersing the many thousand fans on a matchday. Overall, it was a great night at Celtic Park and it was a privilege to have attended this particular game.

Celtic 2 (Wanyama (21), Watt (83))

Barcelona 1 (Messi (90))

Referee: Bjorn Kuipers (Holland) - Attendance: 55,283

Bullywee Beaten At Broadwood

Clyde 1, Montrose 2
Division 2 - Saturday 10th November 2012

FROM THE CHAMPIONS LEAGUE to the Scottish Third Division in the space of three days! The destination for this weekend was Cumbernauld, for our first visit to Broadwood current home of Clyde FC. In the last few months, club officials have been in talks about the possibility of uprooting, to potentially share grounds with Rutherglen Glencairn or East Kilbride Thistle, though no definite timescales have been disclosed for this.

We managed to get complimentary tickets for the game and have had to put a lot of preparation into organising this trip in advance, as the wife is working and some child care arrangements had to be made. I have also planned to meet an old friend of mine pre-match, who lives literally two minutes away from the ground!

The parking options are limited near Broadwood and with kick off approaching and tickets still to be collected, we had no option but to just chance getting parked outside the Main Stand! As we slowed down and approached the awaiting steward, he asked if we were VIP or hospitality, we said we were VIP, he let us in, job done!

I took a couple of pictures from the car park, got the tickets and naturally headed to the first turnstile. An older female employee taking in the money asked us "are you's Montrose fans?" We paused indecisively and before telling her we were just wanting in to see the game, she said "yeez cannae come in here, this is for Montrose fans only", so that was us told!

After finally getting in, right on 3pm, we headed up the stairs to get a seat and stopped just before we reached the top, as it was eerily silent. I suggested it might be a minute's silence taking place for Remembrance Sunday, so we decided to wait. After a few seconds we heard shouts in the distance, so we headed up the steps before quizzically looking at each other, as the game was actually underway! A fortnight ago there were over 7,700 in this very stadium for a live televised match, today however was more realistic, with 468 diehards in attendance.

Clyde manager Jim Duffy is a man of many clubs, both as a player and a manager. He is ably assisted by the colourful character that is Chic Charnley. The 'Bully Wee' had first choice 'keeper, Jamie Barclay, in goal, with the likes of Gavin Brown, Michael Oliver and David Marsh in defence. One of their more experienced players, Lee Sharpe, had to make do with a place on the bench.

In midfield, the main players were Bryan Gilfillan and Paul Hay. The attacking positions were occupied by Kevin Watt, Stefan McCluskey and Stuart McColm.

For Montrose their manager, Stuart Garden, had a couple of injuries and suspensions to contend with, meaning he was without 'keeper Sandy Wood, Stephen McNally and Paul Lunan.

David Crawford deputised in goals, with Ricky McIntosh and Alan Campbell being two of the key men in defence. In midfield, Jamie Winter played in the middle with Lloyd Young and Craig McLeish alongside him. Up front, Scott Johnston and Scott Morton would be charged with leading the line.

The first half was quite uneventful and seemed to pass by quickly, in what were quite difficult, wet playing conditions. McCluskey had an early chance for Clyde but his shot cleared the bar. Montrose 'keeper Crawford, saved well from Watt, before Marsh headed over the bar from a McColm corner.

Lloyd Young tried his luck from distance for Montrose, but Barclay in goal was equal to his effort. On the half hour Montrose created a good opportunity, when Scott Morton just failed to get on the end of a Ricky McIntosh cross from the left.

Just before the break Montrose had a free kick some twenty yards from goal. Winter's kick caused some consternation in the Clyde defence, but the ball was cleared to safety. Both sides had created reasonable chances in the first half, but were lacking a decent final ball and a cutting edge up front, as they went in level at the break.

Not long after the re-start Montrose had a great chance to take the lead when a cross from the left was incredibly headed wide by Alan Campbell, when it seemed easier to score. It was an absolute sitter, but it did seem to spur the away side on and minutes later they took the lead.

Montrose were getting a fair bit of change from the Clyde right back, Gavin Brown, and when another cross from the left bye line fell to McLeish, just inside the penalty box, his shot crept into the bottom corner, with the aid of a slight deflection, to open the scoring. The Clyde defence was static and the goalkeeper, Jamie Barclay, looked a bit unsighted and maybe saw the shot late.

The goal got the home fans fired up anyway and locals of all ages let the manager, Jim Duffy, know exactly what they felt, with an outpouring of really abusive personal slurs and thinly veiled threats! They questioned everything from Duffy's managerial credentials, his team selection, to the tactics and lack of substitutions.

In a reaction to going a goal behind, Clyde did make a change, but it was the double change with fifteen minutes left that was to prove significant, with McBeth and Scullion replacing Sweeney and McColm.

Only two minutes after coming on Pat Scullion equalised. From a corner on the right hand side, the big utility player rose highest and his powerful looping header dropped over Montrose keeper, David Crawford, and into the net.

However, the scores were level for only three minutes, as Montrose went back in front. A cross came in from McIntosh, this time on the right hand side. Two Clyde defenders got in each other's way and the ball broke to Jamie Winter, twenty yards out and his fine right foot volley flew into the bottom left hand corner of the net.

Clyde's best and last opportunity to equalise fell to Kevin Watt, as he was put through on the keeper with two minutes left. As the angle narrowed and under pressure from two defenders, he lifted his shot just over the bar. Watt knew he should have done better and Montrose held out for the narrow victory, as the unhappy Clyde fans vented their frustration and their spleens in some cases! As the final whistle sounded, the tannoy announcer's voice drowned out some of the hostility being directed at the home manager right enough!

This was not the best of games to watch if I am honest, but we enjoyed other aspects of the visit. My mate, Billy, turned to us during the first half and said "I wonder why more people don't come out and support the team?" He was basing this query on some of the lavish looking housing near Broadwood. By full time we got our answer, it is clear that local people do not want to pay their money to watch this level of football.

Clyde originally played at Shawfield, which is situated in Rutherglen, now classified as South Lanarkshire following a boundary change in 1996. They left this ground in 1986 following plans by the GRA (Greyhound Racing Association) to redevelop it for their own means.

The club then spent the next nine years ground sharing with Partick Thistle and Hamilton Accies. Clyde moved to the 8,000 seated, purpose built Broadwood Stadium in 1995. It is an impressive structure and can be seen on the approach as you come off the motorway. It has three decent, similar sized stands and a leisure centre building behind the right hand side goal.

The facilities are very good and with the greatest of respect, it is a venue fitting of higher than Division 3. I never knew the club were now using a modern, all purpose astro pitch which I am assuming will generate more income with other local teams also getting use of it.

The supporters clearly have high expectations for their team on the pitch and there is nothing wrong with that. However, with so few experienced professionals in the side, they may have to accept that the current crop of young players are as good as it is going to get and back them. It is easier for me to say right enough, as I am not the one paying to watch them, week in week out!

Clyde 1 (Scullion (78))

Montrose 2 (McLeish (66) Winter (81))

Referee: G.Duncan - Attendance: 496

TON ROMP AT THE ROCK

Dumbarton 1, Morton 5
Division 1 - Saturday 17ᵗʰ November 2012

WE SET OFF FOR 'THE ROCK', or to give it its Sunday name, 'The Bet Butler Stadium', either way, it is the home of Dumbarton FC. It is a venue that is quite close to home and unfortunately it was wet and miserable, which is something we have become accustomed to in the last couple of weeks! It is a local derby of sorts and as expected, we got a good competitive game.

During the week my eldest lad made up the numbers for our 5 a sides and had played quite well. However, afterwards he said his foot was uncomfortably sore and by the morning he could not put any weight on it. He missed school for the rest of the week, so he was a fitness doubt for this particular tour as well!

On setting off the sat nav said it did not recognise the postcode, so I tried altering it using the address to Dumbarton Castle, still no joy! Good God, it is a national landmark! It left us to do it the old fashioned way of instinct and road signs and after all that, we found it no bother!

No sooner had we parked the car and went to walk the short distance to the entrance, the heavens opened up on us! As we cowered in the rain and the wee man lagging behind on crutches, a female club official shouted on us and asked if we wanted to come in through the main doors. This was probably because we were likely to encounter problems getting the crutches through the turnstiles! It was a decent and considerate gesture, that was much appreciated, however we opted to go in with the ordinary punters!

Dumbarton had originally played their football at Boghead from 1879 to the year 2000. Although it had been the oldest professional football ground in Scotland, it had become run down and was no longer fit for purpose. I recall going there on a couple of occasions in the mid 1980s and being fascinated by the exceptionally small and odd looking Main Stand!

The club moved to their current location, set at the foot of Dumbarton Rock, at the end of 2000. It would initially be known as The Strathclyde Homes Stadium, with a capacity of just over 2,000. As it was not ready to open in time for the start of the 2000/01 season, Dumbarton played their home matches at Albion Rovers', Cliftonhill ground in the interim.

Dumbarton have taken a bit of time to adapt to life back in the First Division and had defender Jack Ross in temporary charge of the team, following the recent departure of Alan Adamson. Morton meanwhile are on a good run of form and would be looking to continue that with three points from this game.

Soaked to the skin, we managed to catch the sides warming up and found ourselves a decent seat in amongst the near 1,200 crowd, albeit in the most uncomfortable of circumstances!

The home team have been changing their goalkeeper in recent weeks, with Stephen Grindlay playing in goal for the earlier games in the season and Jamie Ewings being the number one choice for the last five matches. This would continue again for this match, with Martin McNiff and James Creaney being the main men in his back line.

The midfield would contain Garry Fleming, Scott Agnew and Mark Gilhaney. In the forward positions, the much travelled striker, Bryan Prunty, would be supported by Steven McDougall and James Lister.

For Morton, they kept to a similar set up from the side they fielded at Airdrie. A notable inclusion would be the veteran midfielder, Martin Hardie, in the starting line up. An indication on how this game would be decided was evident after Dumbarton conceded a penalty in the second minute when 'keeper Ewings was adjudged to have fouled Morton winger Graham in the box. Hardie, the veteran midfielder, stepped up and buried the spot kick, to give the Greenock side the lead.

Before twenty minutes had been played Hardie headed in from close range for his and Morton's second, following a corner on the far side. The game was effectively over as a contest when eight minutes before half time, Weatherson's close range header made it three without reply.

Ten minutes into the second half Morton scored their fourth goal in bizarre circumstances. Did he mean it? Well only David Graham can answer that, when his low hit corner seemed to evade everyone in the congested penalty box and travelled into the net! He does have an appalling moustache, which I am sincerely hoping he is sporting for the 'Movember' cancer charity, rather than it being a personal fashion statement!

Not long after that Peter Weatherson grabbed his second and Morton's fifth, with a nicely placed finish into the corner of the net, from a tight angle to seal the win. Although Dumbarton continued to plug away they were getting over run in midfield and not creating many clear cut chances for themselves.

The last fifteen minutes were played out like a training exercise and it was evident which team was near the top and which was near the bottom. There were numerous substitutions made by both teams, the weather continued to worsen and the points were already well on their way back to Greenock.

However, just as it looked like there would be no further action of note, Dumbarton pulled a consolation goal back through Bryan Prunty. He curled a shot into the bottom right hand corner past 'keeper Gaston after Morton's defence failed to clear their lines.

We left during the last minute of injury time and I ran ahead to get the car, so I could bring it closer to our injured tour member! We were in the house for 5.05pm, which is definitely something I could get used to!

This was a good game to catch, though clearly not for the home support! The facilities were good, staff were friendly, including the very well mannered young programme seller who said to me, "that's two pounds please sir, enjoy the match".

The ground only has one stand which runs the length of the pitch and the dugouts are situated opposite. There is nothing surrounding the other three sides, apart from grey fencing. On a decent day you will get a great view of the area surrounding

Dumbarton.

Prior to kick off, stewards did a sweep of the perimeter to make sure there were no free loaders trying to watch the action! During the game there were a couple of delays as the ball went out of play and over the fence, which was almost to be expected. Behind the goal, on the right hand side, there is car parking, but it goes without saying you run the risk of getting a dent from a stray ball!

The 'Sons' were hoping to appoint a new manager in the coming week and I wish them well with that. I am really taken with that white home kit and might even look into purchasing it!

Dumbarton 1 (Prunty (84))

Morton 5

(Hardie (Pen 3) (17), Weatherson (37), (61), Graham (54))

Referee: S. O'Reilly

Attendance: 1,188

No Share For Shire

East Stirlingshire 0, Berwick Rangers 1
Division 3 - Sunday 25th November 2012

WE TOOK ADVANTAGE of the fact East Stirlingshire's home match with Berwick Rangers was on the Sunday afternoon, as Stenhousemuir were playing at the same venue on the Saturday, so it was an opportune moment to continue our 'Grounds Tour'.

I had initially been looking for Sunday's Premiership fixtures and kick off times on Saturday night, when I noticed there was a 3pm Scottish 3rd Division fixture. I said to my two boys, "how do you fancy going to see East Stirling?" and was greeted with faces akin to those who had just been told Christmas was cancelled! I tried, somewhat unsuccessfully, to encourage them and enthuse that we could technically tick two grounds off the list, as the Shire ground share with Stenhousemuir.

By lunch time however, the older one had come round and said he would go, so instead of watching Chelsea v Manchester City, in the warmth of our own home, we set off for the near forty mile journey to sit in the Larbert cold!

We set off quite late but were still parked up, on the main street outside the ground, with about fifteen minutes before kick off. On entering the ground everything is in close proximity, the food bar, the toilets, merchandise, programme seller and half time draw tickets.

The Berwick players were warming up at the goal next to the entrance and we watched them being put through their paces for a few minutes. We then got a programme and something to eat, before taking up seats as close to the centre circle as possible.

The ground has a terrace area behind the goal on the left as you enter and the Main Stand is facing you. Across from this, is where the dug outs are situated and there is limited supporter standing space here for bigger games. It is the same behind the opposite goal, where there is a similar, limited standing area. Both sets of supporters mingled freely, without any animosity and there was a very friendly atmosphere.

As the East Stirlingshire players came off the park, having completed their warm up, two young lads aged approximately eight or nine, waited at the tunnel to collect autographs, which was quite touching to see for this level of football. I am not sure that they would fetch much if they were ever put on ebay!

East Stirlingshire have been playing at Ochilview since the start of the 2008/09 season, when they left their Firs Park Ground, which had been home to them since 1921. It was a ground I never had the privilege of visiting. It was situated among housing and a retail park, with a reputation of being small and somewhat neglected.

With SFA rules on stadium criteria, along with health and safety to consider, it would allegedly not have been cost effective to remain at Firs Park. A decision was made to sell the land and initially groundshare locally with Stenhousemuir for a couple of years at least. Plans to move to a purpose built venue within the Falkirk area, have to date, failed to materialise.

Within the last year I had taken a bit of interest in the Shire, having read Jeff Connor's book, "Pointless", which was the story of him following the team through the 2004/05 season. It would appeal to the average football fan and I would thoroughly recommend it.

Both these teams find themselves in the bottom half of the table, after eleven games played. Shire manager, John Coughlin, was appointed in the summer of 2011 and having finished bottom of the Division 3 table in his first season, he will be out to ensure there is no repeat of this. The irony is, he is an ex player and manager of today's visitors.

I have to confess that I only knew a couple of names from either team and was no more the wiser, even after reading the match programme! Grant Hay is the established first choice goalkeeper for East Stirlingshire, with the likes of Nathan Shepherd, Steven Jackson and Ricky Miller in defence. The midfield contained

David Greenhill, Mark Begg and Michael Herd, with the goal threat being the responsibility of Kevin Turner and Paul Quinn.

For Berwick, they are managed by Ian Little, who initially took over from Jimmy Crease on a temporary basis, after the latter had stepped down last October. He was then confirmed as permanent boss in the summer.

The 'Wee Rangers' had Ian McCaldon in goal, with Devon Jacobs, Dean Hoskins and Dougie Brydon in defence. The creative player in the centre of the pitch was Lee Currie, supported by Steve Notman and Kevin McDonald. In the forward positions, Berwick started with Ross Gray and Darren Lavery.

As the two teams came out, my son remarked how 'ancient' the Berwick 'keeper looked, so out of intrigue I googled him on my phone. On finding out that Ian McCaldon is only a year older than me, it would be fair to say that the boy was bordering on getting a clip round the ear!

Both teams went at each other from the first whistle and there was a lot of football played on the deck, which I was surprised to see. There were not many clear cut chances for either side, though Shire probably had the better of them. Herd shot straight at McCaldon, before a Turner volley went just wide of the post.

Just after twenty minutes Berwick opened the scoring. From a Currie corner on the far side, the ball fell to Ross Gray at the back post and unchallenged, he was able to sweep the ball into the net.

As we were in the Main Stand the club's officials and Directors were sat next to us. The banter between each set of supporters was both funny and good natured. We were surrounded by predominantly older fans and were doubled up laughing at one guy who kept shouting "ring a ding ding, East Stir-ling", along with a group who belted out, "dirty, dirty, dur-teee", every time there was a bad challenge!

Berwick probably had the upper hand going into the latter part of the half. The only other real chance of note for either side was for Berwick, ten minutes from the break, when Hay saved well from a Notman header.

Just before the start of the second half the jovial tannoy

announcer gave the official attendance as 327, which I was surprised at, as it seemed as if there were more people present than that.

Berwick had to play the last half an hour with ten men, when Steve Notman saw red, following an incident in the middle of the park. Manager Ian Little then made a change right away, replacing John Ferguson with Damian Gielty, as they attempted to hold onto their lead.

Moments later Shire blew a great chance to equalise, when McCaldon blocked a Shepherd effort, after he had been put through on goal. Further efforts from Mark Begg and Kevin Turner failed to bring an equaliser, as the game entered the last quarter of an hour.

Shire had given a debut to young Jordan Holt, having signed a one month loan deal from St Mirren. With ten minutes left he connected with a Greenhill corner, but his header drifted just wide of the post.

In the last couple of minutes Paul Quinn twice went close to equalising. The first was a half chance, which he put over the bar. The second came in injury time. As we headed for the exit, Quinn hit the post from twelve yards out, the ball rebounded into the arms of the grateful McCaldon. There was no further action as Berwick left claiming all three points.

Overall, this was an enjoyable day out. I genuinely commend and applaud the staff at the club, who make a matchday possible. The players, although part time and not paid great sums of money, were fully committed and ran themselves into the ground for their team and supporters. It was a very good advert for the Scottish 3rd Division and we will likely see both teams play again this season.

East Stirlingshire 0
Berwick Rangers 1 (Gray (22))
Referee: G. Duncan
Attendance: 327

The Livi Lions Roar

Livingston 2, Dunfermline Athletic 1
Division 1 - Saturday 8th December 2012

THE WEEKEND GAME of choice was at Livingston's Braidwood Motor Company Stadium, though probably better known to football fans as Almondvale and will likely be the last visit of the grounds' tour of 2012.

The club changed their name to Livingston and relocated to West Lothian in 1995, having been known previously as Ferranti Thistle from 1943 to 1974 and Meadowbank Thistle from 1974 up until the change. It was a simple case of rebranding and a hope that they would attract a new fan base in the new town of Livingston.

Following relegation from the SPL at the end of the 2005/06 season, the club have had a number of new owners, not to mention a number of financial difficulties. They were on the brink of closure in 2009 and were demoted to Division 3, but having steadied the ship, they have had successive promotions and are now stabilised in Division 1.

For this game the home team have former Hibernian winger Gareth Evans in temporary charge, following John Hughes' recent departure to take up the unenviable manager's post at League 1 side Hartlepool United. The visitors, Dunfermline, would be looking to take advantage of the fact one of their closest title challengers, Partick Thistle, had their game away at Cowdenbeath postponed due to a frozen pitch.

Not long before we set off, my eldest lad had a pubescent teenager moment and decided not to travel with us. So far this season he has been to the likes of Clyde, East Stirling and Cowdenbeath yet chooses to swerve this game, which on paper is probably this biggest to date. Strange boy, but it is a democracy we live in and it is his loss!

We arrived in good time and found a decent parking space,

near what looked like a high school gym or leisure centre and made the short walk across a bridge down to the ground. After a quick browse of the small club shop we set about getting tickets. Although not a vain person, I really need to consider the hair dye now, as the woman dealing with the parent and child gate asked if I was my mate's old man!! What's the old saying, sarcasm is lowest form of wit! I feel the need to clarify at this point that she was indeed at the wind up!

The stadium is all seated, with a 10,000 capacity, comprising four similar sized stands, with two of the corners enclosed with seats. I found the set up to be very similar to both Falkirk and Hamilton Accies and it is evident that all three clubs have previously modernised their facilities, to meet the old SPL stadium criteria during their respective spells in the top flight. Having established a good vantage point to watch the game, it got underway a few minutes later in front of a 1,495 crowd.

I have seen both teams play already this season, which helped with identifying most of the players. Dunfermline were in their red change strip and probably started the brighter of the two sides. Both had put some crosses into the box and had some shots flash across the goal, but had nobody on the end of them to capitalise and make the break through.

The game was turned on it's head after 20 minutes when Livi's very impressive live wire, Stefan Scougall, wriggled past a couple of defenders and was heading into the penalty box, before being scythed down by Callum Morris. Although our view was some distance away, it was like young Morris had decapitated the boy, as he instantly received his marching orders.

It left the Pars to play 70 minutes with a man less and from the subsequent free kick Liam Fox hit the underside of the bar, though the rebound was cleared to safety.

Not long after Livingston had an even better chance to take the lead, but the chance was passed up again, in what was one of the worst misses I have seen for a while. Striker Marc McNulty capitalised on some slack defensive play by the visitors, dummied the keeper, Hrivnak, leaving him grounded and with the empty goal gaping, he somehow contrived to hit the bar! In fairness I think he simply ran out of puff and was losing his balance as he went to pull the trigger.

Both teams went into the interval on level terms and the second half started much the same as it ended, with Livi doing most of the pressing. A notable incident in the second period was Pars' Craig Dargo being booked for taking a dive in the box, though from our position it looked a legitimate penalty in real time. Then having seen the miss of the season, just after the hour mark we were treated to one of the finest goals of the season so far.

Under no pressure, the Dunfermline players stood off Jesus Garcia Tena as he advanced towards goal and the big defender cracked a shot from a good 30 yards, which flew into the bottom left hand corner of the net. Some fans near us started up the hilarious chant of "we've got Jesus, we've got Jesus, we've got Jesus on our side".

Dunfermline tried to up their game in response to going a goal down and push for an equaliser. They managed a couple of decent efforts on target but without success.

In the closing stages the ball went out of play for a throw in near us and I am ashamed to admit that it had taken me the best part of seventy minutes into the game to realise that the visitor's left back was none other than Stephen Jordan, whom I had seen play for Manchester City on a number of occasions some years ago.

In the last couple of minutes Livingston made their final substitution, bringing on Danny Mullen for the influential Scougall. As he made his way into the box, he was in the right place at the right time, to tap home from two yards out for Livi's second, just at the start of injury time, in what was his first touch of the ball!

Thinking it was job done, we left early to get a head start on the traffic. The radio signal we picked up was Forth FM and now a couple of miles down the road, we looked at each other, confused, as their reporter at the game mentioned two sendings off and three goals!

What went on when we left the ground?! Well, once home, I checked out the 'gospel', aka the sportinglife.com website and established that Andrew Barrowman had scored a consolation penalty and that Craig Barr must have seen red for his part in conceding it.

This was a decent game to watch and we enjoyed the day out. Both teams have a decent blend of youth and experience and although Dunfermline have been near the top of the table throughout the campaign so far, I think Livingston will have a major input on the outcome of the First Division title.

Livingston 2 (Tena (65), Mullen (90))
Dunfermline 1 (Barrowman (Pen 90+5))
Referee: J.Beaton
Attendance: 1,495

Beanos Beaten By The Spiders

Stirling Albion 2, Queens Park 3
Division 3 - Saturday 5th January 2013

SO, ON THE FIRST WEEKEND of 2013 we are back on the road again, to take in the Division 3 fixture at Forthbank Stadium, for Stirling Albion against Queens Park. It was incredibly mild for January and that was most welcome! We had to do a quick pick up in the Maryhill area of Glasgow, so the journey time had to be adjusted!

We got to the ground about 15 minutes before kick off and parked on the main road, along from the leisure centre, which is next to the Main Stand. There was a small trickle of fans heading towards the turnstiles, but we ventured into the main doors of a smart looking building to the left of the Main Stand, which comprised a reception area, a social club area and souvenir shop. We had a brief look in at the latter, with one of the top items for sale being the DVD of Stirling's 1-0 victory over Rangers, from earlier in the season.

We asked where you could buy a programme but were informed it was sold out, so turned to leave, just as the guy said he would go up the stairs and get us one, which was odd! On first glance it looked as though we had been stung, as it is A4 in size and was priced at £3 and looked more like a club magazine than a programme. However, it is packed with features, up coming events, interviews, stats, match reports and is actually both good value for money and an interesting read.

On leaving there we walked over to the car park to take a couple of photos and were eyed suspiciously by one steward in particular! We then went into the stadium and took up seats on the right of the Main Stand, near the front as a lot of the seats were marked 'Reserved' and we did not want to mess with any of the match day regulars!

I was fortunate enough, for want of an expression, to have seen Queens Park in one of Sky television's featured matches the previous week, so I was more familiar with their playing squad than I would have been normally. From Stirling's ranks I knew of Jamie McCunnie, Kieran McAnespie, Bradley Coyne and Graham Weir, although the latter was suspended for this game.

When the game got under way it was set at a very high tempo and Stirling dominated the early openings and should have been ahead in just two minutes. Some nice passing on the left hand side led to a through ball for striker Jordan White to run onto, but he failed to beat Queens keeper Neil Parry and the follow up was cleared to safety.

Albion then forced a couple of corners in quick succession, but could not capitalise, although they remained in control of the first half hour of the game.

It was ironic, then, that the home side fell behind to a freak goal completely against the run of play. From out on the right wing Aidan Connolly whipped in a cross, which was intended for the back post. Although 'keeper Mark Peat initially came out to deal with the cross, he retreated back, anticipating the ball would be cleared by his defence. However the ball evaded everyone and ended up nestled into the bottom corner of the net, to give the Spiders a somewhat unjust lead.

Things got worse for Albion just into the second half. A cross field pass found young Connolly again and he threaded a ball through to the over lapping full back, Paul McGinn who took a touch, before rifling an unstoppable shot, high into the top right hand corner of the net for Queens Park's second of the afternoon. Although we were in the home end, we had no preference for either side and could only applaud the quality of the goal, albeit discreetly, as the goal was befitting of a venue like the Bernabeu or Nou Camp!

The lead did not last long though and just as it looked like the three points were guaranteed to be going to Glasgow, Stirling were back in the game, within four minutes of going two down. Albion broke down the left hand side and from a tight angle, Scott

Davidson saw his shot saved by Neil Parry, but the ball broke out to the penalty spot and Mark Ferry volleyed into the top right hand corner, to make the last half hour very interesting.

Again this was a top drawer finish and eight minutes later we were treated to yet another, when Queens Park were awarded a free kick twenty yards out. Stirling could feel aggrieved, as it was a pretty soft foul, but the referee was right next to the incident. Tony McParland placed the ball down before curling it over the wall and past Mark Peat into the bottom left hand corner, for an impressive strike for the visitor's third.

With a quarter of an hour left Albion reduced the deficit again, when a corner on the right wasn't cleared properly and although a bit scrappy, Mark Ferry headed in from close range to make it 3-2.

The home side did not let up in their pursuit for an equaliser and came close on a couple of occasions, with Michael Keenan passing up two very good scoring opportunities. Despite a late goalmouth scramble right at the death, there was no more scoring and Stirling were unfortunate to not pick up a point from this match.

This was an enjoyable game to watch and gave us five goals, three of which were outstanding and it was a great advert for the Scottish 3rd Division. There were some impressive passages of play at times and there are a couple of players in each side who could play at a slightly higher level.

Stirling Albion had been on the look out for a new ground location in the late 1980s, having decided to leave Annfield, which had been home from 1945 to 1993. Annfield had been the first ground in Scotland to have an artificial surface.

They eventually made the move to the 3,800 capacity, Forthbank Stadium, in time for the start of the 1993/94 season. Coincidently, it was one of the first stadiums built to comply with the Taylor Report in Scotland.

It is quite a neat set up with the Main (West) Stand holding both sets of fans including the 657 in attendance at this game. Opposite is the similar looking East Stand which does not tend to get used that often. Behind both goals there is a small section of terracing which again are used for bigger games.

The facilities are modern, admission prices are fair and provide good value, as does the match programme. Based on that performance I do not think Stirling Albion will be propping up the table for much longer!

Stirling Albion 2 (Ferry (58), (75)

Queens Park 3 (Connolly (29), McGinn (53), McParland (66))

Referee: D.Roache

Attendance: 657

Four Goals In Fife

East Fife 2, Brechin City 2
Division 2 - Saturday 12th January 2013

THIS WEEK SAW US VISIT the Kingdom of Fife again to New Bayview Stadium, to take in East Fife playing at home to Brechin City. The forecasters had predicted snow but there was no sign of it and we had a pretty decent day, which made for a pleasant journey and arrived in good time after an hour and a half's drive.

The chat in the car flagged up a few questions, why is the stadium called New Bayview? What happened to the old ground? Did Steve Archibald not play and coach East Fife? The answer, established once we had returned home, is the club moved to the current location in 1998 and "Archie" played and coached the club between 1994 and 1996.

We found the ground with considerable ease and again got ideal street parking, literally fifty yards from the Main Stand. We bought the match programme then took a couple of photos and had a walk round what we could of the stadium perimeter. I had read that it was situated right next to the sea and it is a very scenic setting. We went through the turnstiles, watched both sides finishing the warm up and found ourselves some pretty reasonable seats, high up in the stand with the home fans, with a decent view of both goal ends.

Both sides had players on their books who were recognisable for playing in the SPL or First Division and from seeing their names on the vidiprinter when watching 'Soccer Saturday'. Names including Collin Samuel, Paul McManus and Liam Gormley for the Fifers and for Brechin, Andy Jackson, Garry Brady, Alan Trouten and veteran goalkeeper Craig Nelson who was on the bench.

When the game got under way it was the visitors who started the brighter and created a couple of early openings, before taking the lead in only the sixth minute. A cross-come shot from McKenna came back off the far post and fell to Trouten who volleyed in the opener. This might have sparked the hosts into life but it failed to make any difference, as they continually gave the ball away cheaply and their passing was poor.

Brechin had a couple of half chances through some of their possession and pressure, but young goalkeeper, Callum Antell, dealt with anything that came his way. Almost against the run of play East Fife equalised just before the half hour mark, following a corner on the far side from Darren Smith, as it was met by the almost unchallenged Collin Samuel and he headed home from close range. The Brechin reaction to losing this goal was swift and it was a double blow for East Fife, as they went behind yet again and lost star striker Samuel to injury.

The home defence were all over the place, as Brechin's Derek Carcary was allowed to get a shot away from inside the 18 yard box, which seemed to go under the goalkeeper, who may have done better with the shot. At this stage you were left wondering if Brechin would go on to extend their lead, but once again East Fife drew level and with a goal you would expect to see in the top leagues in Europe.

A ball was played forward to the isolated Bobby Barr out on the left and with limited options available he held the ball up, keeping the defender guessing, before curling his shot from about twenty five yards out into the top right hand corner. We joined in with the locals and applauded a simply stunning strike. In fact I think we may have commented about it with a couple of complimentary expletives!

The second half saw the roles reversed, as East Fife came out far better organised and the more determined side, as they took the game to their opponents. I am sure manager Billy Brown would have had a few things to say to his players at the break!

Not long after the second half got under way, I happened to glance to my left and saw my two boys with different expressions on their face. The oldest one was wide eyed and the youngest looked terrified, why? The youngest had dropped his large cup of hot chocolate down the full length of my arm! It is funny talking about it now, but I tore strips off him at the time and am grateful that nobody knew us! I can only hope people are more likely to remember the boy sitting in front of us, kicking lumps out the seat next to him, when Brechin scored their second goal, rather than my foul mouthed rant!

Back on the pitch, the home side were the more adventurous and had the better of the chances created, but could not capitalise, as Brechin seemed content for the score to remain as it was. Just as the game looked like it would end in a draw, the visitors carved out the best chance of the half with a couple of minutes left.

The ball was played through to striker Andy Jackson who found himself one on one with the 'keeper. His initial control was perfect, having done everything right, however, with the goal pretty much at his mercy, he slipped the ball past the post, for what was a poor finish. There was not much injury time played and both teams had to settle for a point each.

From all the games I have seen in the SFL this season, there has been some erratic refereeing decisions and to date, I have refrained from commenting. However, I feel compelled to highlight the referee and stand side linesman's performance in this match. There was hesitancy and inconsistency in decision making throughout and East Fife were flagged wrongly for offside, twice in the second half, when nearly through on goal, from an official who looked as if he should have been studying for his pre-lim exams!

This was a really good day out and we enjoyed visiting the ground and the actual game itself. The set up is very similar to Dumbarton's ground, with a Main Stand the length of the pitch and the other three sides lying vacant or as a car park.

On a couple of occasions the ball went over the fence and the game was held up until a replacement was found. Having done a bit of research after the game, I never knew there was a huge power station facing the Main Stand which was demolished as recently as 2011.

The club have decent, modern, clean facilities, a good value programme and very fair admission and catering prices, for which they should be commended. The pre-match and half time music play list needs to be revised though, as in the 21st century 'The Gay Gordon's' will not entice young fans through the gate! It reminded me of the 1980s 'Naked Video' comedy sketch when Gregor Fisher played the Highland newsreader on 'OHBC News', but each to their own! All kidding aside, personally, this was one of my best grounds visited to date.

East Fife 2 (Samuel (28), Barr (37))

Brechin City 2 (Trouten (6), Carcary (30))

Referee: K. Clancy

Attendance: 578

One Goal In Greenock

Morton 1, Raith Rovers 0
Division 1 - Saturday 26th January 2013

I AM NO STRANGER to Cappielow Park, home of Greenock Morton and we are here to take in their home game versus Raith Rovers.

In our normal meticulous fashion the original plan was to go to Alloa v Stranraer, but we opted to leave visiting Recreation Park for a fortnight. We then targeted the home games of either Annan Athletic or Berwick Rangers, but due to the weather changing in the last 48 hours both games were called off earlier in the morning, due to the snow. A text then came through, from my Morton supporting tour comrade, Kenny and we were heading down the M8, Greenock bound at 2.30pm!

Morton are sitting proudly at the top of the First Division and were up against a well organised Raith side, who have done well under their young manager, Grant Murray, who was appointed last summer. The visitors also had former Ton keeper, David McGurn, between the sticks and if memory serves me correctly, he was quite popular down this way when he was at Cappielow.

The home side announced the signing of striker Colin McMenamin, from Ross County, on a short term deal earlier in the week and he was paraded by Chairman Douglas Rae prior to kick off. He will now know in future, that you need to remember the name of the person you are introducing, before wandering onto the pitch asking everyone to welcome "Alan McMenamin!"

The first forty five minutes was not pretty though it did pass by relatively quickly. Both teams played quite high up the pitch, meaning that when the ball was cleared or played over the top, both Assistant Referees were quick to raise their flags for offside. In fact, during one incident early in the second half the far side linesman called a Morton player offside. There followed a kind of rare silence of a few seconds in the crowd, when you hear a lone voice heckle the official which in this case went like, "hey linesman, al shove that flag up your ar★e"!

The official himself found it very funny, as did the rest of the support situated in the 'cow shed' terracing and it was good to see some good natured humour between fans and officials.

There were very few clear cut chances for either side in the first half and not many efforts on target to really trouble either keeper. Rovers probably ended the half the stronger side, having forced a couple of corners in quick succession and a free kick which came to nothing. This left both sides going in at the break goalless and I would imagine the Kirkcaldy boss was the happier of the two managers.

Morton had started out with a cagey formation of leaving one man up front, Peter MacDonald, with the intended support coming from Tidser and Hardie in the central midfield area and from Graham and O'Brien on the wings. This never really materialised and Allan Moore introduced new man McMenamin for Graham at the interval, which changed the home team's approach in the second period.

Only seven minutes after the restart Morton took the lead and what a strike it was. After some inter changing play on the left, between O'Brien and Hardie, the ball was put into the box but cleared by Anderson. It fell to the well placed Michael Tidser who cracked a left foot volley into the net from twenty five yards out, leaving McGurn with absolutely no chance.

Not long after losing the goal, McGurn made a great reaction save to his right, from a McMenamin header, to keep Rovers in the game. Morton were then under a bit of pressure and made a tactical switch with around fifteen minutes left, putting on stalwart Peter Weatherson for MacDonald, in an effort to hold the ball up and try to take the pressure off the rest of the team. In the opposite camp Grant Murray went for broke putting on forward Greig Spence for midfielder Stuart Anderson, in an attempt to get something from the game.

Spence gave Raith a bit more height up front, as well as support to Brian Graham and the latter put a shot over the bar, when he maybe should have done better. Morton lost centre half Kevin Rutkiewicz through injury and the visitors tried to capitalise on this by putting numerous crosses into the box, but Derek Gaston coped admirably with anything that came his way and one save in particular was very impressive.

The home fans were getting anxious but there was not that much injury time and Tidser's wonder strike turned out to be a worthy winner. It was another welcome three points, to extend their lead at the top of the table and ensure the majority of the 2,006 crowd went home happy.

Cappielow is set back just off the main road across from the distinctive blue cranes on the Greenock docks, with car showrooms on either side of it. There is designated car parking which will set you back a couple of pounds and street parking in behind it, though it is useful to know some of the local short cuts to get back onto the main roads.

Adjacent to the official parking area is the entrance to three ends of the ground, the Main Stand, the Sinclair Street uncovered terracing behind the goal and the popular 'Cow Shed' which has both seating and standing areas available. The club do a parent and child gate and the prices are fair and competitive for the First Division.

Away fans get the 'Wee Dublin End', an open end terrace with bench type seating, behind the opposite goal. It is used when opposing teams sell out the away allocation in the Main Stand.

Cappielow is a very compact ground with a playing surface that has a great reputation within the country. No matter where you sit or stand, you will get a decent view of the game, though there are a few pillars in both the Main Stand and the 'Cow Shed', which can obscure your view, but not significantly. There are toilet and catering facilities situated at the side and back of both of these Stands respectively.

The club have invested in the upkeep and improvements of the ground, along with rectifying damage caused by vandalism that sporadically takes place. I have sat and stood in every area of the ground over the years and rarely seen a bad or uneventful game. My eldest son saw his first ever game at Cappielow, in December 2003, when Morton were in Division 2 and they beat Arbroath 6–4 in a fascinating encounter with matching scoreline!

The current team are having a great season and who knows, Cappielow could be hosting Premier League football here next season.

Morton 1 (Tidser (53))
Raith Rovers 0
Referee: K.Clancy
Attendance: 2,006

Fifers Sea Sick In Stranraer

Stranraer 3, East Fife 1
Division 2 - Saturday 2nd February 2013

THIS WEEKEND SAW US HEAD DOWN the Ayrshire coast for a game, as opposed to travelling on the M8 or M80, with our destination being Stair Park, for Stranraer's home game with East Fife.

I had only ever been to Stranraer once before and did not remember it fondly, having got the boat over from Belfast during the Icelandic ash cloud fiasco in 2010. A two day trip to Dublin ended up being six and we had to make our own way home by any mode of transportation possible! We are here for the football though and I hold no prejudice against the town of Stranraer!

It is a very pleasant drive I have to say and following a week of blustery rain, sleet and snow, we got a beautiful day more akin to spring, which made the views along the coast all the more impressive. Although it does not seem all that far away, the 50 miles per hour average speed cameras really slow down your progress. We did however make it in two hours and arrived fifteen minutes before kick off, so we still had time to have a quick look around.

Having discussed coming to Stair Park with a couple of people earlier in the week, I had heard that you accessed a small public park to get to the ground. After consulting the steward where to park we got an ideal space on the side verge, literally seconds walk from the turnstile. We got a programme and team sheet from a booth at the side of the Main Stand, took a couple of pictures and went into the terrace at the corner opposite the main stand.

On the pitch, I remember the Stranraer manager, Stephen Aitken from his Greenock Morton playing days and his brother Chris is also a regular in the Stair Park midfield. The only other ones I knew were striker Michael Moore and Armand One as he played for Partick Thistle and also in the lower leagues in England.

For the visitors, well I saw them play three weeks ago at home to Brechin City in a thoroughly entertaining match that ended in a 2-2 draw. They have the talented Bobby Barr on the wing again and a presence up front in Collin Samuel and Paul McManus. Both teams were going into the match with mixed fortunes, with East Fife coming from behind to earn a point from their 3-3 draw last week against Ayr United and Stranraer losing 4-1 away to Alloa Athletic.

The match got underway with the hosts dominating the early part of the game, though their 'keeper, David Mitchell, had to look lively to save a Samuel shot. The few attacks made by the Fifers after this were closed down by a very organised and resolute Stranraer defence.

It was at this point that we became aware of this intriguing and continual war cry from young Mitchell in the Stranraer goal. It was like the sound of a wounded animal and became increasingly irrititatin as the game wore on! I am not sure what it was he repeatedly shouted to his defenders, but it sounded like "push" or "move". If anyone can shed any light on this, I am all ears!

On nine minutes Stranraer took the lead and it was new signing Darren Gribben who opened the scoring. After a ball into the box from Grant Gallagher, Gribben controlled the ball well before placing it low out of Calum Antell's reach and into the bottom right hand corner of the net.

East Fife were being pressed back into their own half and were not creating anything of note, until just after the twenty minute mark. A mazy run from Craig Johnstone which started in his own half, saw him upended by Michael Dunlop in what was a pretty cynical foul. Dunlop was rightly booked and unfortunately Johnstone could not run off his injury and was substituted ten minutes later. From the resultant free kick Paul Willis put his shot over the bar.

Things then worsened for the visitors just before the half hour when Gribben grabbed his second goal of the afternoon. From our position it looked like the Fifers' defence could have done better throughout the move, from cutting out Sean Winter's pass, to keeping out Gribben, who slid in to force the ball into the net from close range. He may well have had a hat-trick five minutes later but his long distance effort went just over the bar.

Stranraer went into the half time interval with a pretty comfortable lead so the next goal would be crucial to the outcome of the game.

During the break I went for a wander along to the other end, where the visiting fans were housed, to check the view and take a photo of the ground from the 'away end'. At this point I realised how small the crowd was and guessed approximately 400 were present, so I was a bit surprised to see that there was officially only 254 present.

We then changed position again for the start of the second half, going behind the home goal and have to confess that I missed the build up to East Fife pulling a goal back! My two boys were carrying on and talking total hyperactive nonsense and as I was having a word in their ear I turned back to catch the ball flying into the Stranraer net! I am reliably informed that from a set piece Paul Willis turned the ball home to reduce the deficit.

East Fife seem to be slow burners as they have been a few weeks back when we saw them at Bayview, they came out for the second half somewhat revitalised. They appeared to up their game and played with a renewed drive creating a couple of chances before getting their goal.

It was not to last though as once again it all came crashing down, when Stranraer scored their third goal.

As the away side were pushing men forward in search of an equaliser Stranraer broke on the counter, with Darren Gribben squaring the ball back for the impressive Sean Winter to fire past Antell and make it 3-1. The goal knocked the stuffing out of East Fife and I think they knew the game was up from that point.

Stranraer forced a few corners and attacked at will, hitting the post near the end and forced young Antell into a couple of very good stops. When I saw him recently I thought he was a bit hesitant, but credit where it is due, he almost kept this scoreline respectable and prevented a real hiding for his team.

The Fifers had a late flurry of pressure and had a decent chance, when substitute Sean Jamieson headed over from a Barr corner. We left at the start of injury time and heard the final whistle go as we reached the car.

It was a decent, competitive game of football with all the players giving 100%. During the week I had heard a couple of calls on Radio Clyde's Super Scoreboard phone-in, which showed certain supporters up for their ignorance and lack of respect for football in this country. One guy came on to discuss league reconstruction and suggested that "these wee clubs should be forced to merge or be shut down".

I wonder how many football games in general these characters have actually attended, let alone at this level. Not very many I would imagine. Try telling some of these players that their clubs are insignificant, as they push themselves week in week out for the love of the game, or to try and make a name for themselves.

With regards to the ground, Stair Park is a very picturesque venue, especially on a bright sunny day like we had. It is very easy to find when travelling through the town and has reasonable parking for all fans. The Main Stand is very new looking even though it was built nearly twenty years ago. Opposite is an old style enclosure, known as the 'Coo Shed', which is for both sets of supporters. It has benches in it but a lot of fans preferred to stand and watch the game.

Near the entrance to the ground and turnstiles there is a small covered terrace behind that goal, known as the Town End, which was sparsely occupied. At the other end is the East Terrace which is populated by trees and shrubbery and which caused a problem on a couple of occasions when the ball went high over the bar. The facilities are clean and presentable and the staff we encountered were helpful and friendly.

The fans who stood near us spoke about the team enthusiastically and there was some good banter with a few older guys and the far side Assistant Referee, or "Lino" as they all seem to be called in the SFL!

Stranraer are similar to a handful of clubs who have the right idea with regards to admission costs, with adults £12, secondary age kids £3, and primary kids free of charge.

It is not exactly the biggest of towns, so maybe not the ideal club to use as a template or as an example, but if you are going to encourage locals to turn out and support the team, then pricing incentives like this are a step in the right direction.

I am not sure if this is a journey I could do with any regularity. However, I enjoyed the day trip overall and wish the team well in their endeavours of staying clear of the bottom two places in the league.

Stranraer 3 (Gribben (9), (29), Winter (58))
East Fife 1 (Willis (53))
Referee: B. Colvin
Attendance: 254

Wasp Sting For Ayr

Alloa Athletic 2, Ayr United 2
Division 2 - Saturday 9th February 2013

WE BRAVED THE CLACKMANNANSHIRE COLD to watch Alloa Athletic take on Ayr United at Recreation Park. However, in the days following the game there were casualties, with two tour members succumbing to the almost misunderstood of all global illnesses, 'man flu!'

It is another one of those weekends when snow had been forecast and everyone was in a panic about potential travel chaos, but in reality it was actually quite mild and as usual these reports have been exaggerated. We found the ground with relative ease and got an ample spot of street parking, facing the main entrance, about twenty minutes before kick off. After negotiating some complexities at the turnstiles with the adult and concession gates, there was time to have a look around and to take a few pictures.

First impressions of the venue were positive and Alloa are having another good season, with their modern synthetic pitch being used to their advantage. They are currently sitting second in Division 2 and faced a tough test against an Ayr United side at the opposite end of the table.

Both teams have young managers who have had vast experience of playing in all the Scottish leagues. Alloa comfortably won Division 3 last season under the tutelage of Paul Hartley, while his opposite number, Mark Roberts, has been at the Somerset Park helm since being appointed last summer.

The home side have a good blend of youth and experience, with Darren Young in midfield along with Mitch Megginson on loan from Aberdeen. They also have former Celtic youngsters Jason Marr and Kevin Cawley. Similarly Ayr have the experienced Austin McCann, John Robertson, David Winters, Michael Moffat and more recently, Liam Buchanan on their books.

When the game got under way it was Ayr who dominated possession in the early stages although they never really troubled Scott Bain in goal. Alloa were struggling to get any rhythm going and any attempts to move the ball up the park were quickly closed down by a well organised opposition. Both teams tried to play the ball on the deck and rarely opted to play a high ball which was good to see.

After about quarter of an hour the ball was cleared from the Alloa defence, right out the ground and into the (Kentucky Fried Chicken) KFC car park. Impulsively the Ayr fans started singing "Sanders Sanders geez the baw", in reference to the fast food icon Colonel Sanders, whose image you can see from inside the ground and I thought this was very quick witted!

They also gave Alloa's right back, Jonathan Tiffoney, a really hard time for the first half hour of the game and we never knew why. A quick google search revealed that he was signed from Ayr United four weeks ago, which pretty much explained everything!

The visitor's goalkeeper, Ally Brown, made a decent save from a Kevin Cawley strike, before Ayr took the lead ten minutes from the break with a typical opportunist finish from Liam Buchanan. A cross from David Sinclair on the left landed in the six yard box and with Alloa's failure to clear, Buchanan hooked home from close range.

Alloa made a change at half time with Edward Ferns replacing Callum Gallagher up front. They started the second period with a bit more urgency and carved out a couple of openings but ended up going further behind.

A pretty innocuous foul just inside the Alloa half, gave Ayr a free kick which was swung into the box by Davie Sinclair. The cross was met by the unchallenged Neil McGregor at the back post, who headed into the net to make it 2-0.

Moments later it could have been three, when a low cross flashed across the six yard box with no takers. This was to prove crucial as merely six minutes after falling further behind, Alloa were back in the match. A ball played into the Ayr box was mistimed by defender Kyle McAusland and his intended header back to his 'keeper fell short, leaving Megginson to nick in and score from close range.

Ayr had a half hearted appeal for a penalty, when a cross into the box was blocked by what looked like an arm, but there was nothing given by the referee. With quarter of an hour left Alloa missed a great chance to level things when a cross to the back post was sliced wide by substitute Graeme Holmes.

Merely a minute later Liam Buchanan was booked for a challenge near the half way line. It did not look like it merited a yellow card but it was to prove pivotal in the match, as a couple of minutes later he received a second caution, this time for alleged simulation. He had made a good run into the box before taking a tumble and it was hard to confirm either way from our position at the opposite end of the ground, but he was sent off in any case.

Alloa pushed hard for an equaliser but Ayr coped well despite being a man down. With two minutes left on the clock Stephen Simmons might have done better when he headed wide from a left wing cross. Then, Darren Young controlled a ball into the box and despite taking out the defender and goalkeeper, lost his balance and could only hook his shot wide when he should have scored.

As the game entered injury time we started making our way to the exits at the corner of the ground, along with many others in anticipation of the full time whistle. It was lucky we stayed as there were two more key moments left in the game.

Once again a cross from the left had Ayr's defence exposed and a looping header from Ben Gordon dropped over Brown's head and into the net for a very late equaliser.

We expected that to be the last action of the game but despite their numerical disadvantage Ayr almost snatched victory with pretty much the last kick of the game. Although there was a hint of offside, Ayr substitute David Winters raced through on goal and looked like he would score, only for Bain to come to the rescue, blocking the shot with his foot and the ball went out for a corner, to ensure it ended all square.

So overall, a very enjoyable game to watch, especially the second half with some good football, four goals, a sending off and it went right to the wire, proving good value for the 521 fans in attendance.

Recreation Park is situated right on a main road so you really cannot miss it. As you come through the turnstiles there is an open area where a lot of fans seemed to congregate, pre match and at half time. All the facilities are next to each other and I found this ideal. From the food bar, programme sellers, club shop to the toilets, you do not have to venture very far to get the necessities. You also have the option of standing in the corner, behind the goal and also have access to seating in the main stand.

The main stand reminded me of a similar design to that of Dundee United's Tannadice. Opposite is the small Hilton Road Terrace, a small enclosure type stand, which runs the length of the pitch and is occupied by the away fans.

Behind the goal on the right hand side is the Clackmannan Road End, a covered terracing where we stood for most of the game. It is quite new looking and provided a decent view of the game, though there are a couple of pillars which may be a slight inconvenience. Behind the opposite goal there is the Railway End terracing which, unsurprisingly, has a railway line which runs parallel with it and has a limited standing area.

The people and staff we encountered were quite friendly and there is a good local support ethic about the place. Special mention must go to Robert Wilson from the club for his assistance and courtesy in the days leading up to the game which was very much appreciated.

There were people of all ages at the game, including a healthy number of young fans who the club must try and hold onto for the next generation. To ensure that, it may be beneficial to consider having a parent and child gate, probably more so if the club achieves promotion next season, so it can hold onto, and expand its current fan base. I wish them the best of luck between now and May.

Alloa Athletic 2 (Megginson (63), Gordon (90))
Ayr United 2 (Buchanan (36), McGregor (57))
Referee: B. Cook - Attendance: 521

No High Five For Annan

Montrose 5, Annan Athletic 1
Division 3 - Saturday 23rd February 2013

THIS WEEKEND'S MATCH CHOICE was a toss up between Montrose at home or Brechin City at home, so either way we were due East!

Towards the end of the week we decided to take in Montrose hosting Annan Athletic and it proved an inspired choice, as Brechin's game versus East Fife was called off due to drainage problems with the pitch.

After recent car repairs and an MOT, the 'tour bus' was in good shape to take us the two and a half hour distance to Links Park. It was overcast and pretty cold which meant there would likely be calls from the kids in the latter stages of the game to leave early, and this proved to be the case!

There were a couple of occasions when I thought the satnav was taking us off course through some dodgy looking back roads, but we got there with about twenty minutes to kick off. Not for the first time, we got street parking literally outside the ground and it is something I could really get used to!

There was some kind of Irn Bru sponsored kick about at the small space outside the home turnstiles and there were some people hanging around watching, while others headed into the ground. We went for a wander round the main stand first, then round to the away end and it was strange to find no sign of life! No stewards, no Police and no fans! In fact, the only person nearby was the Annan Athletic coach driver, lying back with his feet up! He made a wise choice to stay on the bus and not watch the visitors' performance!

Once you pay in at the turnstiles you are met with people selling the match programme and half time draw tickets. First port of call for us though was the toilet! We then opted to walk round the perimeter of the ground then take up a position behind the goal in the home end covered terrace to watch the game.

I saw Montrose play Clyde in November last year and they have a couple of decent players. Since then their most notable acquisition in the January transfer window has been the signing of Martin Boyle, on loan from Dundee and he was to play a significant part in this game.

In the away camp I would have to concede that with the exception of Scott Chaplain, who I remember seeing play for Partick Thistle a few years ago, I am not very familiar with any of the Annan playing staff. Both clubs have the most up to date astro pitches in their respective grounds, so neither team had a particular advantage and I anticipated a lot of the play to be on the deck.

Just before kick off the club mascot "Monty", mingled with the fans and a lot of the crowd in the Main Stand chanted his name, which resulted in him or her playing to the gallery so to speak!

The game got under way and within a few minutes there was a short sleet storm! Having already stated I thought there might be a bit of football played on this surface, the ball was surprisingly in the air an awful lot of the time, especially in the early stages. The only attack of note in the first ten minutes was from Montrose, when a low twenty five yard free kick by Jamie Winter was spilled by goalkeeper Craig Summersgill, before being cleared by a defender.

The opening goal came in the eleventh minute and it was the start of what proved to be a catastrophic first half for the Annan keeper, Summersgill. A long, high pass from Winter saw the keeper run out of his area and then misjudge the bounce of the ball, leaving Martin Boyle to collect and slide the ball into the empty net.

Four minutes later it was 2-0 and what a shocking blunder by the big number one. It reminded me of the famous Nottingham Forest v Manchester City game from the late 80s, when Forest's Gary Crosby mugs Andy Dibble in the City goal to score! Thinking it was safe to roll the ball out, Summersgill was unaware that Martin Boyle is lurking behind him and as soon as the ball is released from his hands, Boyle nips in front and puts the ball into the empty net! The keeper had his head in his hands and probably wished the ground would open up for him!

Annan could hardly string two passes together and although they had a half chance from Michael Daly, they went further behind in the twenty sixth minute when they conceded a penalty. From the left wing a ball into the six yard box saw defender McNiff go right through the onrushing Ricky McIntosh, leaving the referee, Don Robertson, with no option but to award a spot kick. Jamie Winter stepped up to finish low and hard into the left hand corner of the goal and leave Summersgill with no chance to make it three.

Although the penalty could have given Boyle the opportunity of getting a hat trick, he only had to wait another ten minutes to achieve this on his own. Montrose cut open the Annan defence once again and Boyle found himself in on goal. From a difficult angle he managed to fire a powerful shot low into the bottom right hand corner for four.

Just before the fourth goal was scored we took the time to watch with intrigue, one Montrose fan sing and clap away to himself, with his own repertoire for a good twenty minutes! Egged on by the fans further behind, it was absolutely comical, with him belting out classics like "we'll walk a million miles for one of yer goals oh Mo-ntrose!"

With the game effectively over as a contest at half time Annan made a double substitution, with Ally Love and David Murray replacing Harry Monaghan and Michael Daly. It didn't make any difference, as within seconds of the restart Montrose added a fifth goal.

Some woeful defending by Annan saw them fail to clear the ball despite a couple of opportunities to do so. Under little pressure the full back sliced his attempted clearance only to the edge of the eighteen yard box and that man again, Martin Boyle, placed a low shot past the unsighted Summersgill for his fourth and Montrose's fifth goal of the afternoon.

I know the Annan players will have switched off, but not long into the second half Montrose had a corner and incredibly despite scoring four of the five goals, not one defender even attempted to man mark Boyle! From the resultant kick, the latter fired just over the bar.

The game kind of petered out a bit and the best Annan could offer was a scuffed shot from Ally Love that went well wide of the post. Both teams had various spells of possession, but the ball was up and down the wings without really leading to any creative attacks.

With twelve minutes to go the home side's Jamie Winter fired a shot at goal which curled away from the post at the last minute. A couple of minutes later Annan got themselves a consolation goal, when both the subs combined to conjure up one of the very few positives for them in this game. Murray's free kick on the left was squared for Love and he hooked a shot past home 'keeper John Duncan.

There was nothing really of note after that and Montrose finished convincing and comfortable 5-1 winners . I do not think you could count the Annan fans on one hand, so it was predominantly home fans who made up the crowd of 425 and who went home by far the happier. We got to the car and started the long journey back down the road, ironically passing Arbroath's Gayfield ground which is on the radar for a visit and is only a short distance from Links Park.

This was a decent day out and I was quite impressed with Links Park. The set up is quite similar to Stranraer's Stair Park, in that the Main Stand has been built in the same style and there is a small covered terrace, the Wellington Street End, behind the home goal. Across from the Main Stand is the Union Street Side and behind the other goal is the Beach End. Both are small sections of standing areas and you get a good view of the game from just about anywhere here.

The only criticisms I would have are relatively minor, in fact they are more suggestions than criticisms. I had contacted the club by e-mail the week before this fixture to ask if they had a parent and child gate, as the admission prices were not jumping out at me on the club website. Unfortunately I never received a reply.

Six goals and a reasonable game proved good value on this occasion, but would suggest that to charge £23 for an adult and two concessions is excessive for a 3rd Division fixture. You can get into Scottish First and Second Division games for considerably less than that figure.

Montrose 5 (Boyle (11), (15), (35), (47), (Winter (Pen 26))
Annan Athletic 1 (Love (81)),
Referee: D.Robertson
Attendance: 425

HONEST MEN GET THE POINTS AT GAYFIELD

Arbroath 1, Ayr United 4
Division 2 - Saturday 2nd March 2013

WE WERE UP THE A90 again this week, to Gayfield for Arbroath's home match against Ayr United and got another great day of weather for travelling and watching football. We actually passed the ground on the route home from Montrose last week, so it was a less complicated journey than normal!

Anyone not familiar with the location may not know that the ground is situated right next to the sea, which is similar to the grounds of East Fife and Stranraer, which we visited recently. Again, street parking is available yards away from the Main Stand and an amusement arcade and we got a space in between the two, a good half an hour before kick off. After taking a couple of pictures of the ground and a few scenic shots too, we paid in and went for a wander.

As you enter the turnstiles all the facilities are pretty much facing you. From the young lads selling the match programme, the couple of people selling the half time raffle tickets, the food bar to the toilet facilities. The club shop is also there and although small, it is well stocked with Arbroath merchandise like strips, scarves, badges and old programmes. Impressively, the club still sell 'Danny McGrain's Bearded Army' memorabilia, twenty years after he was the manager here!

We have seen Arbroath this season already and also saw Ayr United play at Alloa last month, so we have a bit of knowledge about the playing staff of both sides. Unfortunately for the hosts they would have to do without the services of the impressive forward Steven Doris through injury. Ayr had their recent signing Graeme Smith in goal, having signed a deal until the end of the season, following a short spell at Partick Thistle.

When the game got under way it was Arbroath who dominated

the opening exchanges and took the lead as early as the second minute. A move down the left hand side saw the ball crossed low into the box by Ross Chisholm and was dummied by player boss Paul Sheerin. This completely duped the Ayr defence, leaving the onrushing Derek Holmes to sweep the ball high into the net to open the scoring.

Arbroath continued to have most of the possession and were creating most of the openings. There were a couple of close calls with regards to possible offside decisions that were not given, much to the chagrin of the Ayr defence and in particular goalkeeper Smith. He let out a verbal volley at the far side Assistant who was near us and I was surprised he was not booked for it.

From a Sheerin corner, Alex Keddie headed over the crossbar for Arbroath, before an offside decision against Michael Travis shortly afterwards spared Derek Holmes' blushes. He should have finished from close range before the Assistant flagged but he blazed his shot wildly over the bar.

Ten minutes from the break Holmes got himself into a very good attacking position again. I am not sure what he was trying to achieve, but it resulted from a good Euan Smith cross from the right hand side into the box, this time it came off his knee from six yards out and trundled harmlessly wide for a goal kick.

Three minutes later Ayr's Liam Buchanan hit a shot from the edge of the box that forced the home 'keeper, Scott Morrison, to turn round the post for a corner. It was one of their few attacks on the home goal and from the resulting corner, proved to be a turning point in the game.

Arbroath had dominated but had only converted one chance and when this happens you sometimes know what is round the corner! As the corner kick was taken Keddie was alleged to have fouled Neil McGregor and the referee, Andrew Dallas, awarded Ayr a penalty. Michael Moffat stepped up and placed his kick high into Morrison's top left hand corner to equalise.

Two minutes from the break Arbroath were attacking down the right hand side, and as we were well placed, thought there was a foul on Euan Smith. The Assistant was standing next to it but never flagged to the referee. The play continued and the ball was cleared down the line, as Ayr started a counter attack. The ball was then played short to Michael Moffat on the left hand side and he impressively curled a shot from about twenty yards, high into the top right hand corner, to put Ayr in front.

Straight from the re-start Arbroath were up the park looking for an equaliser. Travis put an excellent cross into the box but there were no takers. It was picked up by Hamilton who put it back into the danger area and Travis' header was saved by Smith and the onrushing Sheerin could not connect with the loose ball. So after a hectic finale to the first half Ayr went into the break with the lead, despite being outplayed for most of the game.

I have been to many games and many grounds in the last thirty years, but I cannot recall ever seeing what happened at Gayfield as the half time whistle blew. unprompted, a majority of the 651 crowd seamlessly swapped ends, so that both sets of supporters were behind the goal their team was attacking for the second half! Quite bizarre.

The second period got under way and started the same as the first one had ended, with Arbroath on the offensive. A Travis cross into the box saw Sibanda fire in a shot that was saved by Smith and before anyone could follow up, the play was halted for an offside flag.

The home side continued to press but their hopes of an equaliser took a major blow, when ten minutes after the re-start they were reduced to ten men. A minor skirmish in the middle of the pitch saw a couple of players involved in some pushing and referee Dallas deemed that Brian Kerr had overstepped the mark, meaning he picked up a second yellow and first use of the carbolic!

Both teams made substitutions shortly after the hour mark and it was Ayr who benefitted from a very fortuitous refereeing decision on seventy one minutes. Scott Robertson was penalised for the merest contact on Liam Buchanan, from a right wing cross and the forward hit the deck like he had been pole axed!

It reminded me of the old McDonald's advert, where the guy takes a theatrical run and jump and the referee does not hesitate to award the penalty! Michael Moffat stepped up again and this time he kept his kick low, into the bottom left hand corner for his and Ayr's third.

The Arbroath players knew the game was lost and three minutes later Ayr sealed the win with a break away fourth goal. A sweeping move down the left hand side found Buchanan in space and he picked out the scourge of Arbroath, Michael Moffat, with a superb pass across the box. He then coolly slipped the ball past Morrison, for his and Ayr United's fourth goal.

Arbroath threatened to score from a Sheerin corner in the last couple of minutes and Ayr also had a chance from a David Sinclair shot, which went well wide of the left hand post. That effort proved to be the last action of the game and Ayr United ended up 4-1 winners, a scoreline that maybe flattered them.

Arbroath failed to capitalise on their first half possession and chances. They had a couple of harsh penalty decisions given against them, plus Brian Kerr's red card, which meant they could feel justifiably aggrieved. We got to the car and were zooming out the town within a few minutes! Just as we were settling in for the long road back, I realised I had lost the match programme. I had kept it under my arm for most of the game and must have dropped it as I opened the car door. School boy error!

With regards to the ground, it is like a traditional old fashioned stadium with four stands consisting of a Main Stand and three covered terraced areas. To the left is the Harbour End for the home fans and the Seaforth End is for the away support. The East Terrace, which faces the Main Stand, houses both sets of fans. We stood in the home end, at the corner of the Harbour End, with a stunning view of the sea and which also provided a decent vantage point to watch the game itself.

The people we encountered were friendly and the catering is well priced and very good value. So much so, that my eldest boy's pal, Cammy, who came with us, made quite a few visits to the food kiosk!

The game itself was a decent contest with five goals, a red card and a couple of debatable refereeing decisions, so the £15 parent and child admission also proved excellent value.

Arbroath have lost their last two games, ironically both at home, but they are still well placed to get a play off place at the end of the season. From what I have seen of them on the pitch this season, I do not think they could be grudged if they achieved this, come the beginning of May.

Arbroath 1 (Holmes (2))
Ayr United 4 (Moffat (Pen 41), (43), (Pen 72), (75))
Referee: A. Dallas
Attendance: 651

HOME ROMP FOR WEE RANGERS

Berwick Rangers 4, Montrose 0
Division 3 - Saturday 9th March 2013

THE INTENDED GAME for this weekend had been Brechin City at home to Forfar Athletic, but it was postponed having failed an 11am pitch inspection on the Saturday morning. Although a couple of tour members light, we managed to salvage the situation by heading for Berwick Upon Tweed to take in Berwick Rangers home fixture with Montrose, well so we thought anyway!

On looking at the up and coming fixtures for March, the intention was to visit Berwick's Shielfield Stadium on Saturday 23rd March, for their home game with Peterhead, so we have effectively brought it forward by a fortnight! I had recently read on the SFL website that one of the Berwick fixtures had been brought forward to 2pm due to a Speedway meeting at the ground, but could not remember what particular fixture this would affect.

With the time at 1.55pm and us still thirty miles from Berwick, I felt compelled to check the kick off time. My lad confirmed, via a quick check of the club's official website, that the kick off for the Montrose game was indeed 2pm. After getting a few expletives out my system, we continued on course and reluctantly accepted that we would miss most, if not all, of the first half. I would normally put this kind of incident in the "school boy error" category, but in all honesty it was just bad luck!

The directions we had led us out East through Edinburgh and then on arrival at the ground, into a very nice looking housing estate. We parked in a cul-de-sac overlooking the Main Stand at 2.30pm and after negotiating a small fence and a very saturated grassy area, we wandered round looking for a possible way in. As the game was well under way the turnstiles had naturally been dubbed up.

We peered through the fence behind the goal for a couple

of minutes and thought we would wait until half time before chapping the front door! Just as we got back round there, someone came out and we took the opportunity to ask about getting in to see the game. He left us with club official, Dennis McCleary who gave us a discount for admission and sorted us out with a match programme, which was much appreciated.

He told us Berwick were 1-0 up, before we were led down the tunnel area and out to the Main Stand. A couple of minutes later the half time whistle went and we realised we were sitting among the handful of Montrose fans present!

After taking a couple of pictures, we walked the length of the Main Stand over to the far side where the toilets, catering and club shop were situated. The shop is well stocked with old programmes and various bits of merchandise, including current kit and leisure tops. There were some shirts from last season also available in the sale and I ended up buying an old away one for the boy!

We took up seats in the home end for the second half and sat among some locals who were very passionate about their team! By all accounts the game had been quite even in the first period, with Berwick taking the lead in twelve minutes when Fraser McLaren turned home a Darren Lavery pass. The home side then went on to dominate the latter stages of the half and continued in the same vein for the second.

Seven minutes after the restart Berwick doubled their lead. Gielty fed the impressive Dylan Easton down the left hand side, his low cross into the box was cleared only as far as McLaren, about sixteen yards out and his shot sneaked into the bottom left hand corner for Berwick's second goal.

Only a couple of minutes later Berwick were on the offensive again, when Lavery held the ball up well to play in Easton on the left, but he was crowded out by two Montrose defenders.

Some hesitancy in the Montrose defence on the hour mark saw McLaren nearly grab a hat trick when their central defenders left the ball to each other, allowing McLaren to nip in and run through on the 'keeper, John Gibson. The latter did enough to recover the situation when he managed to smother the ball, as the striker attempted to round him, after the ball seemed to hold up slightly in the mud.

Montrose then had a rare foray up the park but Berwick comfortably cleared the danger before the game was turned on it's head on sixty nine minutes. The Montrose 'keeper Gibson's attempted clearance from the edge of the eighteen yard box, ricocheted up in the air, off the back of Berwick's Darren Lavery. With the goal gaping, his strike partner, Scott Dalziel, went to follow up with a header, but took a kick to the face as defender Jonathan Crawford attempted to clear.

The referee, Colin Steven, deemed it to be preventing a goal scoring opportunity, so he sent the defender off and awarded a penalty. Up stepped Fraser McLaren to grab his and Berwick's third goal of the afternoon. He struck his kick straight down the middle and though it was saved by John Gibson, McLaren was not to be denied his hat-trick, when he was first to respond and tucked away the rebound to make it three, without reply.

Lavery nearly got in on the goals himself a couple of minutes later when he controlled a long ball over the Montrose defence and his attempted lob over the keeper went just over the bar. Berwick then changed it around by freshening up the front line, replacing McLaren and Lavery with Philip Addison and Dean Carse.

With fifteen minutes left Montrose had an opportunity to reduce the deficit, when they had a free kick just in from the right hand corner flag. Paul Watson floated his cross to the back post and it was met by substitute Scott Morton but his header crashed off the bar, before being cleared.

With ten minutes left the ball went out of play down Berwick's left hand side. Everyone wondered why play had not resumed, as the players looked around for the ball boys, only to see the comical sight of the two ball boys behind the goal, almost sword fighting with the plastic chairs they sit on during the game! Berwick 'keeper Marc McCallum was left to retrieve the ball himself, but at least he saw the funny side of it.

In the last five minutes, Montrose's Lloyd Young had a shot from eighteen yards out, but it was saved comfortably by McCallum.

There then followed a bizarre exchange between the Berwick number one and Montrose sub Craig McLeish.

McCallum, naturally wasting time, invited McLeish to charge the ball down, knowing that the Montrose forward had no chance of getting it and he would pick it up as soon as he got near it. There was a coming together between the players as they shoulder charged each other and although McCallum was probably more of the aggressor, it was McLeish who was booked for his trouble!

As some fans headed for the exits there was time for one more Berwick goal. Both substitutes combined, when Dean Hoskins' cross from the left was touched in by Dean Carse for Berwick's fourth goal of the afternoon and ended a pretty comfortable afternoon for the hosts.

We saw Montrose take Annan Athletic apart three weeks ago, but they were a shadow of that side in this game and missed their talisman, Martin Boyle, up front. This league is quite competitive, with not much between the teams and it is incredible how some sides can look like Dortmund one week and Dukla Pumpherston the next! We left right on the final whistle, got back across the grass again, sorted ourselves out and set off for the long journey home.

With regards to the ground, Shielfield reminds me a bit like Cowdenbeath's Central Park, due to its multi purpose lay out for both football and speedway, though Shielfield has fewer obstructions in the way for viewing the game.

It has an all seated Main Stand with two floodlight pylons which slightly obscure the view of the pitch. Across from that there is the very small, covered Ducket Enclosure, which leaves a good bit of open terrace on either side of it. There is standing space behind both goals, the East and West Terraces, though due to the speedway track you are a considerable distance away from the pitch.

To the right of the Main Stand sitting on its own in the corner, is a very small enclosure which is like an enlarged dug out or bus shelter. As it is situated on steps you get a reasonable, diagonal view of the pitch, though people passing by to use the facilities on a regular basis may intrude your enjoyment of the game!

As I write, Berwick have a game in hand at home to Queens

Park through the week and this may put them right in among the other play off contenders. The fact we were caught short with the kick off time did not detract from what was an enjoyable ground to visit. The people we spoke with were friendly and welcoming, which always adds to the overall experience.

Although the pitch was heavy, both teams still tried to play a passing game, with some good interchanging play, especially from Berwick and the 478 fans in attendance were certainly entertained. It was somewhat ironic that on the way home we heard a pundit on BBC Radio Scotland mocking the standard of the Scottish 3rd Division. I'm not really sure why he felt it necessary to be so overly critical, especially with the individual being an alleged St.Mirren fan.....!

Berwick Rangers 4 (McLaren (12), (52), (70), Carse (90))

Montrose 0

Referee: C.Steven

Attendance: 478

THE DERBY OF DUNDEE

Dundee United 1, Dundee 1
SPL - Sunday 17ᵗʰ March 2013

IT WAS AN EARLY SUNDAY morning start, as we travelled up to Tannadice Park for the last Dundee derby of the season. The ESPN cameras were there to cover the midday kick off and like the previous fixtures between the sides this season, it did not disappoint.

There had been a couple of weather warnings on the Saturday and although the pitch was not at its best the game went ahead as scheduled. We encountered all four seasons on the journey up to Dundee and feared the worst when, upon reaching Perth, we were confronted with heavy snow. However, a couple of miles on it was totally clear.

On consulting the old grey matter I think the last time I visited Tannadice was for the last game of the 1998/99 season which coincidentally saw United goalkeeper, Sieb Dijkstra, make his last appearance for the club. The big Dutchman lapped up the friendly taunts from the supporters who chanted about him looking like a pornstar!

We got decent street parking just off Tannadice Street and went for a walk round the area and tried to take a picture that would capture just how close the ground is to their neighbour's, Dens Park. After collecting the pre-booked tickets we had a browse round the club shop and then headed to the Jerry Kerr stand to familiarise where we would be sitting.

Despite the early kick off time and the miserable wet weather the pre match atmosphere outside the ground was excellent. The fans mingled freely as ESPN staff randomly stopped people for interviews and any banter or goading between them appeared to be good natured. Although not qualified to comment about any potential post match disorder, there did seem to be an excessive Police presence outside the ground.

As you go through the turnstiles it is a bit of a tight squeeze, as you head up a narrow staircase, although the montage on the walls of the club crest and former players is very impressive. The seats were located two rows from the front of the stand above the players' tunnel, giving you a great view of the pitch.

This was home manager Jackie McNamara's first home derby and he had to do without several key players through injury and suspension, the most notable of them being Willo Flood, John Rankin, Gavin Gunning and Johnny Russell. In the blue corner, interim manager John Brown gave a debut to former Everton goalkeeper Steve Simonsen who had signed a short term contract replacing this seasons ever present Rab Douglas.

When the game got underway it was United who were quicker out the traps. They forced a couple of early chances from Mark Millar and a nice flick at the front post from Jon Daly was deflected for a corner, as Dundee were camped in their own eighteen yard box. The game was a bit stop start as Dundee continually gave away free kicks all over the park and on twenty minutes the dimension of the game changed completely.

Richie Ryan, who had been given the role of controlling the centre of the United midfield, jumped for a high ball with Dundee right back and captain, Gary Irvine. In real time and from referee Bobby Madden's position, it did look like there was some intent, as Irvine led with his arm into the neck of Ryan. It maybe made up for a poor challenge made on Mackay-Steven moments earlier that went unpunished, but in any case Irvine was given a straight red card, leaving Dundee to see out the remaining seventy minutes a man lighter.

This was unfortunate as Irvine had started the game well and had the defence organised in dealing with United's main threats in Jon Daly and Gary Mackay-Steven. Manager, Brown then sacrificed midfielder Nicky Riley for defender Kyle Benedictus.

Dundee never let their numerical disadvantage affect them and they continued to press up the park. They forced a couple of corners and had a Gary Harkins shot from distance that went just wide.

United moved the ball around well and retained possession, but lacked a decent final touch. Gary Mackay-Steven had tormented Dundee on that left side and hit the bar from a close range header following an excellent Barry Douglas cross. Ten minutes from the break he forced Simonsen into a good block following another mazy run.

Mark Millar's delivery from corners caused some problems for the Dundee defence, as they attempted to deal with the aerial threat of Daly. Millar also saw a twenty yard shot flash just wide of the left hand post with Simonsen beaten. However, both sides went into the break all square.

Before the restart we managed to source a couple of better seats. It would appear that this part of the ground does not seem to have seats to cater for the larger or taller gentleman!! I think the guy in front of us would appreciate a second half without my left knee being jammed against his back!

United started the second period in the same manner they had started the first. Daly had the ball in the net from a header but the referee had already blown the whistle for offside. Dundee were defending well and as much as United had a lot of the ball, they were restricted to very few attacking opportunities. A Brian McLean header and a half chance for Ryan were the only ones of note.

On the hour Jackie McNamara made an interesting substitution, introducing seventeen year old Ryan Gauld for Richie Ryan. Seven minutes later, the visitors took a surprise lead and what a way to do it. An over lapping run from Brian Easton on the left, saw his cross controlled inside the box by Ryan Conroy. His first touch was excellent allowing him space on the defender to power a left foot shot, high into the net past Cierzniak.

Conroy celebrated at the corner flag in front of the home end and earned a caution for his actions. He also risked serious injury as someone in the home end launched a camera at the jubilant group of Dundee players!

United's reaction to the goal was to bring on Michael Gardyne for Rory Boulding. The latter had held the ball up well but tended to do a lot of work outside the box, meaning he rarely looked like troubling the Dundee defence. Gardyne on the other hand is a bit more direct and had a point to prove, after receiving a head knock very early on in the last derby match.

The home fans were beginning to get frustrated by the team's inability to break down their neighbours' defence, especially as they had gone behind and had an extra man advantage. Tame efforts from Gauld and Gardyne were easily saved by Simonsen, before Jon Daly missed one of the best chances of the second half. His powerful shot was saved and his attempted lob on the rebound drifted over the bar.

Daly again went close with a header before another strange substitution from McNamara, when young Robert Thomson replaced the tired legs of Gary Mackay-Steven with two minutes left. It proved inspired however, as within seconds a long ball up to Daly was flicked on by the Irishman as it evaded two players in the box. It landed at the feet of Gardyne, who hit a right foot shot high into the net to equalise from close range.

With four minutes of stoppage time to play, United went in hunt for a winner and they almost got it, with a carbon copy of the equaliser. The same two players were involved again, with Gardyne taking a Daly knock down first time on his left foot, but he sliced his shot just past the right hand post.

It ended all square and I think Dundee would be the happier of the two sides given the fact they were down to ten men so early in the game. It was a thoroughly entertaining game and I am sure the 10,731 crowd felt they got value for money. We got away quite smart and I cannot say I am used to staff holding the door open for you when exiting the ground and bidding you farewell!

The stadium itself is quite homely, with the old West Stand terrace behind the goal, all seated and predominantly used by the away fans. The Main Stand which was renamed 'The Jerry Kerr Stand' in the last decade, is almost vintage and is evidently the oldest on view. It is used by both home and away fans, depending on the opposition and ticket sales.

Across from this is The George Fox stand, a two tiered structure, built twenty years ago, which runs the length of the pitch and is what you mainly see of any televised matches at Tannadice. Behind the other goal the Eddie Thompson Stand is used by the home support. Again it is built similarly to the George Fox with the two tiers.

Any time I have been here I have enjoyed the visit. Coupled with a decent game and genuinely friendly people, this has been a particular highlight of the grounds visited to date.

Dundee United 1 (Gardyne (89))
Dundee 1 (Conroy (67))
Referee: B.Madden
Attendance: 10,731

Goalless In Govan

Rangers 0, Stirling Albion 0
Division 3 - Saturday 23rd March 2013

RANGERS' HOME FIXTURE with Stirling Albion was chosen by ESPN for their Live 12 noon kick off on the Saturday afternoon, presenting a unique opportunity for us to fit two games into the one afternoon!

It appears I was not alone with this line of thinking, as a few Welsh fans had a similar idea, having stayed on past the International fixture at Hampden Park to watch this from the away end judging by the flags on display!

I would not proclaim to be like the next David Icke, with some far out predictions, but surely something is wrong when one week from Easter, you have to endure weather more akin to Moscow in December instead of a Scottish Spring!

It was a relatively early start but timed well, parking just off Shieldhall Road, leaving ample time to cover the short walk down to the stadium. It is an area I am well aquatinted with, due to my parents being brought up close by and having once worked in the Ibrox area for five years.

It is also a ground that I have visited many times before and have sat in three of the four stands in the past. I have never sat in the seats we were allocated for this game though, which were located in the corner of the Govan and Copland Road stands.

In the build up to this match there was a possibility that Rangers could claim the Division 3 title with a victory over Stirling Albion. However, the early kick off and the fact Annan Athletic v Queens Park was postponed earlier in the morning, meant that any celebrations would have to wait.

The hosts lost their last home fixture to Annan Athletic a fortnight ago so there was possibly a bit of trepidation with this game. It could maybe explain the somewhat muted atmosphere inside and outside the ground, as there seemed a real apathy in every aspect. From my reckoning I would say there were more than 10,000 fewer people in attendance than the official 44,608 figure suggested.

The football on display is a far cry from SPL fixtures and European ties which were the norm at Ibrox for decades. Following events from last summer which saw Rangers enter administration in February of 2012 and then liquidation in the June, the fans have rallied to support the next generation under new owner Charles Green.

On the pitch, manager Ally McCoist had a selection headache due to injury and suspension and started with probably only three recognisable experienced players in Neil Alexander, Lee McCulloch and Lee Wallace. He had to make do without the services of David Templeton, Dean Shiels and Andy Little through injury and Ian Black through suspension, following his sending off at Elgin City last week.

The team also had striker Francisco Sandaza missing in quite odd circumstances. He was suspended by the club earlier in the week after disclosing details about his salary to someone claiming to be an agent, in what transpired to be a hoax telephone call.

Stirling are one of the form sides in the division just now, having climbed off the foot of the table to a more respectable seventh place. They had Sam Filler in goal, with the experience of Jamie McCunnie in defence and Mark Ferry in midfield. Young Jordan White played as the main striker with Scott Davidson partnering him up front and they proved a handful throughout.

When the game got under way there was not much between the teams, but it was Rangers who carved out the best opening in six minutes. Kane Hemmings was leading the front line, wearing the number nine shirt and was back at Ibrox following a recent loan spell at Cowdenbeath. He held the ball up before slipping it into the box for the on rushing Lee Wallace to collect. However, Albion's 'keeper, Filler, stood up well to block his shot.

From a Barrie McKay cross out on the right wing Hemmings' header went over the bar, when he should have hit the target at the very least. Minutes later he then mis-hit a shot wide of Filler's left hand post when put through on goal and again he should have done a lot better.

Stirling were impressively composed on the ball when they had it and looked to retain possession and not panic. Their first real chance to threaten the Rangers goal came five minutes before the break. From a Davidson corner on the far side, the ball reached Jordan White first and his headed effort was goal bound, only for Fraser Aird to head off the line.

At this point I did notice a lot of fans criticising a couple of the younger players and this was maybe down to frustration in some instances, given the two or three decent goal scoring opportunities that they failed to take earlier in the game.

Midway through the first half I thought I was seeing things when the Rangers centre half, Emilson Cribari, ducked to avoid the ball when he should have attacked it with his head! With defending like this, it is not surprising the amount of goals the team have conceded this season.

Albion came even closer right on the stroke of half time when the two strikers combined again, but this time the roles were reversed. Jordan White found himself breaking down the right and his cross was delivered to the back post where Davidson controlled with his chest before firing just over the bar.

He was under pressure from the onrushing Neil Alexander but given the time and space he was in, he maybe could have done better. The home fans made their feelings known as they booed the team off the pitch as the half time whistle went.

Rangers started the brighter of the two sides in the second half and went close when Fraser Aird's low shot from outside the box was turned round the post for a corner by Sam Filler.

The home side had linked well in patches during the first half but this seemed to be absent in the second and they gave away possession quite cheaply at times. On one such occasion they were nearly punished when Aird was too casual in trying to pick out Lee Wallace. Stirling broke down the right flank and Alexander had to react to a mis-hit shot from Davidson.

A good run and cross from Rangers' Robbie Crawford, on the right hand side, was initially blocked and on the follow up he managed to square for Hemmings, who fired just wide of the 'keeper's left hand post. In an attempt to get a winner, Rangers introduced Kal Naismith and Anestis Argyriou for Barrie McKay and Fraser Aird.

Stirling Albion continued to frustrate and worked extremely hard in closing down the ball when they did not have it, while looking dangerous on the counter attack. I can only assume that Scott Davidson was substituted just after the hour due to being on a yellow card as he was the key to the majority of Albion's best moves.

The game fizzled out as fans drifted to the exits and the only other notable chance came in injury time, when Argyriou's diving header went wide of the right hand post.

The game ended goalless and again the fans who were left in the stadium let their feelings known, with a chorus of booing! Since going round the grounds over the last six months we had yet to encounter a goalless game until today. I suppose with the law of averages we had to get one somewhere along the way, I just never expected it to be at this venue!

Despite events at Ibrox in the last twelve months the stadium remains an impressive structure. Composed of four modern stands, the significant change made to it being the 'Club Deck' which was like an extension built on top of the Main Stand in the early 1990s. A couple of the corner areas have been filled in over the years, which have provided more seating and slightly increased the capacity.

The away support is allocated to the corner between the Broomloan Road and Govan stands, apart from when Celtic visit as their fans are allocated the full Broomloan Road end. This is not likely to be an issue over the next couple of seasons, unless the two clubs meet in domestic cup competition.

Each stand provides a decent view of the pitch, apart from the higher up seating in the Club Deck. From experience, you cannot see the touchline unless you stand up and lean over!

The seats we were in for this game were low down and it was hard to make the players out at times on the far side touchline against the dark blue seats in the Main Stand.

The match programme is a good read for home fans with plenty of pictures of games and players, past and present. If there was any criticism to make, it would be that there are absolutely no details on the opposition, outwith both squads listed on the back page.

Ibrox has played host to many famous matches over the years for domestic, European and International football. The fans have bought into the new owner's vision for the future and bought season tickets to support the club, but it may be some time yet before the club experiences a full house for a significant high profile game.

Rangers 0
Albion Rovers 0
Referee: C. Thomson
Attendance: 44,608

No Thrill At Firhill For Livi

Partick Thistle 6, Livingston 1
Division 1 - Saturday 23rd March 2013

IT WAS HARDLY PHIL COLLINS at Live Aid in 1985, with two gigs back to back either side of the Atlantic but a quick freshen up and we were on our way from Glasgow's South Side to the North of the city. The day's second game was literally a 'thrill at Firhill', as Partick Thistle took on Livingston, in Division One's game of the day and it did not disappoint.

Only twenty four hours previously Thistle announced that Alan Archibald had been given the manager's post on a permanent basis, which was a decision that had the unanimous backing of the 'Jags' supporters. The team have been unbeaten since "Archie" took over the reins when Jackie McNamara departed for Dundee United earlier last month, so it was an almost inevitable appointment.

I used to work in this area and my in-laws live here, so it is a venue I am very familiar with and I have seen a few games here over the years. I pass the ground often but think the last time I was here for an actual game was in 2007. I took my eldest lad to all three of Thistle's pre-season games against Ayr United, Falkirk and Leicester City, which were all played a few days apart.

The club have had their ups and downs over the last decade, but have been on a more stable financial footing over the last six or seven years. They have had the added income of local rugby being played at Firhill, up until last summer and some decent sponsorship deals with Puma, Ignis, Macb and Greaves Sports.

We have not seen Thistle play so far this season but have taken in two of Livingston's games, away at Hamilton last October then two months later when they were at home to Dunfermline. On both occasions they won and have been quite impressive, but not so in this game! They were missing two key players in Stefan Scougall and Jesus Garcia Tena, but I am not sure if even they could have prevented what turned out to be a proverbial 'hiding'!

Thistle are in great form and proved to be far superior to their opponents. They were pretty much at full strength and have a young, enthusiastic and skilful side, that have a great chance to be playing Premier League football next season. When the game got underway both sides had a bit of possession but it was Thistle who struck first, with the first clear chance of the game on five minutes.

A close range shot by Steven Craig was palmed away by Andy McNeill for a corner and that should have proved to be an inspirational moment for the goalkeeper. Instead, it proved to be the start of a horrible afternoon for the Livi man and that is without mentioning the bizarre looking pony tail he was sporting!

Outwith a direct Steven Craig free kick there were no real goal scoring opportunities until Thistle got a lucky break on eighteen minutes. An attempted shot by the lively Steven Lawless from the edge of the box caught defender Paul Watson on the arm and referee George Salmond awarded a penalty. It was a harsh decision, as Watson had turned his back on the shot but Aaron Muirhead stepped up and drilled his shot straight down the middle, to give the hosts the lead.

Three minutes later Thistle doubled their advantage. A corner on the right hand side from James Craigen evaded everyone and the ball was picked up on the far side by Sean Welsh. He lofted it back in and found the unmarked Steven Craig in the six yard box and he headed home past McNeill, who went down to it in installments!

As we were near the stewards and Police cordon separating both sets of supporters, the early goading got too much for two fans, one from each side and there was a comical stand off between them! Guys in their forties still wanting to fight, good God!

Back on the park, the Livingston players' body language was of a team that knew they were beaten, yet it was not over by a long shot. Ten minutes from the break Partick Thistle got their third and you had to blink, to double check and confirm, if what you saw did actually happen! Lawless played a pass to James Craigen who went on a run and hit a decent shot from twenty yards out. It bounced in front of McNeill and into the net but it was like there was no goalkeeper between the sticks!

Three minutes before the break the game was as good as over, when Thistle grabbed their fourth of the afternoon. From a Livingston free kick in a dangerous position the ball was cleared up to the half way line and picked up by the highly impressive Chris Erskine, who tried to play in Steven Craig. As he would have been flagged for offside had he touched the ball, he cleverly left it, and Erskine continued his run and collected, before playing in Lawless. The diminutive attacker side-stepped two challenges before casually lifting the ball over McNeill to make it four without reply.

It was a really well-worked goal and was reminiscent of Gio Kinkladze's goal of the season in the English Premiership some years ago. He may have to work on his goal celebration though, poor effort!

The hosts were forced into a change at the interval with Kris Doolan replacing Steven Craig in attack. One minute after the restart Livingston pulled a goal back. A free kick was floated into the box and headed into the path of Paul Watson, who volleyed high past Scott Fox from six yards to reduce the deficit. It failed to inspire any kind of fight back from the visitors though and Thistle continued to dominate proceedings.

Just before the hour the Jags made it five and quite possibly one of the best goals I have seen this season. It was a case of possession football, as some patient play gradually found the home side sweeping up the park. A nice chipped cross was held up by Doolan who nodded the ball into the path of Erskine. They then played a one-two with each other and Erskine calmly slotted a low left foot shot out of the reach of McNeill in goals. There was at least twelve passes made in the build up and if this was a more high profile league, people would be raving about the quality of this goal.

Five minutes later a Livi move down the left resulted in a ball into the box, which was controlled by substitute Danny Mullen. He had the space to turn and get a shot in that clipped the corner of the bar. Thistle then had a chance to add to their tally when a corner on the right found its way out to Lawless, who fired in a twenty five yard shot that dipped just over the bar.

With twenty minutes left the hosts added a sixth goal and again it was stunning. Aaron Sinclair was allowed to charge a good twenty yards up the park unchallenged, before lifting a neat cross into the six yard box. It found Kris Doolan who controlled the ball on his chest and as it dropped, he volleyed it into the net, all in the one move.

The game was long over as a contest, Thistle kept the ball while Livi wished the clock would quickly hit ninety minutes. There were no real chances of note thereafter, it finished 6-1 and a valuable three points were collected. Elsewhere, Morton came back from two goals down to win 4-2 at home to Cowdenbeath, ensuring the Division One title race will go right to the wire.

This was a great advert for the Scottish Football League and the 2,897 fans in attendance were thoroughly entertained. Partick Thistle seem to have all the right ingredients in their side to be successful, with a mixture of ability, height, youth, experience and a will to win. All the players played their part in this result, but I thought Erskine and Lawless were exceptional at times and the club will do well to hold onto them in the summer.

I've always enjoyed coming to watch football at Firhill. The club have an intriguing history and have unfortunately lived a lot of it in the shadows of two other teams in the city. The stadium is quite accessible, being next to two main roads leading into the city centre and you are also only a ten minute walk from the Underground at St.George's Cross.

Street parking is available near the ground, with several streets on either side of Maryhill Road, giving you only a short distance to cover walking to and from the stadium. For this game we parked up on the hill just off Murano Street, giving us not even a five minute walk down to the turnstiles.

The Main Stand at Firhill is quite traditional and distinctive and can be seen from some distance. It is only used on occasion and I am unsure if there is an issue with it meeting certain SFL criteria. Opposite is the Jackie Husband Stand which was built twenty years ago and is predominantly used by the home supporters.

In the last decade, new flats and a new stand were built behind the goal to the north of the stadium, both of which are very modern in appearance. Opposite this, there was an open terrace which was not used for some time and was later cleared in anticipation for a similar build to that on the north side.

I have a couple of friends who work just down the road in the local Housing Association, who suggested that the club may have had an issue with the council's Planning Department over certain permissions. It has lain vacant as a grass embankment now for possibly six or seven years and I am unsure what the future holds for this part of the ground.

There is a good community feel about Firhill and the club in general. The staff are welcoming and friendly and the club have done a lot of work locally to encourage families along to the games. The club's decision to let kids under the age of sixteen into the ground for free a few years back is a great incentive to the next generation of fans, while making it affordable at the same time.

Partick Thistle 6
((Muirhead (Pen 19), Craig (22), Craigen (36), Lawless (43),
Erskine (57), Doohlan (69))
Livingston 1 (Watson (46))
Referee: G. Salmond
Attendance: 2,897

Poignant Pause For Pars

Dunfermline Athletic 0, Falkirk 2
Division 1 - Wednesday 27th March 2013

IT HAS BEEN A TURBULENT TIME for Dunfermline Athletic over the last couple of months and we were through in Fife, for the re-arranged midweek fixture with Falkirk at East End Park to show some support. The game was brought forward due to Falkirk's Scottish Cup Semi Final with Hibernian in two weeks time.

Following recent reports that the staff were not receiving their salaries, the team's form has coincidentally faded, going from title contenders to mid table obscurity in recent weeks. On almost a daily basis more and more information has been emanating from the club in relation to the financial position and very little of it has been positive.

There was the possibility that the club could have been liquidated, due to an outstanding tax bill in the region of £134,000, putting this game in doubt. However, merely hours before kick off, the club applied to put themselves into voluntary administration, buying them some time to sort things out off the pitch.

The last time I was here was in November 1997 when the away end had an open terracing. A lot of changes have been made since then, with the club now having four all seated stands. I have to say that the cameras do not do it justice, as it looks better when you are physically in the ground than the television images portray.

We got up here in an hour and parked in one of the local side streets, about ten minutes walk from the stadium. I had called earlier to buy tickets over the phone, so the first port of call was to pick them up. I actually could have got complimentary tickets for this game, but in light of the circumstances it would have been morally wrong in every sense to have taken up this option. Having walked round the perimeter of the ground, we then headed to the Norrie McCathie Stand which is the home end behind the goal.

The pitch still had some snow on it and clearly was not at its best, but it was deemed playable. It was a bitterly cold evening and after all that has been going on at the club, I think everyone was just pleased that the focus could shift back to the football, even just for ninety minutes.

As we found out earlier in the season when these two teams met, this is a popular game for both sets of supporters. There was a disappointing crowd of 2,879 present, somewhat low I thought, given the perilous position Dunfermline found themselves in.

The Pars fielded a strong side for what was likely to be the last time this group of players would be together. They could call upon the experience of Gallacher in goal, Dowie, Jordan, Husband, Barrowman and Dargo, who was on the bench.

Falkirk who have Alex Smith in charge, following Steven Pressley's recent departure to Coventry City, have a very young side in comparison. The main men for them being McGovern in goal, veteran defender Darren Dods and their top scorer this season, Lyle Taylor up front.

There was very few notable moments in the first ten minutes of the game, until Falkirk got a free kick on the right wing, some twenty five yards from goal. Thomas Grant floated the ball in and Lyle Taylor rose highest, to head the ball past Gallacher and open the scoring.

Dunfermline had a decent chance to equalise four minutes later when they had a direct free kick but Chris Kane fired it wide. The home side had a couple of good spells of play but their final ball let them down. On twenty two minutes the Pars had a claim for a penalty, when Ryan Wallace broke free from Flynn and although there was contact, it would have been a soft award had it been given.

Only a couple of minutes later Wallace was involved again. He picked the ball up on the left hand side and managed to get a shot off, but he went for power instead of composure, meaning it went over the bar and he really should have scored. Falkirk had a couple of tame efforts at goal that failed to trouble Gallacher, but had a great chance just after the half hour mark to extend their lead.

Thomas Grant stepped up to hit a direct free kick from twenty yards out, following Husband's foul on McGrandles, but it went just over the bar.

Three minutes later some careless passing in the Dunfermline defence gave Alston a chance, but he failed to capitalise and he hit his shot wide. Gallacher was forced into action again on thirty eight minutes, expertly turning another Taylor header away for a corner, following a Grant cross on the left.

Taylor's tenth minute header proved to be the only goal of the first half and they took their lead into the interval. Dunfermline tried to turn the game around when they replaced Chris Kane with Ryan Thomson. Falkirk had the first chance of the second period when Grant collected the ball on the right, but flashed his shot wide of the post. Some nice link up play by the hosts almost resulted in an equaliser in the fifty fifth minute, when Barrowman's knock down saw Falkingham get a decent strike on target, but McGovern saved.

The game then hit a bit of a lull with play being stopped or interrupted due to petty fouls and both sides giving away possession. There were a couple of free kicks at each end, though both teams lacked a decent final touch and there were no scoring opportunities until the latter part of the match.

In the last eight minutes Lyle Taylor nearly ensured the three points for Falkirk, when he turned in the six yard box, but he hooked his shot over the bar. Two minutes later Taylor was in again, only this time his effort was blocked by Jordan McMillan

With two minutes left on the clock, the game was effectively over when Falkirk claimed a second goal. Duffie's throw in was held up well by Taylor who turned, wriggled away from a couple of defenders in the process and headed for goal. Blair Alston, who was almost running along side Taylor, seemed to cut in and take the ball off Taylor's toe, to crack a low shot into Gallacher's left hand post and make it two.

As the game headed into injury time we made our way up to the exit and watched the last couple of minutes from there. There was no further incident and the visitors claimed the victory. We headed to the car, very slowly I may add, having nearly seized up due to the exceptional cold!

The atmosphere was decent during the game, as both sets of fans taunted each other with the customary obscenities! The Pars fans were quite upbeat throughout, with the majority of the noise coming from the Norrie McCathie stand. It was quite a somber moment at the end of the match, watching the Dunfermline players walking off the pitch, not knowing if they would have a job in the coming days when the administrators got down to business.

This was not the best of games but it was still an enjoyable visit. The Main Stand is relatively old fashioned looking, but very impressive from outside on the main road. The players' tunnel is situated in the corner between it and the Norrie McCathie Stand.

Behind the opposite goal is the East Stand which is pretty much identical and houses the away support. Running parallel with the Main Stand is the North Stand, an old terrace which has been seated in recent years and not used that often. Round the back of it is a big car park area which is a bit dirty underfoot if it has been raining!

Dunfermline Athletic are a well known established Scottish club of 128 years. They are suffering like many other clubs in the country, through the current recession and bad financial decisions. With a lot of work going on in the background, hopefully an amicable agreement can be thrashed out with the administrators. I sincerely hope there is a positive outcome for all concerned at East End Park.

Dunfermline 0
Falkirk 2 (Taylor (10), Alston (88))
Referee: G. Salmond
Attendance: 2,879

LATE SHOW AT SOMERSET

Ayr United 2, East Fife 1
Division 2 - Saturday 30ᵗʰ March 2013

IT WAS A CHANGE OF SCENERY AGAIN, as we headed to Ayrshire and Somerset Park, for Ayr United hosting East Fife. We have seen both teams a couple of times this season and given our experience to date, there would likely be goals in this game.

I have not been here since the mid 1980s, but it is what I would describe as a likeable, traditional Scottish stadium, with a Main Stand and the other three ends of the ground being terraced.

Some of the road junctions near the ground proved tricky, and I will admit to cursing the sat nav woman more than once! We got a parking space down a street at the side of the railway line, a few minutes walk from the ground. We went for a quick look in the club shop which was quite busy, mainly due to a couple of special offers on merchandise the club were doing. We collected tickets and went for a walk round the outside of the ground.

When I came here many years ago we were in the Main Stand, so I was keen to check out the terracing on this occasion. For the first half we stood on the open terrace across from the Main Stand and then went behind the home goal, as Ayr United were shooting into this end for the second period.

Ayr had January transfer signing Graeme Smith in goal, with the ageing defenders John Robertson and Austin McCann in the full back positions. With Michael Donald grafting on the wing, they had the deadly duo of Liam Buchanan and Michael Moffat up front. According to the kids the latter looks like Dimitar Berbatov from a distance, but I think that's were the similarity ends!

While Ayr's form and performances have improved since the turn of the year, East Fife's seem to have gone in the opposite direction and they are currently sitting second bottom of Division 2. They have changed their goalkeeper in recent weeks, replacing

Calum Antell with Michael Brown and can rely on the experience of Collin Samuel and Paul McManus in attack. The Fifers also have the benefit of having the speed and trickery of Bobby Barr, who I have liked the look of in the games I have seen him play in this season.

The game got under way and the ball spent a lot of time in the air during the opening few minutes. Paul McManus had a shot blocked for East Fife on five minutes before his team mate, Robert Sloan, was short with a pass back on the left flank which let Michael Moffat in on goal, but he was penalised for hand ball.

Ayr could not get any rhythm to their play at all and the best they could muster in the first quarter of an hour was a run and shot from Mark Shankland, which failed to trouble the keeper. Moments later Ayr fell behind and it was from a lovely move and finish. Bobby Barr made a great run down the left, just keeping the ball in play and put in a cross to the back post. Lurking in the area was full back Scott Durie, who steadied himself before volleying high into the net to give East Fife the lead.

Both teams distribution and delivery from set pieces were somewhat disappointing and Ayr's only response to going behind were two half chances from Buchanan who linked well with Moffat. The Fifers in turn had a chance with a run and shot from Samuel at the edge of the eighteen yard box, which was deflected for a corner.

Just before the half hour mark Ayr missed a great opportunity to equalise, when Mark Shankland put a cross over from the right. It cleared the heads of the defenders and landed at the feet of Liam Buchanan six yards out, but he did not anticipate the ball coming to him and his shot was hurried and went high over the bar, when he should have buried it.

Ayr were beginning to dominate and pin East Fife back in their own half, but some poor crossing and over passing the ball at times, meant the opposition back line were comfortable with anything that came their way. From an Ayr corner ten minutes before the break Michael Moffat flicked the ball on for Chris Smith, whose shot was blocked and cleared.

Right on the stroke of half time East Fife won themselves a free kick near the left hand corner flag following a foul on Paul McManus. The delivery was poor though and the ball travelled out for a goal kick and it proved to be the last action of the first half, as Ayr went into the break a goal down.

The home side were out the traps the quickest at the start of the second half, with the main threat being Michael Moffat. In the first five minutes of the restart he was put through on goal, but was flagged for offside, before seeing a header drop just over the bar from a free kick.

East Fife then had a spell of possession and got a foothold in the game. From a Bobby Barr cross the Ayr defence had to come to the rescue as Graeme Smith spilled the ball. He did redeem himself though, minutes later, saving from a Samuel header from a dangerous McManus cross.

The Fifers had another good break with twenty minutes to go when Paul Willis got himself into a decent goal scoring position, but his shot from just outside the eighteen yard box went well wide. Ayr responded with a break up the park and Liam Buchanan showed some nice control down the right side, but his intended cross failed to trouble the visitor's goal.

From an Ayr corner three minutes later East Fife broke quickly up the park and McManus' cross found Barr breaking into the box, but he was tackled cleanly by John Robertson, as the Fifers appealed in vain for a penalty.

Ayr had just replaced Mark Shankland with David Winters and it proved to be an inspired substitution by manager Mark Roberts. With twelve minutes left the scores were level, when a Winters cross was controlled in the box by Liam Buchanan. It was not the tidiest of finishes but he managed to turn and power a shot into the net at the second attempt to equalise.

Two minutes later Michael Moffat had a great chance to give the home side the lead when he was put through on goal, but he couldn't get any real power in his shot and it was saved by the feet of 'keeper Michael Brown.

East Fife then made a like for like change, when they replaced

McManus with Liam Gormley, as they chased a winning goal. They then had another penalty claim turned down, when Bobby Barr went down from a challenge in the box, but referee Don Robertson waved away the claims and booked the winger for simulation.

Ayr then had an opportunity to score themselves, when a well flighted cross from Robertson on the right was met by the head of Michael Donald six yards out, but it was expertly turned away by 'keeper Brown for a corner.

With four minutes left it was Ayr who grabbed the winner and surprisingly Michael Moffat was not involved! Buchanan again found space to get a shot in on goal, it looked relatively comfortable for the goalkeeper, but he could not hold onto the ball and as it spun in the air, David Winters followed up to score.

A minute later Ayr nearly scored again, when Michael Donald played in Moffat, but this time Brown managed to block the shot and the ball was cleared.

In the fourth minute of stoppage time East Fife had a great chance to equalise, when Liam Gormley attempted to lob his shot over Smith in goal, but he managed to save and that proved to be pretty much the last action of the game. A vital three points in the end for Ayr, as they chase the last Play Off spot in Division 2, but East Fife acquitted themselves well and can feel justifiably aggrieved that they left with nothing.

This was an enjoyable, competitive game of football for the 956 fans present. The fans on the open terrace were quite critical of the team in the first half and they let the players know about what they thought of some of the performances on the park! As we went behind the goal in the second half, the fans in this area were slightly more supportive.

I would say that in the two games we have seen Ayr United this season, at Alloa and Arbroath, their fans have been the noisiest and the wittiest yet, with their songs and chants. However, on their own patch they were quite subdued, with not much in the way of singing going on, which was a bit of a surprise.

As mentioned about Somerset Park already, it has a Main Stand with an open terrace opposite and two covered terraces behind both goals, the Somerset Road end for home fans and the Railway End for visitiors.

It is next to a railway station and about half a mile from the town centre, meaning that it is not far to walk and you are near all local bus routes in and out of the area. The main motorway junctions in and out of Ayr are also only a couple of miles away, making it quite an accessible venue.

I can only assume that the down turn in Scottish football is affecting Ayr United the same way every other club has been. The attendances have dropped to under 1,000 some weeks, depending on the opposition and this is surprising given the large catchment area.

The team's current league position may have some kind of input to that, with some fans maybe finding this level unappealing, and I would suggest that the admission prices may also be a contributing factor to this also. With no parent and child or family gate on offer, the basic adult and concession gates priced at £15 and £8 respectively, is over priced in my opinion, especially for the third tier of Scottish football.

Maybe the locals here can afford this outlay, but on top of transport, food, programme, a venture into the club shop and admission money, it is not something I could do personally with any regularity.

This was a good day out all round, but I would like to think the club are open to suggestion about enhancing people's match day experience and give the latter comments some consideration.

Ayr United 2 (Buchanan (79), Winters (87))
East Fife 1 (Durie (15))
Referee: D. Robertson
Attendance: 956

Point A Piece In Paisley

St Mirren 1, Celtic 1
SPL - Sunday 31ˢᵗ March 2013

IT IS EASTER SUNDAY, I am sitting in the living room ready to watch Sky TV's football offerings, when the phone rings at 12.20pm. It is my young cousin, who is still inebriated from the night before, on to tell us that there are tickets available in the St.Mirren end for us.

I politely declined them initially given nobody in the house was ready to go and the fact that it was twenty five minutes before kick off! However, after some deliberating with the kids, we decided to hot foot it over to Paisley and got there for just after kick off.

We met up with our contact and collected the briefs, before getting a couple of pictures of the stadium on our way round to the West Stand area, where we would be sitting.

I pass this ground three or four times a week and have visited twice previously with the boys in the last couple of seasons, for games against Falkirk and Hearts, when the local schools were giving away tickets. The irony is, I also pass the now vacant Love Street site, the former home to St.Mirren for over one hundred years, with similar regularity.

As this was one of Sky television's featured matches, there was also radio coverage, meaning we could hear the team news in the car which was useful, as we were not likely to catch it before kick off! St.Mirren boss, Danny Lennon, has made very few changes to the starting eleven in recent weeks and their general form has been decent, culminating in a League Cup Semi Final win at Hampden Park in January, over their opponents in this game no less.

The Saints went on to lift the League Cup two weeks ago, having defeated Hearts in an epic Final and this was the first game at home since that triumph. Just prior to kick off the team were applauded onto the park by the Celtic players, a gesture which I am sure was appreciated by all fans and officials at St.Mirren.

Craig Samson between the sticks has been steady all season and has a defence well marshalled by skipper Jim Goodwin. The main men in midfield are former Celtic player, Paul McGowan, who was on loan here for a spell before making the move permanent in 2011. There is also promising youngster Paul McGinn and Conor Newton, who is on loan from Newcastle United until the end of the season.

Up front, the Saints can call upon experienced hit man Steven Thompson and the impressive Esmael Gonçalves, who is another player on loan from Rio Ave in Portugal.

For the visitors, manager Neil Lennon had threatened to ring the changes, following some erratic results and performances, yet he continues to stick to the same group of players. For this game Celtic would be missing full backs Lustig and Matthews, along with longer term absentees Scott Brown and James Forrest. The defence has made a lot of uncharacteristic errors this term, with one of the main offenders, Efe Ambrose, deputising at right back in this game.

The midfield was a physically strong one, with Wanyama, Ledley and Kayal in the centre to break up St.Mirren's passing game. Samaras and the inform Kris Commons rotated playing on the left and supporting Gary Hooper in attack.

All the games between the sides so far this season have been very keenly contested and this one had the added edge to it, due to St Mirren's cup win less than two months ago.

There were still a few stragglers like us heading into the turnstiles as the game had kicked off. We entered onto the concourse just as Celtic had a corner on the far side and waited as the ball landed out at the edge of the box, where it was neatly dinked back in by Ambrose. Kris Commons, who had made a run into the danger area, rose high almost on the run, to powerfully head past Samson and give the away side the lead after only six minutes.

From the restart the Saints had a couple of corners and goalkeeper Fraser Forster made a comfortable save from Dummett, before a Newton shot went over the bar. Celtic had a couple of corners themselves and remained relatively comfortable in possession of the ball. A weak header from Commons and a shot high over the bar from Gary Hooper were all the Champions elect could muster.

St.Mirren were dangerous on the break though and Celtic's defence struggled with some of the balls being played into their box by Van Zanten, Dummett and Teale. Saints best chance came after eighteen minutes, when Steven Thompson's glancing header went just wide, following a great run on the right, again by Gary Teale.

The game did not have any real flow, as referee Bobby Madden continually stopped play for petty fouls, which tended to upset the home support. On the half hour mark we had the first real controversial moment in the game, when the Saints thought they had equalised, only for a foul to be given on 'keeper Forster.

Again it was from a Teale cross, this time on the left to the back post, where Dummett rose with Forster and Izaguirre. The ball dropped into the net, before the referee blew for a foul. There did not appear much wrong with the goal from our position and television replays showed later that it looked like Dummett was pushed by Izaguirre into Forster and that the goal should have stood, or St Mirren should have been awarded a penalty.

Just before half time Kris Commons landed awkwardly following a challenge involving Gonçalves and his team mate Beram Kayal. After initially receiving treatment, we had the unfortunate scene of the stretcher being called for. While Celtic played on with ten men, the game then faced its next controversial moment, when the home side's claims for a penalty were waved away.

A Teale corner from the left cleared everyone in the area and as Wanyama went to head it, he mistimed his jump and the ball appeared to hit the arm of Georgios Samaras. The big Greek striker was a bit unsighted and it would have been harsh as there was no intent, but it is a situation when you have seen a penalty being awarded.

During the interval the League Cup was paraded round the track, which went down a treat with the home fans who scrambled

Ground no. 1 - Cowdenbeath's 'Blue Brazil' souvenir shop and (below) the stock car racing that seems to attract more punters to Central Park than the football.

(Above) Cliftonhill - home of Albion Rovers and (left) Dumbarton Rock, which dwarfs The Bet Butler Stadium home of The Sons.

Bayview - home of East Fife with a view across the Firth of Forth.

Cappielow Park, Greenock where we took in Morton's 1-0 win over Raith Rovers in January.

Above: My boys engrossed in the action at Stair Park, Stranraer as the Fifers attack the Blues goal.

Left: The entrance to Recreation Park, Alloa for The Wasps' Second Division encounter with Ayr United.

Below: I find a convenient parking space close by Links Park, Montrose.

Gayfield, Arbroath - a ground bordered on one side by the North Sea and Arbroath beach, it was also the venue for one of the most famous games in football history as The Red Lichties beat Bon Accord 36-0 back in 1885.

At last a picture of the much-maligned 'Lino', subject of ritual abuse, most of it light-hearted, the length and breadth of Scotland.

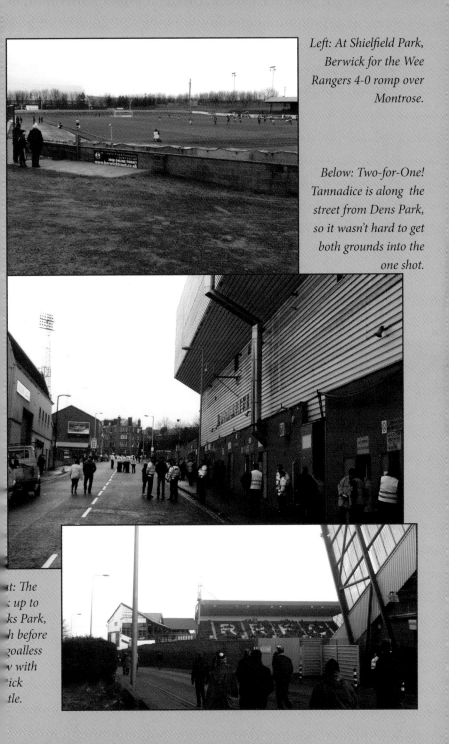

Left: At Shielfield Park, Berwick for the Wee Rangers 4-0 romp over Montrose.

Below: Two-for-One! Tannadice is along the street from Dens Park, so it wasn't hard to get both grounds into the one shot.

...t: The ... up to ...ks Park, ...h before ...goalless ... with ...ick ...tle.

Top: My son Ry[...]
races to inform me [...]
Elgin being awar[...]
a penalty at Borou[...]
Brig[...]

Middle: Our Cor[...]
playing it cool at [...]
entrance to Ann[...]
Athletic's Galaba[...]
grou[...]

Left: The calm bef[...]
the storm at Gle[...]
Park before Brecl[...]
City's four-goal thri[...]
with Stranra[...]

Left: Loons Indeed! Forfar's club shop attracts pre-match attention.

Middle Left: Fir Park, Motherwell.

Middle Right: Pittodrie, Aberdeen - still one of the finest stadiums in Scotland.

...ther sea ..., this time ...n Inverness's ...edonian ...ium.

Stairs leading to an unused section of terracing that still remains at Dens Park, Dun

A lone piper welcomes me for the final leg of my odyssey at Peterhead for the Play-Off Final Second Leg on Sunday May 19th 2013.

to get pictures of it.

Anthony Stokes was the replacement for Commons as the second half got under way. There was not much between the sides in the first ten minutes before the card happy Madden altered the game with his next blunder.

Near the halfway line Victor Wanyama went in for a challenge with Paul McGowan. It did look like the Kenyan had tried to pull out of the tackle at the last minute, but there was some contact and the Saints midfielder came off second best. Referee Madden was close by and pulled out the red card, leaving the Hoops with over half an hour to play with a man less. It did look a harsh decision and a yellow card may have sufficed.

The Saints were looking to capitalise and probably looked the more threatening going forward. They had opportunities through Teale and Van Zanten, but neither of which troubled Forster. Both sides made changes with Carey replacing McGinn for St.Mirren and McGeouch was introduced in place of Hooper for Celtic.

The visitors were sitting deeper, as they tried to hang on to their slender advantage and this left St.Mirren with more of the possession. Neither side carved out any clear cut chances, with Thompson heading over from another Teale corner for Saints and a Mulgrew free kick at the other end came to nothing.

With ten minutes left it was time for the fourth and final controversial incident of the afternoon. The Celtic defence failed to clear their lines, starting with Izaguirre on the left of the eighteen yard box. The ball ended up with Stokes, who seemed to lose his footing, Gonçalves picked up the ball and headed into the box, where he was clumsily challenged by Izaguirre. Referee Madden did not hesitate in pointing to the spot and from nothing, St Mirren were thrown a lifeline.

We were seated looking right in line with where the challenge was made and thought the referee had blown due to simulation by Gonçalves. There seemed very little contact and if there was, it had taken place outside the box.

Having taken a penalty against Celtic in the League Cup Semi Final at Hampden, Paul McGowan had a chance to score against his former side once again. He faced Zaluska the last time, but he was up against the intimidating frame of Fraser Forster, who would surely prove to be a sterner challenge. What do I know, the confident midfielder went for power and smashed his kick down the middle, to equalise and make the closing minutes very interesting.

If there was going to be a winner, it looked like it would come from the home side. They had a great chance when Gary Teale was allowed to run at the Celtic defence almost unchallenged, but his drive went just over the bar. The Saints brought on their latest signing, Estonian midfielder Sander Puri, and he nearly had a dream debut with a goal, but he could not convert a shot from close range, after Forster fumbled a Carey cross.

This proved to be the last real action of the game as both teams had to settle for a point, which was probably fair based on possession and chances created. It is not often you hear both managers bemoaning decisions made by officials, but this was the case in this game and referee Bobby Madden's ears will be burning for days! To say the official made a few errors of judgement is a major understatement.

Even though this was a very short notice visit, it was quite an enjoyable game to watch and maybe helped change my opinion of St.Mirren's new ground. The club moved a quarter of a mile along the road from Love Street to here in January 2009. For the previous two visits here, we were in the South Stand behind the home goal. The atmosphere was almost non existent, I did not think the view was great and the standard of football was not any better. Having walked round the perimeter before and after this game and sat in a different end, I saw it in a new light!

For anyone passing the main East Stand, either in the car or on foot, the façade is very impressive, with the large club crest leaving you in no doubt of who plays here! The offices at the front look quite lavish and I like the fans' names engraved on the walls, either side of the main doors.

Adjacent to this is the West Stand which is the home end, though for certain opposition, a small section is used for the away fans, who are normally allocated the North Stand behind the goal. Opposite this, the South Stand is used as the family area and the club do good deals including Under 18 s priced at £5 and Under 12's at only £2. The club also do a lot of school and community work, occasionally giving away tickets to Renfrewshire Primary schools, in an effort to encourage locals to come out and support the team.

Over time, the new ground will develop its own character and maybe then the club could look at re-naming a couple of the stands with the names of former legends. In the last couple of seasons St Mirren have seen their attendances increase as a result of Danny Lennon's football philosophy and with the style of football he likes his players to play. Their league position is a strange one and probably does not do them justice, but the League Cup win gives the club a great platform to build on.

St Mirren 1 (McGowan (Pen 81))
Celtic 1 (Commons (6))
Referee: B.Madden
Attendance: 6,066

All Square On April Fools!

St Johnstone 1, Dundee United 1
SPL - Monday 1ˢᵗ April 2013

WHAT BETTER WAY TO PASS the evening of a Bank Holiday Monday, than by taking in a game and ticking another ground off the list in the process. We travelled to McDiarmid Park, Perth for the Live ESPN match between St Johnstone and Dundee United. Both are targeting a top six finish and a potential European place as well, so it was bound to be a competitive match.

We arrived in good time and opted for street parking some ten minutes walk from the stadium. The last time I visited here was back in August 1997 and used the official parking area, but it took over forty minutes to get out, so I was determined not to let that happen again! I can also recall a visit to St Johnstone's old ground, Muirton Park, back in the mid 1980s which is maybe giving my age away slightly! As a stadium enthusiast and a Scottish football fan, I can at least say that I have visited both venues.

Apart from the fact both teams could be doing with a win, this is also a local derby fixture of sorts and I wondered what kind of crowd would turn out. Pre-match it was busy with people milling around outside, and I could sense the anticipation of the supporters. Before going into the stadium we walked round the perimeter of the four stands, taking a few pictures along the way and paid a visit to the small club shop as well.

Both sides were able to field strong sides for this one, though it would be fair to say United were probably at more of a disadvantage, following an injury to Gary Mackay-Steven on recent international duty and still without long term casualty Johnny Russell.

The Saints have had a great season and have benefitted from a solid back line, starting with Alan Mannus in goal, Dave Mackay, Frazer Wright, David McCracken and the veteran Callum Davidson in defence, though the latter two were missing for this game.

In midfield there is a mixture of ball winners and creative players, with Murray Davidson, Liam Craig, Paddy Cregg and Chris Millar. This season the Saints manager, Steve Lomas, has a welcome headache with a number of forward players to choose from including Rowan Vine, Steven MacLean, Nigel Hasselbaink and target man Gregory Tade.

For the Tangerine's, their boss, Jackie McNamara, recalled Michael Gardyne in place of Rory Boulding up front, while their newest star, Ryan Gauld, was almost a direct replacement for Mackay-Steven and Willo Flood returned from suspension.

When the game got under way it was hard going on the eye, with a lot of high balls being played up the park with no specific targets. Passes went astray and the distribution from both sides was below par.

The two sides had headers that did not trouble either goalkeeper, Murray Davidson for Saints and Keith Watson for United. A Gardyne run and cross into the box saw Daly narrowly miss the cut back and the chance was gone for the visitors.

The opening goal arrived midway through the first half and it was the impressive United youngster, Ryan Gauld, who broke the deadlock on twenty three minutes. Liam Craig was robbed of possession in the middle of the park by Mark Millar, who then threaded the ball through for Gauld and as 'keeper Mannus advanced from his area, the midfielder poked the ball under him and it rolled into the net, as the St Johnstone defenders looked on helplessly.

The referee, Ian Brines, made himself unpopular with both sets of supporters by continually holding the game up with petty fouls and the game never got a chance to flow. St Johnstone were struggling to break the United defence down and all they could muster was a weak shot from Vine, which did not trouble the goalkeeper. Then a direct free kick from Liam Craig, five minutes from the break, went just over the bar.

Craig again, right on forty five minutes, had a shot blocked following a counter attack and just before that United's Mark Millar should have done better with a direct free kick, which hit the wall and was cleared. Although the visitors led, I am sure both managers will have been glad to hear the half time whistle, so they could reorganise and look to improve for the second half.

Neither team dominated the early part of the second half, but it was St Johnstone who then went on to have a reasonable spell of dominance. Rowan Vine's poor first touch saw a good move come to an end, before complacency in the United midfield just before the hour nearly led to a Saints equaliser. The United players tried to take a quick free kick following a foul on Gauld, but it was intercepted, leaving Tade bearing down on the United goal. Cierzniak narrowed the angle and Tade's shot went wide of the left hand post.

The only effort on goal for United in the second half came from Stuart Armstrong, but his shot posed no threat to Alan Mannus' goal. Again St Johnstone pressed and came close twice in a matter of seconds. Liam Craig's well struck shot was superbly saved by Cierzniak, who turned it away for a corner. From the resulting set piece, Keith Watson cleared Murray Davidson's header off the line.

Nigel Hasselbaink then replaced Gregory Tade on the hour mark for the home side, as the Saints continued to pursue an equaliser. After only a few minutes on the park the substitute had a glorious chance to score when his header from six yards out was comfortably held by Cierzniak. As the game entered the last quarter of an hour Murray Davidson put a header just over the bar from a Vine corner.

Jackie McNamara then used all his substitutes a couple of minutes apart, before seeing his side reduced to ten men, after Stuart Armstrong was given his second yellow card of the evening. He was a bit unfortunate, as I initially thought that United had been awarded a penalty. Having received the ball, he turned in the box and appeared to be fouled, but Ian Brines' interpretation was that he had dived and after a caution early in the first half, Armstrong was off.

St Johnstone were throwing everything at their opponents and with ten minutes to go Steve Lomas gave Gwion Edwards a run out when he replaced Rowan Vine. After good hold up play by Murray Davidson, his shot was saved by Cierzniak, before Edwards himself saw a shot go wide of the right hand post.

As the game entered injury time Steven MacLean looked odds on to score, when he was given time and space to shoot inside the eighteen yard box. Maybe he had too much time to think about it, as his shot cleared the crossbar when he should have scored.

As a lot of fans made their way to the exits St Johnstone forced a corner, having desperately claimed for handball in the United penalty area. From the resulting kick the ball found its way to the back post, where Liam Craig powerfully headed high into the net from a standing jump to equalise. The place erupted and we felt compelled to almost join in with the celebrations as it would have been discourteous not to!

I thought at the time United's defence may have dealt with the corner a lot better and that Jon Daly may have been at fault, but he was just over powered by Liam Craig.

There was not much time left for either side to grab a winner and both managers would probably have been satisfied with the draw, as they each chase that top six finish before the SPL split this weekend.

This was a really entertaining game of football, especially for the neutral, watched by 4,613 fans, played at a fast pace with two good goals and scoring opportunities at both ends of the park.

I was not sure about McDiarmid Park, I had always been put off by television images of it half empty and because of that official parking set up I had experienced before! On this visit it gave me a chance to review it again in finer detail and a bit like St.Mirren's new location, I left with a totally different perception.

The stadium is set back just off the motorway and close by a shopping centre. As there are houses on the main road leading into the ground, the area can get congested at peak times and on a match day.

Although more than twenty years old now, McDiarmid Park is still a modern looking venue with four adequate sized stands with a total capacity of over 10,000. Part of the Main and all of the North

Stand are for away supporters, with the home fans occupying the East and Ormond Stands.

The stadium is well maintained and caters well for fans, with facilities readily available, signposted and easily located.

The club has been criticised in some quarters for some of its low attendances. This is despite making shrewd signings in the transfer market, showing good form in the league and achieving qualification into the Europa League in recent seasons.

If you are a local thinking about taking kids or grandkids to see the football, you will not find many clubs offering such affordable admission prices like St Johnstone. We were in the Ormond Family Stand which is behind the goal at the home end, to the right of the Main Stand. It is priced at £15 for parent and child which is tremendous value for the Premier League.

The club cannot be faulted for trying to bring in the next generation of supporters. I think many other clubs could be doing with taking note of St Johnstone's strategy both on and off the park.

St Johnstone 1 (Craig (90))
Dundee United 1 (Gauld (24))
Referee: I. Brines
Attendance: 4,613

Sand Dunes At Starks Park

Raith Rovers 0, Partick Thistle 0
Division 1 - Tuesday 2nd April 2013

A MIDWEEK VISIT TO STARKS PARK, Kirkcaldy, was our fourth game on the road in as many days, for the rearranged fixture between Raith Rovers and Partick Thistle.

It has been a hectic schedule for Thistle, as they have been running behind with games in hand following some adverse weather that affected not only their own pitch but those of Cowdenbeath and Raith Rovers. They also had one eye on the Ramsdens Cup Final against Queen of the South coming up at the weekend.

We got a reasonable run through the rush hour traffic and made good time, with the only thing really slowing us down being temporary traffic lights near the ground. After a quick scout around the local streets, we opted for a space facing in the direction of the motorway, which would be ideal for the road home.

There are only really two ways to enter the ground, by the away stand or by passing the Main Stand, which also leads you to behind the home goal. We went into the club shop which is a small container located just outside the home end turnstiles, but there was not much to see, so we went in to get something to eat and get seated prior to kick off.

I have only visited Starks Park once before, which was for a Scottish Cup tie in early 1987 if memory serves me right. In a recent Partick Thistle game at Firhill that we had attended, we focused on how Alan Archibald had taken up the reins, following Jackie McNamara's move to Dundee United at the beginning of February. Similarly, Rovers have Grant Murray in charge as player manager, for what is his first managerial post having replaced John McGlynn last summer.

The Fifers have had a reasonable season and showed recently that they are a more than capable side following their recent televised Scottish Cup 5th round game at home against Celtic. They have David McGurn in goal with the aforementioned Murray and Simon Mensing as the centre halves, and Grant Anderson, Stuart Anderson and Joe Hamill as the main men in midfield. Up front Rovers had the height and presence of both Brian Graham and Greig Spence, with Eddie Malone and new signing, Joe Cardle, recently released by Dunfermline, on the bench.

Despite the Cup Final being on their minds, the number one priority for Thistle is the league title and the only notable change Alan Archibald made for this game was keeping Kris Doolan in ahead of Steven Craig in attack.

I was looking forward to seeing Steven Lawless and Chris Erskine again, but it is worth mentioning that the success so far has been a collective team effort, that has seen 'the Jags' top the league table through most of this season.

The weather was very mild, the sun was out too, so the conditions made for a decent game of football, though the pitch looked to be heavy with sand in some areas. Right from the start both teams showed they were keen to get the upper hand and after only a minute on the clock, Thistle 'keeper, Scott Fox, had to turn a Brian Graham shot from the eighteen yard box round his left hand post for a corner. Rovers were having most of the early possession and had a decent chance when Mensing headed over the bar from a corner.

The visitor's first chance came when Chris Erskine found space and got a shot away, however it came off Doolan's backside and went out for a goal kick! Just after that we had possibly one of the defining moments in the game, when Spence capitalised on some casual play by Lawless in the middle of the park. He found himself breaking clear of the Thistle defence and heading for a one on one situation with Fox, but he dithered, attempted to go round him and the young keeper bravely came out to smother the ball and avert the danger.

Raith Rovers had another good effort on twenty two minutes when Joe Hamill fired a shot from the left of the eighteen yard box which was deflected for a corner. Five minutes later it was Thistle who had a great opportunity to take the lead following a mix up in the home defence. McGurn thought his defence were going to clear the ball, while they thought he was going to do it, meaning the keeper reacted late, diving at the feet of Lawless, taking both ball and player. The ball rebounded out to Doolan at the edge of the box and his shot went just wide and out for a goal kick.

Both teams were getting efforts in on goal and just after the half hour Grant Anderson held the ball up well, before turning and getting a shot in that went high over the bar. A couple of minutes later the Rovers defence were alert to clear from an Erskine cross, as Doolan waited to pounce.

Just before the break Fox saved well from a powerful Jason Thomson drive and from the follow up Joe Hamill fired wide of the right hand post. Grant Anderson then put a decent cross into the box which Brian Graham just failed to connect with.

The half ended with a chance for Thistle as Erskine again managed to get a shot in, but it went wide of McGurn's left hand post. At the break, Rovers manager Grant Murray will have been the happier of the two bosses and the hosts probably shaded the first half in terms of possession and clear cut chances.

As was the case in the first half, Rovers were possibly the hungrier looking side at the start of the second. The Thistle defence were kept on their toes when a long ball over the top for Spence was read by goalkeeper Fox, who reacted quickest to clear. A cross intended for Graham was then cleared, before the pivotal moment in the match, when Partick Thistle were reduced to ten men.

Having received a caution five minutes after the restart for a foul on Grant Anderson, centre half Aaron Muirhead then saw red, when just before the hour mark he scythed down the same player. It was an extremely foolish challenge and left referee Calum Murray no option but to send him off.

Unfortunately this incident changed the dynamic of the game, as Thistle looked to see the game out and avoid defeat by sacrificing the flair of Steven Lawless with new defensive signing Jordan McMillan from Dunfermline.

The irony was, that instead of capitalising on the numerical advantage, it was not Raith Rovers who created the next few scoring chances. With fifteen minutes left James Craigen went on a great run, linking with Erskine who played a one-two with him, but McGurn saved his shot comfortably. Then, from a run on the left wing Stuart Bannigan managed to cut into the area before firing a right foot shot which was well held by McGurn.

Raith made a double change when new signing Cardle replaced Hamill and Eddie Malone went on for player boss Murray. As expected the last ten minutes were dominated by Rovers as they went for a winner. Brian Graham had a great chance when the ball landed in the box, but it seemed to sit up too high for him and his shot went over the bar, when with a bit more composure he maybe would have scored.

Allan Walker then had two chances to make himself the hero, when his shot in the box was blocked and cleared in the last five minutes and then again in injury time. A long Rovers throw in from Malone saw the ball land with Walker, but he blazed his shot over the bar and this proved the last action of the match.

A point a piece in the end and I am sure both managers will be happy enough to take the positives from the game, especially Alan Archibald given his team played more than half an hour with ten men.

Despite the scoreline this was a decent game to watch and an enjoyable venue to visit. In the last two decades the club have invested in the ground by building two impressive single tiered stands behind each goal. The design of them both inside and out reminds me of the stands behind each goal at Rugby Park, Kilmarnock, with the exception of the external staircases the latter has.

The North Stand is for the away fans and the South for the home support and it is incorporated into the old Main Stand. It is unique in its lay out in that it runs less than half the length of the pitch and almost slots into the corner to sit with the South Stand. Opposite this is the unused Railway Stand and it is pretty self explanatory why it is called this, as the train line runs behind it and it is quite a busy line! There are currently no seats in it, but I am sure there were seats in it at one point. To help fill the current void, there are a couple of large supporters' flags on display.

When watching any games from Starks Park on television, the gap next to the Main Stand looks as if the houses are literally peering into the ground. Although the locals will be able to see a good bit of the action, when you are outside, you can see there is actually a main road between the ground and the houses, with a wall that has quite a steep drop.

The match programme on sale was from the original fixture date of Saturday 9th February 2013, although I will admit it took me a bit to realise this! I never sampled the food personally but got a few things for the kids and they were not overly impressed. It appeared to be a lot of home made things like rolls, burgers, tea and coffee and based on the lack of change they returned with, it was a little over priced.

On a more positive note, the club's admission price of £20 for parent and child is reasonable and is in line with a number of other clubs in Division One. It was therefore a bit of a surprise when the crowd for this game was announced over the tannoy early in the second half as 1,761, which was lower than I expected.

I would clarify this in saying that this is not a criticism of either club's fans, as there was a good travelling support from Glasgow who were vocal throughout. The highlight being David McGurn getting singled out over the colour of his goalkeeper kit at the start of the second half, with a chant of "who's the f*nny in the pink"!

Raith Rovers 0
Partick Thistle 0
Referee: C. Murray
Attendance: 1,761

KILLIE PIE BUT GRIM ON THE EYE

Kilmarnock 1, St Mirren 1
SPL - Wednesday 3rd April 2013

ANOTHER NIGHT, ANOTHER GAME, as we headed to Ayrshire again for Kilmarnock versus St Mirren at Rugby Park. This is the Paisley side's game in hand, following their recent League Cup Final win over Hearts. It is also the tour boys' sixth game in a week, so fatigue and stadium overdose is creeping in!

Thankfully the venue does not involve too much travelling and we were able to set off post rush hour. Again, this is a ground I have been to a few times before, but not for a good fifteen years and when trying to park anywhere near it, I got a flashback to previous visits!

After a few dodgy turns up streets that were gridlocked with cars, and some 'amber gambler' moments at the traffic lights, we got a space maybe ten minutes or so walk away from the ground. As it goes, it worked out well for the return journey home, as we were on the main route out the town and onto the M77 motorway.

As we approached the ground it was merely minutes before kick off, but I still managed to buy a programme and meet an old work colleague who works as a steward at Rugby Park. I then had to meet another friend who got us a couple of complimentary tickets through the league sponsor, Clydesdale Bank.

We encountered a bit of a jobsworth on the turnstiles, but the situation was eventually resolved and got in just after kick off. We were located in the Moffat Family Stand behind the goal, to the right of the Main Stand. As the game was now already underway we just took up seats anywhere and opted for a spot to the right of the goal, which provided a decent view.

Kilmarnock were looking to cement their place in the top six, before the final round of fixtures occur this weekend when the league splits into two. Manager Kenny Shiels has once again blended in some useful signings, like Sammy Clingan and Kris Boyd, with the talented young players who have broken into the first team this season. The home fans have already seen the likes of Mark O'Hara, Rory McKeown, Jude Winchester and Ross Barbour become regulars in the starting eleven during this campaign.

For this game defender Jeroen Tesselaar played against his former side, Clingan was the midfield anchorman, while Borja Perez supported the forwards Boyd and Paul Heffernan, meaning Cillian Sheridan started on the bench.

In the opposite dugout, Saints boss Danny Lennon was looking to continue the feel good factor with the Paisley side and their fans, after the recent cup triumph. They were at full strength with possibly their strongest available eleven starting this game. Jim Goodwin is the focal point of the defence, with key men in the middle of the park McGowan and Newton along with young John McGinn, and veteran Gary Teale providing the ammunition for Gonçalves and Thompson.

The game was a bit dull for the first quarter of an hour with the first real goal scoring opportunity falling to Kilmarnock on eighteen minutes. A Perez corner on the left was met by the head of Boyd, but the ball went over the bar and the striker knew he maybe should have done better.

No side were really dominating proceedings but it was Killie who were creating the better chances. Saints 'keeper Samson had to look lively when he had to charge out his box to clear a long ball that had been played over his defence. Mark O'Hara then had a shot that went wide of the left hand post without troubling the goalkeeper.

Just before the half hour St Mirren had two great chances to score. First of all, after a run by Dummett on the left, the ball flashed across the goal and Steven Thompson who was sliding in, just failed to connect. Then a ball played through for Gonçalves left him with a great chance to open the scoring, but his low shot ended up going wide of 'keeper Bell's right hand post.

Ten minutes before the break it was the visitors who took the lead and in similar circumstances to the opportunity that was missed just minutes before. A fantastic pass from Van Zanten cut through the centre of the Killie defence and found Gonçalves in space. This time he had the composure to slip the ball under Cammy Bell and into the net to open the scoring.

Instead of getting a reaction from the home players, St Mirren then had a couple of great chances to add to the scoreline. Gonçalves linked well with Thompson, leaving the latter with a clear shot on goal, but he lacked composure and his awful mishit shot went well wide of the target.

Then three minutes before the break it was Gonçalves again who fired a shot from inside the eighteen yard box, which was superbly turned away by Bell for a corner.

Killie ended the half with another chance from a Perez corner, this time from the right hand side and similar to his earlier miss, Boyd put his header wide of the post.

The second half was barely sixty seconds underway when Kilmarnock were level. A defence splitting through pass from Perez put Boyd clean through on goal, and he had the composure to clinically finish low into the bottom left hand corner of the net, leaving Samson with no chance.

The home side dominated the early stages of the restart and nearly scored again moments after equalising, when Dummett cleared the ball for a corner as Boyd was ready to pounce. Killie were getting balls into the box but failing to pick out Boyd or Heffernan. Just after the hour it was Kilmarnock again who threatened to score, when Perez fired a shot just wide from a Garry Hay cut back. Only a couple of minutes later Hay himself got in on the act when he cracked a shot from twenty yards out which dipped just over the bar.

With twenty minutes left St Mirren nearly took the lead again on the counter attack. A Kilmarnock corner was cleared out the penalty area and found McGowan. His run and cross found Gonçalves, but he rushed his effort and it went aimlessly wide of the goal.

With Killie really needing all three points, they pretty much dominated the last fifteen minutes. A ball into the St Mirren box found Boyd, but his close range header was mishit into the ground and was saved by Samson when he really should have scored.

With five minutes left and the Saints camped in their own half, Garry Hay hit another fine strike from just outside the penalty box that Samson did well to save. In the last minute James Fowler found himself with a great chance when he burst into the box, but the onrushing Samson blocked both player and ball, as the home fans screamed in vain for a penalty.

In injury time a Boyd free kick was again well held by Samson and it proved to be the last chance of the game. It ended level and although both managers will each claim they should have won, a draw was probably a fair result over the ninety minutes.

Rugby Park is a decent stadium and certainly one of the best in the Premier League in my opinion. However, despite winning the League Cup in 2012 the club does not seem to get the support it deserves from the locals, meaning some games are poorly attended and there can be a lack of atmosphere.

My first visit here was in the early 1990s when the ground was predominantly terraced, a bit like most football grounds around the UK were at that time. In the last two decades Kilmarnock have heavily invested in the stadium which has seen the rebuilding of three ends.

The East Stand which runs opposite the Main Stand, the Moffat Stand for home fans behind one of the goals and the Chadwick Stand which is used for away supporters behind the opposite goal replaced the old terracing. The latter two are pretty much identical and have a scoreboard on the roof facing.

Once through the turnstiles you have to climb a quite unique set of spiral staircases to get up to your seats.

In recent years the club have utilised the Moffat Stand for families, with reasonable pricing for the top league. The adult price is £17 and a concession is £5. The match programme is also excellent value at £2.50 and contains a lot of good information on the club, the opposition and season statistics past and present.

Depending on the direction you approach the stadium parking can be found close by on local streets or in our case for this game, slightly further out!

Given the venue we could not have visited without sampling the famous 'Killie Pie', which lived up to expectations and the catering is reasonably priced.

I did find some of the local fans we encountered a bit odd though, and some of their language was pretty choice and sometimes unnecessary, given we were in the designated family area!

The game itself was a reasonable spectacle it was still a good ground to visit again and take the kids to.

Kilmarnock 1 (Boyd (47))

St Mirren 1 (Gonçalves (36))

Referee: C.Allan

Attendance: 4,494

ELGIN EDGE THE POINTS

Elgin City 3, Montrose 2
Division 3 - Saturday 13ᵗʰ April 2013

A WORK COLLEAGUE and an avid follower of the grounds tour has been saying that we have been 'playing it safe', alleging there has not been many long distance games attended! Well, the match choice for the second weekend in April saw us head to Borough Briggs, Elgin, for the game between Elgin City and Montrose, which pretty much dispels that myth!

This is quite possibly the furthest place in Scotland I have ever visited, and concede it was not a venue that I approached with much enthusiasm due to the length of the journey. However, it turned out to be a long, but worthwhile day out and we were even home in time to collect the wife from work. Easy!

A lot of pre-match preparation was put in for this one, and morale in the camp slumped when both the AA route planner and the satnav said the run time was four hours, thirty six minutes! As it goes, we actually got there an hour less than that and ended up parked across from the Main Stand at 1.45pm. It would be high fives all round, if I manage to escape receiving a letter from the authorities!

So, with time to spare we set about getting fed and having a walk about. Just along the road is a huge Tesco store and some other shopping outlets. We had a brief scout round both the shops and the ground, before opting to go in early after each tackling a sandwich 'meal deal'!

Elgin City are in their thirteenth year of being a Scottish Football League club, having played in the Highland League throughout most of their one hundred and twenty year history. This season has been quite progressive and they, like their opponents for this game, Montrose, have an excellent chance of getting a Division 3 Play Off place.

We have seen Montrose several times this season, so I am quite familiar with their playing squad now, but Dennis Wyness apart, I am not very knowledgable on the Elgin team. I would highlight however, that I remember the manager, Ross Jack, as a player in the 1980s when he played for Dunfermline Athletic and Kilmarnock. I would also add that, apart from his goal scoring record, I remember him well from the Panini sticker albums of that era!

The home side had Joe Malin in goal, club captain David Niven is the right back and one of the key figures in defence. Brian Cameron and Craig Gunn seemed to be the main men in midfield with Paul Harkins providing support for Daniel Moore and Stuart Leslie.

For Montrose, well they had John Gibson in goal and he seems to have ousted Sandy Wood for the number one jersey in recent weeks. The main men at the back are Stephen McNally and Paul Watson with Lloyd Young and Terry Masson in midfield.

In the games I have seen 'The Gable Endies' this season, one of their key players has been Jamie Winter in the middle of the park and he seems to make them tick. In attack they have Scott Johnston on the wing and also the luxury of the free scoring Martin Boyle, on loan from Dundee.

The sun was out, but it was a bit windy. Both teams knew the importance of a win, so as expected the players on either side were wholehearted in their commitment in trying to get the three points.

Elgin forced an early corner and a free kick but neither really troubled the Montrose defence. At the opposite end, a ball into the Elgin penalty box by Paul Watson found Garry Wood, but his hooked shot from close range went over the bar.

The hosts had a good chance after ten minutes when Montrose attempted to play offside, which left Paul Harkins to fire in a shot that was saved by John Gibson, then cleared to safety by Paul Lunan.

Moments later Elgin nearly opened the scoring when Craig Gunn shot just wide of the left hand post, when the ball landed to him from a Gavin Morrison free kick. Merely seconds later Montrose broke up the park and from close range, Scott Johnston toe-poked his shot just wide, from a Watson cross on the left.

Montrose were starting to press a bit further up the pitch and had a sustained period of pressure. A long ball into the Elgin box saw Sean Crighton clear for a corner to avert the danger, as Wood and Boyle waited to pounce. Home 'keeper Malin then spared skipper David Niven's blushes when he was dispossessed on the right touch line. The ball found its way into the penalty box and Malin saved superbly from a Boyle shot.

Then, from a Montrose corner on the right, the ball bobbled in the box as the Elgin defence struggled to clear their lines. A Garry Wood header forced Malin into another excellent save, before the ball was cleared for a throw in.

Just before the half hour mark we got the first goal of the afternoon and Elgin could have no complaints. A nicely weighted pass by Garry Wood cut through the home defence and was latched onto by Terry Masson. As 'keeper Malin advanced, Masson knocked the ball under him with the outside of his foot to open the scoring.

Elgin hit back minutes later when a shot from the edge of the eighteen yard box by Paul Harkins was well held by John Gibson. Five minutes from the break, Elgin had another chance when a Niven throw in on the right found Stuart Leslie, who turned in the box, but again Gibson was equal to his left foot drive. Two minutes before the break Elgin's perseverance paid off, when a good move down the left hand side resulted in an equaliser. Daniel Moore played a ball through for Paul McMullan and from a relatively tight angle and only the goalkeeper to beat, he buried his shot into the far corner of the net to even things up.

The sides went in level at the break in what was a really entertaining first half. A draw was probably about right, based on possession and goal scoring opportunities. There were problems though for Montrose who were forced into two changes at the break. Jamie Winter, who was toiling in the latter part of the first period, was replaced by Ross McCord and goalkeeper John Gibson, who had a good half, made way for Sandy Wood.

It probably had nothing to do with the substitutions, but it was Montrose who started the brighter at the start of the second period. Two minutes in, Lloyd Young tried a speculative over head shot that was saved by Joe Malin. On fifty minutes Montrose were back in front and it was a well-worked goal. Some nice hold up play in midfield resulted in a pass from Masson on the right, through the centre of the Elgin defence. It was picked up by Scott Johnston and he clipped the ball over Malin and into the net to make it 2-1.

Both teams were trying to move up the park but tended to cancel each other out. The game hit a spell when play was constantly interrupted by petty fouling and a couple of bookings for Masson and Johnston of Montrose.

Just after the hour Elgin City were level again, and what a strike it was. A move on the right wing saw the ball played to Stuart Leslie about twenty five yards from goal. He controlled the ball but had maybe taken on too many players. As he was about to lose the ball, he stretched to get a pass into the path of Paul Harkins, just outside the eighteen yard box. Hitting the ball first time and with little back lift, it crashed high into the net leaving 'keeper Sandy Wood with no chance.

Seven minutes after the equaliser Elgin had a good half chance from close range but Craig Gunn put his shot over the bar. Five minutes after that, Gunn was involved again, as his shot inside the box was blocked by Alan Campbell and from the rebound, McCord did well to block Paul Harkins' follow up.

Elgin dominated most of the second half but their decision making and final ball let them down at vital times. With the scores level, I think some fear of losing crept into both teams play and neither side really forced any clear cut chances, until three minutes from the end.

An Elgin attack saw captain David Niven in unfamiliar territory, up supporting the forwards. He had the ball in the box, turned, and although there was maybe some contact, I am unsure if it was enough to give a penalty. The referee, Matt Northcroft, thought otherwise and awarded the spot kick.

We made our way round behind the goal, along with many other fans, before it was taken. Paul Harkins stepped up and buried his kick into his bottom right hand corner, sending Sandy Wood the wrong way to give Elgin a 3-2 lead.

Apart from a Paul Watson shot for Montrose that went over the bar, there was no further action and the game ended with all three points staying at Borough Briggs, which delighted a majority of the 777 in attendance.

I always have an open mind when visiting a ground for the first time, and as previously stated, the only thing putting me off Borough Briggs was the travelling. This was an excellent venue, coupled with a really decent game of football, and is definitely one of the best visited to date.

We opted to stand behind the home goal, and latterly at the corner next to the covered terracing.

As you enter the ground there are people handing out team sheets and selling the half time draw tickets. Tucked away in a corner was a guy taking in season ticket vouchers and selling the match programme, yet some say men cannot multitask! Next to this there are toilets and a food outlet, so again, like some other grounds visited this season, all the facilities are quite close together.

In all four corners of the ground there are open spaces where young kids played football, with one side even having small goal nets! It was great to see so many of them wearing Elgin City home and away kits and inviting other locals of similar age to join in. Behind both goals there is some new looking terrace area on grass embankments.

The terracing opposite the Main Stand runs pretty much the length of the pitch, but it has a lot of supporting poles underneath the roof, which partly obstruct your view of the pitch.

The Main Stand is small and quite unique looking, with it situated centrally, leaving standing room or limited terrace space for spectators on either side of it. The dug outs are also intriguing as they are placed either side of the Main Stand and it looked like the Elgin back room staff were sitting in with the home fans!

I found the town a pleasant, clean and quiet place, with the people we met friendly and helpful. From our position inside the ground we could see the car, so it meant we were on our way home, literally seconds after full time.

After a few miles down the road, I was busy listening to BBC Sportsound when I became aware of the kids counting. I eventually asked what they were doing, only to be told they were counting the vast assortment of dead birds and animals at the side of the road! Each to their own I suppose.

Elgin City 3 (McMullan (43), Harkins (62), (Pen 88))
Montrose 2 (Masson (28), Johnstone (51))
Referee: M. Northcroft
Attendance: 777

Stenny Stun South

Stenhousemuir 2, Queen of the South 1
Division 2 - Tuesday 16th April 2013

WE WERE BACK AT OCHILVIEW AGAIN, to take in Stenhousemuir's re-arranged midweek home game against newly crowned Division 2 champions and Ramsdens Cup winners, Queen of the South. This is a venue that was visited in November last year, when East Stirlingshire were playing Berwick Rangers, however, having seen the tenant, there was a compulsion to visit the landlord as well!

We went a slightly different way on the approach to the ground this time, not through choice you understand, the woman on my phone app guided us! With the road next to the ground quite busy, we ended up parking further away than the last time, but it was still a relatively short walk and we got there a good fifteen minutes before kick off.

After a quick bite to eat at the snack bar, there seemed to be more space over on the far side of the ground, which is normally for the away fans, so we sat in there.

Stenhousemuir, known as 'The Warriors', are still in contention for a Play Off place, while Queens have won the league at a canter, but were wanting to keep their winning sequence going. The host's manager is former Motherwell and Kilmarnock defender, Martyn Corrigan. He has a good squad made up of young players and experienced pros in key positions like Chris Smith in goal, David Rowson in midfield, Darren Smith on the wing and John Gemmill their target man up front.

Unfortunately for Corrigan, he had to to do without the services of Brown Ferguson and Stuart Kean who were absent through injury.

We saw Queen of the South play in the Ramsdens Cup Semi Final last October and they just grew stronger as the season wore on. Their management duo of Allan Johnston and Sandy Clark have proved a very good combination and they too have a fine blend of players for this division or higher.

Lee Robinson is the regular goalkeeper, Chris Mitchell and Chris Higgins are two of the main men at the back, with Stephen McKenna and Danny Carmichael influencing the midfield. The goal threat would be from top scorer, and son of the Assistant Manager, Nicky Clark, who would be partnered by Derek Lyle in attack. The veteran defender Ryan McGuffie was on the bench while former Aberdeen midfielder Derek Young was not in the squad.

As the game got under way both teams started purposefully and it was the visitors who had the first chance after five minutes. A ball played through for Derek Lyle to chase, saw Stenny 'keeper Chris Smith react quickest and he smothered the ball from the striker's feet.

Darren Smith had a half chance for Stenhousemuir a couple of minutes later but his right foot shot went over the bar. Just before a quarter of an hour, it looked to be business as usual for Queens. Nicky Clark had the ball in the net with a header from a free kick, however the stand side Assistant had already flagged for offside.

Along with really bright sunshine on one side, there was also a strong wind which was affecting the players ability to pass the ball at times. The strange thing was, that in spite of this, both teams continued to play long passes, which was not pleasing either set of supporters.

The tactics by both teams saw them press high up the park, meaning that when balls were played up to the forwards, there were quite a few offside decisions made. Nicky Clark then had a shot blocked and Derek Lyle fired wide for Queens, while at the other end Nicky Devlin was unlucky with a drive from twenty yards out after a good passing move.

Just before the half hour mark Stenhousemuir opened the scoring and it came out of nothing. A ball was played through to Darren Smith, at the edge of the box and with his back to goal, he swivelled and fired a low, left foot shot into the net past Lee

Robinson.

Queen of the South were slow to respond but ten minutes from the break Nicky Clark collected the ball on the left and got a shot in that was deflected wide for a corner. Five minutes later Stenhousemuir nearly doubled their lead when Jamie Reid's right wing cross had Robinson scrambling but the ball dropped just over the bar.

Just before the break Queen of the South created another chance when a good run by Lyle on the right saw him square the ball to Patrick Slattery, but his effort at goal was comfortably held by Smith.

It looked as though Stenhousemuir would be taking their lead into the half time interval, but they gave away a foul some twenty five yards out. Chris Mitchell calmly stepped up and curled an unstoppable free kick into the top left hand corner to equalise, giving Chris Smith absolutely no chance. Over the balance of play it was probably no more than they deserved.

During the break my youngest turns to me, and out the blue, says that he would reluctantly consider playing for Norwich City! Where it came from I have no idea, but he clearly has ideas well above his station!

Having lost that goal right on half time it would have come as no surprise if it had affected the Stenhousemuir players. As it goes, the players came out as hungry as they had been in the first half and nearly took the lead again seconds after the restart. A ball was played through for John Gemmill but Robinson got there ahead of the striker to clear.

Just after that Queen of the South had a good opportunity to score, when Nicky Clark brushed off a defender and unselfishly squared a ball back for Derek Lyle, but he shot wide of the post. Danny Carmichael, for the visitors, also took the ball for a run and squared it, when he really should have taken a shot himself.

Stenhousemuir's only real notable chance came from Darren Smith, when he shot just over the bar from a David Rowson pass. Both teams were having spells of possession without really dominating. With just over twenty minutes left Derek Lyle again had a chance for the visitors from close range but shot just wide of the post from a tight angle.

As the game entered the last quarter of an hour Stenhousemuir took the lead again. Having scored in the first half, Darren Smith then turned provider, when his right wing cross picked out Sean Dickson unmarked in the box. He showed great composure to bullet a header into the top corner past the helpless Lee Robinson. Minutes later Stenny 'keeper Chris Smith twice came to the rescue when he saved from Nicky Clark in a one on one situation, and also blocked the follow up to maintain their lead.

The home defence were well marshalled and reacted quickest to block a Chris Mitchell shot near the very end of the game and deal with the subsequent corner. The ball was bouncing in and around the home penalty box but 'keeper Smith was equal to Lyle's tame header.

Stenhousemuir saw out two minutes of stoppage time and although Queen of the South had a couple more long throw ins and corners, their winning run came to an end, as the Warriors claimed the three points.

Ochilview is quite an accessible venue and easy to find. As mentioned in the write up from the East Stirlingshire game last year, there is not much detailed information to provide. There is really only one way into it, which is like a lane off a side road. Once there, the turnstiles are facing you, or you can walk past the Main Stand to the far side and enter at that end.

The Main Stand is small and does not run the full length of the pitch. A lot of the seats are marked 'Reserved' or with people's names on them, which can potentially limit your seating options. For games that draw small crowds, I am unsure if the club open the terracing behind the goals. There were 504 fans at this game and standing there did not appear to be an option available to fans.

Opposite the Main Stand, there are the dug outs and a high fence, with some car parking spaces and housing behind it. To the right, it is also fenced off with a five-a-side pitch adjacent. For a couple of televised games at Ochilview this season there have been some limited standing space in the above areas, meaning that the ground capacity of just over 5,200 has been fully maximised.

From the two games we have attended at Ochilview, both sets of supporters have mingled without any animosity. Once in the ground the toilets are on your right hand side, the club merchandise is sold from a small hut facing you and there is a programme seller situated next to it. The programme itself is basic but informative and very reasonably priced at £1.50.

The food bar is situated on the left and has a good selection on offer at very reasonable prices. If I had any criticism it would be the admission charges. I did contact the club in advance of the game, but unfortunately received an almost discourteous, unhelpful response. At £13 for adults and £8 concessions, I felt this was over priced, suffice to say it was not the best value we have had in Division 2 so far this season.

Stenhousemuir 2 (Smith (28), Dickson (72))
Queen of the South 1 (Mitchell (44))
Referee: C. Charleston
Attendance: 504

No Glory At Galabank

Annan Athletic 0, Stirling Albion 1
Division 3 - Saturday 20th April 2013

AT THE VERY END OF DECEMBER last year, we had pinpointed traveling down for Annan Athletic's home game against Elgin City. However, it was the Christmas holidays, I had watched the classic Gene Hackman film, "The French Connection", and fallen back asleep again! By the time I resurfaced it left us short of time to get down to the Borders, so the plan to visit the Galabank Stadium was put on hold.

So, four months on, we have finally made it down for Annan's home game against Stirling Albion. We got a decent run in the car and in surprisingly very warm, pleasant conditions. It is not a ground visible from distance but what guided us was the music blaring from the tannoy which could be heard in the distance! It is situated on a bit of a slope, so after a quick pass by we doubled back and parked up a street, merely a few minutes walk from the ground itself.

With a good half hour before kick off, I stopped to take a couple of pictures then headed down to see about getting in. On arrival at the entrance you are greeted by staff signposting you over to a booth to pay cash and get a ticket for entry. The staff on the turnstiles do not take cash payments and the set up is very similar to the one used at Partick Thistle.

As we got through the turnstiles there were some women collecting for a cancer charity. We made a donation and were advised to check out the home baking they were also selling. I left my youngest to choose a few cakes for us all and despite a wide variety available, he proceeded to buy possibly the worst ones there!

We opted to stand in the far right corner of the ground, which was next to the player's tunnel. We caught the latter part of the warm up and the game kicked off shortly afterwards. Both sides are familiar to us having seen them play already this season, and both have had mixed fortunes on the park.

Annan Athletic were formed in 1942, and have played most of their football in English regional leagues and latterly in the Scottish Juniors. They became a member club of the Scottish Football League in 2008, following the collapse of Gretna FC and were then inducted into Division 3.

Last summer the club opted to change the playing surface from grass to a modern generation of astro turf. This would give the club an opportunity to generate funds by hiring the pitch out to local teams in the community.

The team manager is Jim Chapman who has been in charge since the turn of this year, replacing Harry Cairney who had spent six years at the helm. Annan have had some mixed results so far this season, although their form has picked up in recent weeks.

Their main players are goalkeeper Alex Mitchell, centre half Martin McNiff, who is on loan from Dumbarton, midfielder Scott Chaplain and forwards, Michael Daly and David Hopkirk. On the bench they could call upon Harry Monaghan and Ally Love, with the latter player making a significant contribution to the team this season with his goals.

Stirling Albion on the other hand have had a much improved 2013 and after a few weeks of postponed matches in February, due to the weather, they have lost only twice since, to in-form sides Berwick and Peterhead.

Manager Greig McDonald had David Crawford in goal, replacing the recent first choice, Sam Filler. The experienced duo, Kieran McAnespie and Jamie McCunnie were at the back, the industrious Scott Davidson and Josh Flood in midfield, along with Jordan White and Stephen Day, the first choice strikers for this game. Similarly, 'the Beano's' had two useful players on their bench in striker Graham Weir and winger Phil Johnston.

The game was barely two minutes old when, after the first real meaningful attack from either side, we had the opening goal. A Stirling free kick on the half way line was flighted deep into the Annan box, and although a number of players jumped in an attempt to win the ball, it evaded both defenders and forwards. Lurking at the back post was Stephen Day and his header seemed to hang in the air and dropped over 'keeper Alex Mitchell into the far corner of the net to give Stirling the lead.

Annan had a lot of possession after the goal but the best they could muster was a dangerous cross, which was cleared for a corner and a shot from distance by Hopkirk, which failed to trouble the Albion defence.

On the twenty minute mark Stirling then carved out a couple of decent opportunities in quick succession. Scott Davidson tried a chip shot from the edge of the eighteen yard box which went wide of the right hand post, before Mark Ferry shot past the opposite post, following a nice passing move down the left wing.

On the half hour Albion 'keeper Crawford dived bravely at the feet of Annan's Jordan McKechnie, following a cross in from the right wing. The home side put a couple of decent crosses into the box but there were no takers. At the other end, Annan then broke up a decent Stirling move and cleared a Josh Flood cross. Right at the end of the half a nice chest lay off by Annan striker Michael Daly, inside the eighteen yard box, gave McKechnie another chance to score but his shot went just over the bar.

There was no further action as referee Colin Steven brought the first half to an end. During the interval the sparse group of Stirling Albion fans seemed to disappear from behind the goal at the away end, only to re-emerge ten minutes later. They had gone onto the five a side pitch behind the terrace for a kick about!

From the restart it was Stirling who were probably the better of the two sides and having forced a couple of free kicks and a corner, they nearly doubled their lead ten minutes into the second half. Jordan White struck a direct free kick from twenty five yards out against the bar and as players anticipated the rebound, it went out for a goal kick.

Just after the hour both teams made substitutions. Graham Weir replaced the injured Scott Davidson for Stirling and Annan made a double switch, with Ally Love and Harry Monaghan coming on for

Jordan McKechnie and Steven Sloan respectively. The substitutes did not really have the desired effect as chances created were still few and far between. Stirling had a free kick from a similar position to the last one when they hit the bar, but this time it was crossed into the box and cleared.

With fifteen minutes to go Ally Love hit a shot which went well wide and bounced into the terrace. My youngest lad collected the ball and threw it back on the pitch. It made his day and with the exception of the White shot that hit the bar, it was one of the few memorable moments of the second half!

As the game entered the closing stages a Stirling Albion cross on the left was cleared to safety and at the other end a Love corner for Annan caused some consternation for the Albion defence, before being cleared.

In the last minute Annan substitute Andrew Donnelly, who had replaced David Hopkirk just minutes earlier, had a half chance but having initially controlled the ball well, he put his shot over the bar. This resulted in Stirling 'keeper David Crawford screaming at his defence and he took his time with the resultant goal kick. A heckler from the crowd shouted "hurry up you, av got a night oot tae go tae!" Crawford turned round and shouted back "so have I". Given that Annan were losing, it was good to see that some of the support still had a sense of humour!

Just after the goal kick the final whistle blew and Stirling Albion left with all three points. It was not great to watch and it was unfortunate that the fixture happened to be between two sides that were not likely to make the Play Offs, leaving them with not much to play for.

The Galabank Stadium is a modern venue, which is quite compact, with a capacity of just over 2,000. The main entrance leads you through to the home support area and has a different set up to anything seen so far this season.

There is a yellow container which is the club shop and is also where you can buy the match tickets and programme. Across from this, there is a dug out which is also like a bus shelter and was occupied by a handful of older supporters when we passed it!

You also have the toilets and food kiosk on the left hand side. Once through the turnstiles you are on the terrace behind the goal, with the option of going into the Main Stand on the left hand side. It is quite small and does not run the full length of the pitch, with approximately twenty feet of standing space on either side of it. The dug outs are situated on either side of the stand, meaning the supporters are pretty much on top of the back room staff!

Opposite the Main Stand is a large fence and there is no space or capacity to contain spectators. Behind the opposite goal, it is used for away fans and is pretty much identical to the home end, with the five a-side pitch next to it. One thing that was evident during the game was the amount of times the ball went out the ground. I reckon this happened four or five times and may cause frustration depending on how impatient a person you are!

From the people in the local shops to the people we met inside and outside the ground, Galabank is a very welcoming, hospitable place. The attendances are normally around the four hundred mark, but at £10 for adults, £5 for concessions and under 12s going free it is very good value.

On our travels this season we haven't seen Annan take as much as a point and I am sure some fans would probably wish we would stay away! The game was certainly not the greatest seen to date, but proved to be a very enjoyable visit none the less.

Annan Athletic 0
Stirling Albion 1 (Day (2))
Referee: C. Steven
Attendance: 488

Horror Show At Hibernian

Hibernian 0, Aberdeen 0
SPL - Monday 22nd April 2013

FROM ALL THE GROUNDS I have visited over the years, Easter Road for some reason had escaped me! However, we are through in Edinburgh for the ESPN Live Monday night showing of Hibernian versus Aberdeen.

I had been advised by a native from the capital, that I may be better getting the train to Leith due to the traffic. I thought it may be quieter on the roads as it was outwith the weekend, but that was to be a grave error of judgment. I left work early to go home and change, and had a rough idea of when to be on our way, for what was a 7.30pm kick off. What I was also counting on, was that the kids would have been fed, suffice to say that was not the case!

We made good progress through Glasgow but then got snarled up in the Leith rush hour traffic. By the time we were near the ground it was ten minutes before kick off and we still had to collect the tickets. I eventually ditched the car just up from the ground, on London Road and we did a power walk down to the ticket office!

The game was just about to kick off as we queued outside, I took a quick couple of pictures and we went into the Main Stand. The tickets we had were for near the half way line allegedly, but we just took the closest vacant ones available.

The games between both teams this season have not yielded many goals, however it had all the hallmarks of being a decent spectacle due to recent events at both clubs. Last weekend Hibernian came from three goals down to Falkirk at Hampden Park, in the Scottish Cup Semi Final, to eventually win 4-3. It meant a second successive Cup Final appearance for manager Pat Fenlon as he seeks to rectify the shambles that was last season's showpiece against city rivals Hearts.

In the other dug out, Derek McInnes was in charge for the

first time following his recent appointment as Dons Manager, after Craig Brown announced his retirement.

Hibs have relied again on their talisman, Leigh Griffiths, this season, not only for his goals but his presence and all round contribution to the team. At the other end, they also have possibly the best goalkeeper at Easter Road for a few years in Englishman Ben Williams. At the back, James McPake is a regular in the centre of defence, a guy who has impressed me and disappointed in almost equal measure. There have been moments he can control and hold the defence together like a Franco Baresi, then give the ball away, mis-time a challenge and look more like Frank Spencer!

At the end of February this year, midfielder Kevin Thomson returned to Hibernian, the place it all began for him, following his release from Middlesbrough. Having had an injury ravaged couple of years on Teeside, he was initially training with the Hibs first team but signed a contract in March to play for free, until the end of the season.

For this game, Pat Fenlon had to do without the suspended Ryan McGivern, along with Paul Cairney and Scott Robertson, who were injured. Youngsters Alex Harris and Danny Handling started in midfield, with Eoin Doyle partnering Griffiths up front.

Aberdeen made only two changes from their last match, with Clark Robertson and Rob Milsom replacing Gary Naysmith and Scott Vernon. The Dons can call upon the experience of goalkeeper Jamie Langfield, along with Russell Anderson and Mark Reynolds, on loan from Sheffield Wednesday, at the back. Their main player in midfield is Gavin Rae, with the creativity in the side coming from Jonny Hayes and Niall McGinn quite possibly Aberdeen's player of the year.

We got seated, literally a couple of minutes just after kick off, with Hibs starting possibly the brighter of the two sides. The pitch looked a bit dry and rutted in places and the ball spent a lot of time in the air, which was surprising as both managers do tend to try and play on the deck, but this was maybe a 'Plan B' tactic due to the pitch. After a quarter of an hour played there were a couple of crosses into the box for Aberdeen by McGinn and Hayes, neither of which found Josh Magennis or a red shirted player. Hibs then had a half chance when Thomson's free kick on the half way line was flicked on by McPake in the box for Griffiths. However, he went for the spectacular overhead kick which went wide of Langfield's goal.

With twenty-five minutes played Hibs had a great opportunity to break the deadlock. A high ball played over the Aberdeen defence was latched onto by Leigh Griffiths, and although he maybe could have taken the ball in further, his powerful drive was parried by Jamie Langfield, then cleared.

Both sides were playing high up the park, meaning that any decent through pass or high ball over the top, resulted in the Assistants flagging for offside. It was grim to watch, and the thought that this match was being beamed around the globe was enough to give you the fear! It proved to be almost twice as bad for the ESPN camera man on the near touch line. The ball was cleared into the stand and a fan threw it back onto the pitch. With the camera man's focus being on the game, he would have got the fright of his life as it whacked him on the back of the head!

There were no other incidents of note, and referee, Steven McLean thankfully brought the first half to an end. Maybe the half time "10 second challenge" would brighten things up? Unfortunately, no, this proved to be much in line with the first half action! One of the participants was an older looking gent, wearing what looked like various bits of retro kit of the Pat Stanton and Arthur Duncan era! There were no goals produced and it was reminiscent of the episode in 'Father Ted' when they had the over 75s five-a-side football championship!

The second half got underway and it started similarly to the first, with Hibs the better side. Three minutes in, Jamie Langfield made a comfortable save from Handling's side foot shot, following a good cut back from Griffiths on the left wing. Ten minutes later Hibs again threatened when a Clancy cross was met by Doyle, but his shot came off the post and was cleared.

Aberdeen were clearly needing to alter their game plan, and just after the hour Derek McInnes made a positive double change, with midfielder, Peter Pawlett replacing Milsom and Vernon on for Magennis. Alex Harris went close for the home side when his shot from the edge of the box was blocked by Shaughnessy. With fifteen minutes left it was Hibs who again nearly scored. Griffiths' right wing corner was headed goal wards by Paul Hanlon but Pawlett was well positioned on the goal line to clear.

Aberdeen had created very little opportunities in the whole game, let alone the second half, with Niall McGinn bordering anonymous. With ten minutes left, having been involved at one end moments before, Hanlon was back at the other, clearing a Hayes cross before Vernon could get his head on it.

On eighty-six minutes Leigh Griffiths conjured up a bit of magic, when he found himself out on the right hand side some thirty yards from goal. There did not appear to be any danger, but the space opened up and his rasping shot at goal forced Langfield into a decent save. There were no further chances for either side, the game finished goalless and the two minutes of added time could not come quick enough! It meant an unbeaten start and a clean sheet for Derek McInnes, though Hibs probably deserved to win the match based on possession and chances created.

Given it was live on television, this was not the greatest advert for the SPL, yet I have been at worse games so far this season. The crowd of 8,326 was slightly disappointing but some of the patter where we sat was good and the atmosphere was decent I thought, with a lot of the noise generated by Hibs' 'Sect 43 fans' group who were high up in the East Stand.

You could argue that it was end of season fare, post split and nothing to play for, but that was not the case. Hibs have players looking to gain a starting place in the Scottish Cup Final and Aberdeen have a number of players out of contract in the summer and looking to impress the new manager.

I have to say I was quite impressed with the now complete, new look Easter Road stadium. Situated just off busy roads and densely populated housing and shops, it has a very plush, modern look about it both inside and out, befitting of any twenty first century football stadium. It has been a job in progress, with each stand being built at various times and some years apart since the mid 1990s.

During the 1994/95 season work began on both the North and South Stands, which are the areas behind both goals. The North Stand, which is to the left if you were standing at the Main Stand or viewing on television, is for the home support and was renamed "The Famous Five Stand" shortly after completion, as a tribute to the successful Hibernian side of the 1950s.

Both are two tiered and have a slightly strange appearance in the respect that they look as if a corner has been cut off (see photo). I am unsure if this was to do with the angle of where the stadium is situated, building design or planning permission issues. Maybe by having more Perspex than seats, it would allow in more sunlight for the pitch, I will need to clarify with the handful of 'Hibees' that I know!

The old (West) Main Stand was rebuilt and completed in 2001 and is where we watched this game from. Again, this is a two tiered structure that contains corporate seating and is where the tunnel and dug outs are situated. The last piece of the stadium jigsaw was the new 6,500 seater East Stand, replacing the old terracing in 2010. This is a steep, single tier stand designated for the home supporters and given the sound generated from it, this is where the 'singing section' is.

The admission prices were slightly reduced for this game, with adult tickets £20 instead of £22 and concessions £10 instead of £12, which is reasonable by SPL standard. The food prices are also in line with other clubs in the division, which are over priced in my opinion and is a subject that has been covered already in other stadium write ups! The staff we spoke with at the main entrance and the ticket office were helpful and friendly which is always a good start. Getting to Easter Road can be difficult and getting stuck in traffic was probably the only downside of an otherwise very good stadium visit.

Hibernian 0, Aberdeen 0

Referee: S. McLean - Attendance: 8,326

Blues Hedge Their Bets

Brechin City 2, Stranraer 2
Division 2 - Tuesday 23rd April 2013

SO WE FINALLY MADE IT to Glebe Park, Brechin, for the midweek Division 2 fixture between Brechin City and Stranraer. This is one of many recent re-arranged fixtures for the home side, following drainage problems with the pitch, which have led to a raft of postponements and a fixture headache. We had made plans to visit here on three previous occasions in the last couple of months, but each time the game has been called off due to the aforementioned drainage issue. In fact, the situation has been that bad that Brechin had to play a match recently at Station Park, which is the home of local rivals Forfar Athletic.

Again, this was a meticulously planned journey, with an early finish from work to ensure some progress was made through the rush hour traffic. As it goes, it went so well we were parked on the main road just along from the ground at 7pm, giving us ample time for a look around. It was a lovely, bright night, ideal for watching or playing football. Having strolled round a couple of the local shops in town, we then decided to go into the ground early, taking a couple of pictures outside the main entrance beforehand.

Outside the turnstiles it states the admission prices, with parent and child listed as £12. However, the young guy tried to charge us £18 before I highlighted what the sign, which is fastened to the wall outside, said! Another young guy then came up and said the price was £15. I am not sure if they were at it, but we ended up paying it just to get in!

From there, we walked through on the right hand side to the Main Stand and crossed the tunnel area, surprisingly unchallenged by the stewards. This leads you out to the club shop on the far right hand corner. It is a small but adequate sized out-house, that caters for the average Brechin City fan's needs.

It is wall to wall with replica shirts, jackets, old programmes and various other bits of club memorabilia. I was very impressed and in my element! It was at this point I asked about a match programme for this game, only to be informed that they do not do one anymore as it is not cost effective for the club. This is a real shame but the club still provide a decent free colour team sheet none the less.

I then got talking to Fergus, who works in the shop and he regaled us with some of his own football memories. He is something of a grounds enthusiast as well, so it was good to speak with someone with a similar interest.

It was approaching kick off so we went to leave, but before we left, Fergus gave my lad some Brechin City stationery which was very much appreciated. I can confirm that I have since bagged the pen and have been using it at work!

As the game was now under way, we watched on from behind the goal at the home end and gradually made our way along the hedge side touch line. Brechin are under the stewardship of former Dundee United and Nottingham Forest midfielder, Ray McKinnon, having replaced Jim Weir in the post last October. After a difficult start to the season Brechin went on a fine winning run that has put them into third place and almost guaranteeing them a Play Off place.

We saw Brechin play at East Fife in January when both sides fought out a competitive 2-2 draw. For this game, veteran goalkeeper Craig Nelson was between the sticks and the main men in defence being Gerry McLaughlan and Ewan Moyes. The midfield had the industrious pair of Gary Fusco and Johnny Stewart, with the responsibility of scoring goals resting on Andy Jackson and Alan Trouten. Brechin were also fortunate to have some experience they could utilise on their substitutes bench, in David McKenna and Garry Brady. Back in February we were down at Stair Park, Stranraer, when they were also up against East Fife! They were on form that day, comfortably winning 4-1, though they currently find themselves battling at the bottom end of the table.

Stranraer has been home to the current manager, Stephen

Aitken, for some time. He actually lived quite near me years ago, when he was starting out in the game and is in his second spell at the club in all capacities. Having been a player at the club for six years in the early millennium, he was appointed Assistant Manager to Keith Knox in 2009. Aitken then replaced Knox at the helm in October last year

The Stranraer goalkeeper is David Mitchell and even after this game I am still none the wiser as to what it is he shouts at his defence! In front of him are Lloyd Kinnaird and Michael Dunlop, the main men in defence, along with the boss's brother, Chris Aitken, who plays a holding midfield role. The side has some pace on the wing through Sean Winter and good attacking options also, with players like Craig Malcolm and Robert Love.

When we saw them nearly three months ago, Darren Gribben had just returned to the club and he scored two of Stranraer's four goals but he was on the bench for this game. Joining him was crowd favourite, Michael Moore, meaning there was a place up front for the far travelled Armand One. The big Frenchman has played in the lower leagues of both Scotland and England for what seems like years. Now thirty years old, he is a man mountain and although he was a figure of fun at times for some of the home fans, the Brechin defenders struggled to cope with him while he was on the field.

The game took a while to get going, with neither side really stamping their authority on it. The first time a goalkeeper was called into action was after a quarter of an hour when Nelson comfortably held a shot on the left from Stranraer's Mark Staunton.

A couple of minutes later Andy Jackson collected the ball from a Brechin throw in and his left foot drive, from just outside the area, was turned away by Mitchell for a corner. On twenty two minutes Brechin were on the attack again, this time it was Ryan Ferguson with an effort at goal, following good play down the right by Ryan Stewart, but Mitchell was equal to it.

Even though the pitch was not the greatest, both teams did try and play short passes instead of lumping it up field, though there were quite a few stray passes at times. Brechin were playing high up the field and Stranraer were thwarted by their offside trap a couple of times. Ten minutes before the break the hosts had a great opportunity to open the scoring from a Ryan Stewart corner on the right. It was met by the head of Ewan Moyes, who rose highest, but the ball went just over the bar.

Five minutes after that Stranraer created a similar opportunity when Sean Winter's right wing corner found Michael Dunlop, whose shot was saved by Nelson. The visitors were applying pressure to the Brechin back line and Grant Gallagher was unlucky when his shot from distance just cleared the bar.

Then, three minutes from the break, Armand One, whose hold up play and lay offs had been impressive, managed to get a shot in from the edge of the box that had plenty of swerve, but was saved by Nelson. As we entered into the last minute of the first half the Stranraer pressure paid off. Sean Winter's cross on the left found Armand One in the box and with his back to goal, he controlled the ball before turning to hook a powerful shot high past Nelson's left hand post to make it 1-0.

It was maybe harsh on Brechin who deserved to be at least level going into the half time break. We had stood at the half way line, next to the famous Glebe Park hedge, to watch the game during the first half. We went over to the food bar next to the big stand, which is behind the home goal and opted to sit in there for the second half. Just before the game resumed one of the Stranraer substitutes fired a shot that hit a seat along from us and it smashed into about forty pieces. I very much doubt he could have achieved this had he tried it again!

The light wind that had been prevalent earlier had died down, which would hopefully help the players too. Brechin made a switch at the break with David McKenna replacing Gary Fusco, but it was Stranraer who asserted the early pressure. Craig Malcolm found himself in a great position to score when he was charging through on Craig Nelson five minutes after the restart. His shot was blocked by the 'keeper and the rebound from Lloyd Kinnaird looked goal bound, but was cleared to safety by Moyes.

Armand One nearly grabbed his and Stranraer's second goal

on fifty five minutes, when his header dropped just over the bar from a Chris Aitken cross on the right wing. The visitors would rue their missed opportunities as Brechin equalised just before the hour mark. A good run and cross by Jonathan Brown on the left was picked up by Andy Jackson whose low right foot shot beat Mitchell at his right hand post to make it 1-1.

Mitchell then turned a Trouten shot away for a corner and a Moyes header went wide of the post, as Brechin pressed for more goals. At the other end, Stranraer had their claims for a penalty waved away by referee Stephen Finnie, after an alleged hand ball in the box from an Aitken cross.

As we entered the last quarter of the game Stranraer made two attacking substitutions a few minutes apart, with Darren Gribben replacing Sean Winter and Michael Moore on for Armand One. Both sides forced a couple of set pieces but did not trouble either defence. With fifteen minutes left Jackson's twenty yard shot was comfortably dealt with by Mitchell in the Stranraer goal. Brechin then made their second change of the evening when Garry Brady replaced Jonathan Stewart, before taking the lead two minutes after that.

A cross on the right was headed against the bar by Andy Jackson. The ball spun up high in the air and Alan Trouten reacted quickest to head in from a yard out and put Brechin into the lead. With the goal coming so late in the game and Brechin looking relatively comfortable, it looked as though they would close the game out. However, there was to be a sting in the tail and it came from a lack of concentration and maybe a bit of complacency in the home defence.

Kinnaird's throw on the right near the Brechin eighteen yard box was not dealt with and the tenacious Craig Malcolm managed to get the break of the ball and bury a shot past Nelson from a very narrow angle to equalise five minutes from the end. It meant the home side's lead lasted only three minutes and it was a moment savoured by the handful of travelling fans.

In the second minute of stoppage time Stranraer again had the ball in the box, but as Craig Malcolm shaped to shoot, the whistle had already gone for a foul. This incident upset the Stranraer bench and it required referee Finnie to go over and calm things down.

With no further action both teams had to settle for a point. Brechin had all but guaranteed their place in the Play Offs beforehand, so the draw cemented this and a third place finish in the table. For Stranraer, it was a vital away point in their battle to avoid the drop into Division 3.

This was a long, almost overdue ground visit, but it was certainly worth the wait. It is an intriguing venue which offers a good view of the pitch no matter where you choose to stand or sit. As you enter through the turnstiles on Trinity Road it takes you to the back of the newest David H. Will Stand, which is all seated with a 1,000 capacity. It has bright coloured seats in yellow, red and blue with BCFC printed on them.

The Main Stand is on the right hand side of this. It is small in size and is almost like a cricket pavilion in appearance. It backs onto the player's tunnel and changing rooms, along with both dug out areas. The club shop is in the right hand corner and there is a covered terrace behind the opposite goal, known as the Cemetery End, as there is a cemetery located directly behind it!

Across from the Main Stand is the famous Hedge Side end. This is a standing area which runs the length of the pitch and has a ten foot hedge running parallel with it and provides an adequate view to watch the game. On the half way line there is a small, elevated television gantry for showing any live matches or highlights.

This was an enjoyable experience and not as rushed as some other midweek fixtures we have attended so far. The staff and people we met were welcoming and friendly, the food was decent and well priced, as was the admission cost. Along with a good game of football, Glebe Park ticks all the boxes with regards to affordability and entertainment and goes down as one of the favourite grounds visited to date.

Brechin City 2 (Jackson (57), Trouten (83))
Stranraer 2 (One (44), Malcolm (86))
Referee: S. Finnie - Attendance: 401

Dens Men Defy The Drop...

Dundee 1, Hearts 0
SPL - Saturday 27th April 2013

LAST MONTH WE TOOK IN our first Dundee derby at Tannadice. We are back in the City of Discovery, this time though we are along the road to Dens Park, for Dundee's home fixture versus Hearts, as they continue their battle to avoid relegation.

Like so many of the SPL stadiums, this is one I was last at in 1998, before the kids were born! Since that time a lot of refurbishment has taken place at Dens, with all the terracing being replaced behind the goals with new all seated stands.

Dundee are a club who I have never really had an opinion on. My memories of them as a kid are of their 1980s strip made by Admiral, and players who graced the jersey like Bobby Geddes, Cammy Fraser, Ian Ferguson, George McGeachie and Jim Duffy. They had some great strikers in their time later that decade, with free scoring players like Tommy Coyne, Keith Wright and Billy Dodds. I always loved listening to long term Dundee supporter and Radio Clyde reporter, Dick Donnelly, referring to the 'Dark Blues' in his distinctive tone.

The club have had two spells in administration since the early Millennium, but have managed to come out at the other end on each occasion. The club finished runners up to Ross County in Division 1 last season and were thrust into the SPL late in the summer to replace Rangers, who had been liquidated.

They were ill prepared for the step up and did not start the season well. By Christmas the team were adrift at the bottom of the table and in early February manager Barry Smith was relieved of his duties. He had done an exceptionally decent job, in very trying circumstances, guiding a young and depleted side through the second spell in administration, but the board felt it was time for change.

The weather was surprisingly great and we had a pretty decent journey getting here, though I damaged an alloy trying to park the car on a side street! The kerb was high, I rushed it, school boy error and lesson learned!

There was a good vibe around the stadium as we wandered round three of the stands and browsed in the club shop. Interim boss, John Brown had been given the job on a permanent basis, twenty four hours earlier and the club had also announced that tickets for this game would be half price. This was a coup for me, as instead of costing £40 for me to get in with the two boys it was only £20. It meant that I could put some of that saving back to the club by buying a couple of things from the official shop.

The tickets we had were for the South Stand, known locally as 'The Derry'. The queues to get in were long and slow and I managed to keep it together, having initially been advised by a young female on the turnstiles that we were in the wrong stand! We eventually did get in and had pretty decent seats to be fair, giving you a good view of both ends of the pitch.

Although the team are anchored at the bottom of the table, momentum has gathered among the Dundee faithful in recent weeks, as optimism about staying in the SPL continues to grow. While the 'Dark Blues' have been in good form and picking up points, second bottom St Mirren have been in free fall since their League Cup win against Hearts last month.

One of Dundee's most consistent performers in the last few weeks has been goalkeeper Steve Simonsen. Having come into a struggling side, under new management and replacing a club legend in Rab Douglas, he has been in excellent form. In front of him, the defence has a good blend of experience, youth and pace with players like Matt Lockwood, Kyle Benedictus, Brian Easton and Lewis Toshney who is on loan from Celtic.

Unfortunately, Gary Harkins, who has been probably the key player in the Dundee midfield recently, was suspended for this game. John Brown could still call upon the likes of Jim McAlister, Kevin McBride and Iain Davidson. Up front, Carl Finnigan started, having missed a lot of the season through injury and he was partnered by John Baird. On the bench, there were options with Colin Nish and new signing from Dunfermline, Andy Barrowman.

For the visitors, well they continue to make more headlines for events happening off the park. The new Hearts manager, Gary Locke, has done a good job of keeping the players focused on their own individual responsibilities, which is playing football.

Jamie MacDonald continues to improve in goal for Hearts, and he was protected by Darren Barr, Andy Webster, Kevin McHattie and Jamie Hamill, who has missed most of the season through injury. The main man for them in the middle of the park is Ryan Stevenson, along with youngsters Jamie Walker, Dylan McGowan and Jason Holt. The front men selected were John Sutton and Michael Ngoo, who is on loan from Liverpool until the end of the season. Neither side had the upper hand in the early stages of the game and it did not get flowing due to a number of petty fouls committed by both sets of players. With just under ten minutes played it was Hearts who had the first real effort on goal, when Jamie Hamill's low effort from twenty yards out was well held by Simonsen.

Just after a quarter of an hour Andy Webster was in possession of the ball for Hearts on the halfway line. He did appear to dwell on the ball and was dispossessed by Finnigan. Webster felt he was fouled, the referee, John Beaton, did not agree and as Finnigan broke away, Webster hauled him to the ground. The Hearts stopper picked up the first yellow card of the game for his troubles and it was to prove significant.

From the resulting free kick, Kyle Benedictus' vicious effort was heading into MacDonald's top left hand corner, but he managed to produce a superb save, turning the ball away for a corner. Less than fifteen minutes after receiving his first booking, Andy Webster was involved in another challenge that earned him his second caution and an early bath. In a similar position to the first incident, he crashed right through the back of Finnigan as they both contested a high ball. Both players received treatment and when Webster was back on his feet, Beaton issued him with the yellow and red cards, leaving Hearts to play more than an hour of the game with ten men. As Webster trudged off the park, he got some friendly chants from the home fans due to him being an ex-Dundee United player!

Sometimes these kind of flash points can make a game interesting, but I find it has the opposite effect in the modern game. Hearts sacrificed Michael Ngoo as they reshuffled their side and basically set the team out not to concede a goal, which tends to be brutal to watch.

Hearts fans then started goading the Dundee fans with chants of 'going down' before they retaliated with 'Hearts are going bust' and 'Albert Kidd' which is in reference to their much publicised financial issues and losing the league title at Dens Park in May 1986.

Dundee forced a couple of corners ten minutes before the break which were taken by Jim McAlister. From the first one, the Hearts defence could only clear the ball to the edge of the eighteen yard box. John Baird managed to get a decent shot in that was deflected wide. McAlister himself then had a tame header at goal, from a cross on the right, which was comfortably saved by Jamie MacDonald.

The last action of the first forty five minutes was a half chance for Hearts, as Jamie Hamill hit another long range effort which went well wide. As much as Dundee maybe had the upper hand, they were lacking a bit of creativity and they had to win to maintain any chance of staying up. The Dundee fans were still in good spirits, more so when news filtered through from Easter Road that Hibernian were leading against St Mirren.

Both managers made changes during and just after the break. Dundee replaced Matt Lockwood with Ryan Conroy, while Hearts introduced Dale Carrick for Jamie Walker. Less than five minutes into the restart it was Dundee who nearly took the lead from an inswinging corner by Conroy. The ball was met by the head of Brian Easton, whose header crashed off the face of the bar before being cleared. Hearts had a couple of breaks up the field and although the Dundee defence looked slightly nervous at times, they never really threatened. I am unsure if the referee, John Beaton, was trying to almost even things up, but he went through a strange ten minute spell where he seemed to penalise Dundee players for the merest of fouls.

Just after the hour mark Dundee made a double change a couple of minutes apart. Colin Nish and Nicky Riley came on for Iain Davidson and John Baird respectively. I think the home side were looking at utilising Riley's trickery and Nish's height as they went in search of a winning goal.

With a quarter of an hour left to play Finnigan shot high over the bar for Dundee, before Ryan Conroy nearly scored with a long range drive. Having collected the ball on the right from a throw in, he strangely moved the ball over to his weaker right foot, before seeing his powerful shot go just wide of the post.

This should have been a warning to Hearts as Conroy was instigating most of Dundee's attacks. As the news came through that St Mirren were now winning against Hibernian, a winner was absolutely essential now for the hosts. With ten minutes remaining they were provided with a decent opportunity, when Stevenson fouled McAlister some thirty yards from goal.

The distance was not ideal but Ryan Conroy stepped up and went for pure power. Keeping his shot low, the ball took a slight nick off the Hearts wall, but it was enough to deceive Jamie MacDonald and the ball ended up in the net. Dens Park erupted, some fans from the South Stand were on the pitch, as stewards attempted to get them off and you could see how much that goal meant to the supporters. The remaining minutes were filled with Dundee trying to keep possession and run down the clock. A roar then went up as news came through that Hibernian had equalised, with the scorer none other than former Dens wonder kid, Leigh Griffiths, with another goal to make it 3-3.

With two minutes left the home side were reduced to ten men themselves as Nicky Riley saw red, following an altercation with McHattie next to the far side corner flag. It looked petulant but Riley lifted his hands and left John Beaton with no alternative but to issue a red card. After four minutes of stoppage time the game ended, with the three points staying on Tayside. St Mirren dropped points, meaning the survival dream remains a possibility and Dundee live to fight another day. We got out promptly and were on our way home, after a short hold up at traffic lights on the way out of town.

The stadium has two ends that are old fashioned and traditional looking, with both areas behind the goal being rebuilt over the last decade. The North Stand is the Main Stand which has a distinguished design and blue roof. It looks as if there is a kink in the middle of its structure, similar to the Main Stand at Wolverhampton Wanderers' Molineux stadium. There are also quite a few supporting pillars which may obscure part of you view. The dug outs are situated at the front of this stand, with the players tunnel in the corner, next to the away end which is the Bob Shankly Stand.

The South Stand is like an old terrace which has had bucket seats fitted and is where we sat for this game. This is where the hardcore support go, I am reliably informed! We were parked up on a street only a few minutes walk away from the Main Stand. Three ends of the ground are all on the same level, however, to get into the South Stand you need to walk down a steep hill that runs behind the Bobby Cox Stand, which is the home end. It is a busy road at the bottom of the hill and is where the turnstiles are located.

The newer stands are single tiered and hold approximately 3,000 each. Today, Dens Park has an all seated capacity of just over 12,000. Similar to Tannadice along the road, there are remains of the old terrace and stairways at either side of the South Stand, which gives it a bit of nostalgia. I think so anyway!

This proved to be a very enjoyable day out in all aspects, from the journey time, pre match wander, the game itself and the drive home. We also caught a break with the discounted ticket prices for this particular match. Dens Park is a decent football venue, with the locals and the staff that we spoke to inside and outside the ground very friendly and helpful. It is definitely more of an SPL stadium than that of a Division 1 side.

Dundee 1 (Conroy (82)), Hearts 0
Referee: J. Beaton - Attendance: 5,896

Celts Well Beaten

Motherwell 3, Celtic 1
SPL - Sunday 28ᵗʰ April 2013

AFTER A FINE DAY OUT in Dundee the day before, it was almost back to normal as we made a visit to an extremely wet Fir Park, Motherwell, for the live Sky Sports lunchtime game. The first time I was at Fir Park was in the early 1980s and again, like so many grounds mentioned before now, the last visit I made here must have been around 1999.

This is a relatively local game, so there was not much traveling involved. It was busy trying to get off the M74 motorway, then again as we got nearer the ground. Although the side street we left the car on was only about five minutes' walk away from the Main Stand entrance, we were soaked through in that time, which made for an uncomfortable experience watching the game.

I had booked the tickets online a fortnight ago, but still had to collect them. The queue was out the door, but thankfully it was for people buying, not collecting, so we waited only a couple of minutes to get served and be on our way. As the damage had already been done with regards to being wet through, we walked round the four stands and took a couple of pictures along the way.

Once we knew what turnstiles we were entering, a small queue had formed. A couple of minutes had passed and it was not moving very fast. Some fans were beginning to lose patience and there were some raised voices with a couple of stewards. It transpired that the turnstile operators were questioning the age of some people trying to gain access to the Family Stand! The extended wait meant that we just got drenched even further!

We got something to eat at the curiously located food counter, which is situated right at the top of a busy stairwell, before going up to our seats, which were near the back of the stand, next to one of the Sky cameras. Just before kick off it was announced over the tannoy that the game would be delayed for fifteen minutes due to one of the 'Cash Converters' advertising hoardings coming loose on the East Stand across from us.

Motherwell have been on a great run of form and are unbeaten since the end of February, leaving them in a strong position to finish second in the table. They have a good team spirit, with a number of key players in the side and were pretty much at full strength for this game. Goalkeeper Darren Randolph has been the regular number one for a couple of years now and is now getting international recognition with the Republic of Ireland.

They have experienced full backs in both Steven Hammell and Tom Hateley, with Shaun Hutchinson being the focal point of the defence. The midfield has the tough tackling pair of Keith Lasley and Nicky Law in the centre, with the pace and skill of Chris Humphrey and James McFadden in the wide areas. The latter has hardly played any games in the last couple of years due to long term injuries, but his form has picked up in recent months and he has been influential in this Motherwell team.

Up front, the industrious Henrik Ojamaa is partnered by SPL top scorer and PFA Player of the Year contender, Michael Higdon. He is taunted about his weight by opposition fans and occasional fellow professionals, but I am a fan of his. There is no doubt about his scoring record, he has a presence in attack, is good in the air and on the deck, and as he has proved already this season, he can score from distance too. The only attribute he is missing is maybe some pace, but he certainly makes up for that with his goals return.

In the opposite dug out Celtic manager Neil Lennon had publicly stated that with the league title now won, his intention is to give some of his players a rest. Those given a break included Kelvin Wilson, Efe Ambrose, Joe Ledley and Kris Commons. Lennon also had to do without the services of long term casualties Adam Matthews and captain Scott Brown along with James Forrest who sat this one out, despite playing last weekend.

Fraser Forster was in goal, Thomas Rogne replaced Wilson in the centre of defence alongside Charlie Mulgrew. The holding midfielders were Beram Kayal and Victor Wanyama, with the width provided by Georgios Samaras and Australian Tom Rogic. Tony Watt started up front with Gary Hooper, meaning that Anthony Stokes was on the bench.

The kick off was not delayed as long as originally thought and the game got going only five minutes behind the original kick off time. Celtic seemed to come out the traps quicker and moved the ball around well.

The first decent chance came in the opening couple of minutes when Rogic received the ball midway through his own half, before hitting a fine long pass over the Motherwell defence. It found Tony Watt in space on the right, though he looked to be at least two yards off side. The young striker controlled the ball well but, under pressure, he put his shot just over the crossbar.

Five minutes later Motherwell then had a great chance to take the lead from a corner. It was taken short between Hateley and Law, before the ball was whipped across the six yard box from Hateley's delivery, but Hutchinson failed to get on the end of it. In fairness to the big defender, I think he anticipated that Wanyama would clear it, but instead the Kenyan made no attempt to win the ball, which put Hutchinson off.

Some good interchange play from Celtic, after quarter of an hour, saw the ball moved across the eighteen yard box from Rogic to Samaras and he laid it off for Kayal, who fired a clean shot at Randolph which the keeper comfortably parried.

At this point there was a farcical situation going on near us with some fans in the stand. A small minority of fans had chosen to stand instead of sitting at kick off, meaning that a lot of others, mainly kids, could not see the game. After a couple of requests for them to sit down, from stewards and nearby supporters, everyone did sit apart from three individuals.

It dragged on for the majority of the first half and they eventually moved seats, but it overshadowed what was a decent start to the game. Had this been any other area of the stadium, I am quite sure someone would have pointed out the error of their ways and the matter would have been resolved!

We were then treated to a moment of magic from James

McFadden, as he rolled back the years. Having received the ball on the left of the Celtic half, he ran at two defenders before cutting into the box, however, he then moved the ball onto his right foot and sliced his shot wide of the right hand post.

The next chance of the game fell to Celtic on the half hour and it was from a set piece in a dangerous position, following a foul by Higdon on Samaras. Charlie Mulgrew on his favoured left foot curled a free kick some twenty five yards from goal but Randolph made it look more difficult than it actually was, with a somewhat theatrical save.

Tony Watt was having an excellent game and again he held the ball up well on the left, before putting in a cross that landed in the six yard box. It fell for the on rushing Hooper, who took it first time, but his side foot volley was expertly blocked by Randolph.

Five minutes before the break Celtic eventually made the breakthrough and it was down to the tenacity of Watt down the left wing again. From inside his own half, Wanyama slipped a ball through for Watt and he accelerated past Simon Ramsden. As the angle narrowed, he managed to clip the ball over the onrushing Randolph to the unmarked Hooper. The Englishman's six yard header hit the face of the bar, but he readjusted his body for the rebound and volleyed into the net past a couple of despairing Motherwell defenders.

It looked as though that would be the only goal of the half, but with one of the last kicks of the ball Motherwell were level. A long pass to the half way line found Lasley, whose first touch was exquisite, taking the ball away from Rogne who foolishly dived in. The midfielder then played a nice pass through for Ojamaa, who held off the attentions of Lustig and Mulgrew to fire past Forster at his near post to equalise.

Based on the chances and possession in the first half, Celtic maybe edged it, but their slackness was punished by a team who were not likely pass up the opportunity to take advantage.

The equaliser seemed to galvanise the Motherwell players and it looked to have had almost the opposite effect on the Celtic team. The second half was only a couple of minutes old when the hosts were awarded a penalty. You could argue it was fortuitous, but none the less it was a penalty every day of the week. A ball played down the right for Ojamaa to chase, saw him get in on Charlie Mulgrew's blind side and as the defender moved for the ball he made contact with the Estonian striker and both players hit the deck. Referee Euan Norris did not hesitate and immediately pointed to the spot. Michael Higdon took the kick and placed it high into the top right hand corner, leaving Forster with no chance and put Motherwell ahead.

Six minutes later the home side extended their lead even further. Some patient play on the right saw Nicky Law roll the ball out to Hateley and he floated a deep cross to the back post from about forty yards out. There was a suspicion that Higdon was offside as the ball was played across, however he had put Lustig under pressure and the big Swede's header came back off his own post, then off the back of the diving Forster and into the net. The Motherwell fans were ecstatic, while the Celtic players and fans looked on bewildered. Having taken the lead, they were now 3-1 down with less than an hour played.

On sixty five minutes Motherwell then had a chance of a fourth goal on the counter attack. Ojamaa collected the ball inside his own half before playing a defence splitting pass down the right for Humphrey to latch onto. The winger cut inside and his shot was deflected off the covering Mulgrew and when the ball spun up in the air, Forster had to look lively to palm the ball away to safety.

Neil Lennon made his first substitution just after this incident, bringing on Paddy McCourt for Thomas Rogne, in an attempt to create more from midfield. The big Norwegian defender had a poor game by his own standards and failed to cope with numerous Motherwell breaks.

Again, Motherwell had a golden opportunity to score on seventy minutes, when they broke up a Celtic corner and raced up the pitch. Ojamaa again collected the ball and knocked it low and long for McFadden on the left to chase. He burst through on goal, but maybe had too much time to decide what to do with the ball and he opted for power, and blasted his shot straight at Forster.

The Celtic defence was almost non existent and McFadden may have been better squaring the ball to Humphrey had he looked up.

A last throw of the dice by Celtic saw McGeouch on for Rogic and Stokes on for Samaras, but they never looked like threatening the home goal. Motherwell themselves made a couple of changes as they looked to close the game out, with Carswell on for McFadden and Francis-Angol replacing Ojamaa.

A Celtic break in the last minute saw Mulgrew play a pass through for Stokes on the left, he held the ball up well and his trundling shot came off the base of the right hand post before it was cleared. There were no further incidents and Euan Norris whistled to end the match. A dominant performance by Motherwell, a pretty dire one from Celtic and the result ensures European football for the Lanarkshire club next season.

We had left right on the final whistle as I wanted to get a match programme from the shop. At least getting it from here ensured I got a dry copy! The wet weather, queue at the turnstiles and the fans standing during the game was unfortunate, however Fir Park remains a decent venue to watch football. The attendance for this game was just over 7,500 which is a lot lower than normal for this fixture, but it meant the traffic was quieter!

The stadium is set in amongst some up market housing and is made up of four individual stands, each different in size and construction. The oldest is the Main Stand, renamed in recent years, The Phil O'Donnell Family Stand. It does not run the full length of the pitch, as to the right of it there is a partially built frame, which has been untouched for years, due to the club having a dispute with a local resident over land issues I understand.

On the left, behind the goal, is the Davie Cooper Stand, which is a single tiered structure for home supporters. Next to this and running parallel with the Main Stand is the East Stand. This was an old terrace that was seated in the 1990s and again this is for the home support only. On the right corner, near the away fans, is where most of the noise within the stadium is generated. There are also some executive boxes located at the back of this stand.

Behind the opposite goal is the domineering South Stand. This is a decent sized two tier stand, with a scoreboard situated in the middle and is for visiting fans. Fir Park is suitable to the club's needs and they depend on local support and business to help finance the running of it. Motherwell have looked at various initiatives to encourage fans of all ages to come along and support them.

The staff in the ticket office were helpful and efficient. The official programme is a decent production and the admission price of £25 for parent and child is reasonable for the top division.

Motherwell 3 (Ojamaa (45), Higdon (Pen 50), Forster (og 55))
Celtic 1 (Hooper (40))
Referee: E.Norris
Attendance: 7,503

LATE JOY FOR LOONS

Forfar Athletic 2, Ayr United 1
Division 2 - Saturday 4th May 2013

IT IS THE LAST DAY of the Scottish Football League season and
we are at Station Park, Forfar, where the home side hopes to sneak
the last available Division 2 Play Off place. We have made it here in
good time, despite a horrendous and uncharacteristic wrong turn
at Perth!

Normally when you approach any given venue you can spot
the floodlights in the distance, but having negotiated some intricate
roundabouts and been told by the satnav "you have arrived at your
destination" we still could not see the ground! We parked on a busy
main road and then spotted fans heading down the one street, so
like sheep, decided to follow them!

To encourage more locals to come out and support the team
for this game, the club announced earlier in the week that the
admission prices would be halved. That meant £5 for adults and
£3 for concessions, which was a welcome bonus for us. With about
twenty minutes before kick off, we had a brief walk past the Main
Stand side before going back round to the terracing turnstiles.

As we paid in and got through, programme sellers were notable
by their absence. We asked someone selling half time draw tickets
where we could get one, before hearing the dreaded words 'sold
out'! We asked at the club shop but they did not have any left
and tried our last option, the pie stall. Again, they had sold their
allocation too. This is the first game we have attended without
getting either a teamsheet or programme, disaster!

I then thought about asking the Forfar Chairman, Alastair
Donald, via social media site, Twitter. I had been communicating
with him and Radio Clyde Sports Reporter, not to mention
Forfar Athletic fan, Alison Robbie, in the lead up to this fixture.
Fortunately for us, the Chairman came good having got us a

programme from the boardroom and I agreed to meet with him at full time!

The opposition for this game are the now very familiar Ayr United. They are safe from relegation and are just off mid table, so it was an opportunity for their manager, Mark Roberts, to tinker with his side. Forfar on the other hand are managed by the well known, bunnet wearing, Dick Campbell and it appears there are quite a few of his family in the playing squad too!

Forfar play on a modern synthetic surface and have had a good season. They have Darren Hill in goal and he has been the number one choice for most of this calendar year, replacing veteran Derek Soutar. The key men in defence are captain Mark McCulloch, Iain Campbell and Michael Bolochoweckyj. The industrious midfield includes Gavin Malin, Danny Denholm and Dale Hilson, with Ross Campbell supporting the far travelled Chris Templeman up front.

Unfortunately for Dick Campell, he had to make do without the services of Steven Tulloch, Martin Fotheringham and the influential Gavin Swankie. For Ayr United, players like Kyle McAusland, Jackson Longridge, Aaron Wylie and Anthony Marenghi got starting places. They replaced the very experienced John Robertson and Austin McCann along with Liam Buchanan and David Winters.

As the game kicked off, it was surprising to find the ball played in the air, especially against a relatively strong wind. Forfar created the first decent chance after five minutes when Ross Campbell's shot from six yards out was deflected for a corner following an Iain Campbell free kick.

With twelve minutes gone we got the opening goal of the game and again it started from an Iain Campbell set piece. His twenty five yard direct free kick was fired in at goal and it required a smart save from Graeme Smith, as he turned the shot away for a corner. Gavin Malin's out swinger on the right was flicked on by Danny Denholm, for Athletic's own version of Peter Crouch, Chris Templeman, to head the ball into the net from close range.

Ayr struggled to get going and they never put the hosts under any real threat. A Scott McLaughlin run and cross which drifted harmlessly over the bar was all they had to show for their early efforts. Forfar then created two chances in quick succession on twenty five minutes. Gavin Malin's shot from the edge of the box was cleared for a corner and from the resultant kick, Ayr managed to clear their lines under pressure, despite what looked like an infringement on their goalkeeper.

After half an hour Ayr were beginning to get a hold of the ball more. Anthony Marenghi floated a dangerous free kick into the box, but it was cleared, before Jackson Longridge's shot was comfortably saved by Darren Hill.

At the other end, Forfar nearly and quite possibly should have doubled their lead following a counter attack. Danny Denholm burst clear on the left, but he opted to square the ball into the centre when he may have been better getting a shot away himself. The move broke down and within seconds Ayr were level, albeit very fortuitously.

Robbie Crawford's cross on the left was intended for the back post, but Forfar's centre half, Michael Bolochoweckyj, attempted to intercept it and only succeeded in slicing the ball past his own goalkeeper. The big stopper was very unlucky and only moments earlier he had expertly controlled a difficult bouncing ball, under pressure from two Ayr forwards with a piece of skill of which Franco Baresi would have been proud!

Ayr were struggling with some of the high balls being played into their box by Forfar. Two minutes before the break they blocked another attempted shot for a corner, before we had a defining moment in the game, right on the half time whistle. A long ball into the box for Templeman saw him tussle with Darren Brownlie. The Ayr stopper was alleged to have bundled the striker to the ground and referee Craig Charleston awarded the penalty. It was a relatively soft award, which Brownlie was also red carded for, leaving the away side to play the full second half with a man less. Iain Campbell stepped up and smashed his shot low into Smith's right hand corner to restore Forfar's lead.

We had started watching the game from just below the Main

Stand, but decided to move round to the opposite side of the ground, just before the penalty was awarded. Similar to the procedure at Gayfield, Arbroath, the fans switched ends at the break, so they were behind the goal their respective team was attacking in the second half.

Ayr made a change following the red card, with Chris Smith on for Anthony Marenghi. Two minutes after the game restarted Forfar replaced Bolochoweckyj with Mick Dunlop. Ayr came out the traps hungry for an equaliser and nearly got one from the normally deadly Michael Moffat. He controlled a through ball just inside the Forfar half as the home team attempted to play offside. He was bearing down on goal, then stalled, as if he was unsure what to do with it next. His hesitation bought the Forfar defence time to track back and the chance had gone.

Forfar then forced a couple of corners but did not threaten the Ayr goal. At the other end, Darren Hill comfortably handled a couple of tame efforts at goal from the visitors. As Forfar had to win the match to have any chance in participating in the Play Offs, a slight nervousness crept into their play and Ayr could almost sense it.

With twenty five minutes to go Ayr had a great chance to equalise following Scott McLaughlin's corner on the right. Nobody in the Forfar defence seemed to pick up Chris Smith and his header went just over the crossbar. Ayr went even closer five minutes later when another McLaughlin corner, this time on the left, was delivered to the back post and was headed across goal by Michael Donald. He picked out Kyle McAusland and his shot went just over the bar.

With thirteen minutes left Darren Hill had to look lively again when he was forced to tip a Neil McGregor header over the bar from a McLaughlin free kick. Anything Ayr created, McLaughlin seemed to be at the heart of it. In the last quarter of the game he hit a shot from twenty yards out that Hill easily held. The midfielder then put a dangerous cross to the back post, but there were no takers, following a poor refereeing decision to award Ayr a free kick in the first instance.

Forfar were uncomfortable with the ball in possession and latterly tried to run the clock down. They created a couple of attacks which led to corners, but none of them threatened the Ayr goal. Some nice hold up play down the left for the home side saw Templeman cut into the box and his shot was deflected for a corner.

At the other end, Hill parried a McLaughlin shot but it was cleared to safety, before the moment when every Forfar supporter held their breath. With four minutes left an Ayr cross on the left was not cleared by the Forfar defence, the ball broke to Michael Donald who had a clear shot at goal. Instead of a composed finish, he went for power and blazed his shot over the bar. The irony was that word had filtered through that Alloa had scored at Arbroath, meaning that if Forfar could hold onto their lead, fourth place and the last Play Off spot was theirs.

Forfar managed to see out two minutes of stoppage time and win the game. As the players left the pitch, a hush descended among the supporters as it was announced over the tannoy that Forfar would be at home to Dunfermline during the week in the first leg of the Play Off. We made our way round to the Main Stand to meet the Chairman and collect the match programme. After a brief exchange, we then left and set about getting back on the road home.

Station Park is quite a basic ground but homely and traditional at the same time. The Main Stand runs for approximately half the length of the pitch, with a seated upper tier. There are approximately eight supporting pillars which may obscure your view slightly, depending on where you sit. Instead of a bottom tier, there is a kind of sharp drop, with an all brick facing that gives some standing space below, like an old enclosure.

The dug outs and players tunnel are situated in the centre of the Main Stand and there are two floodlight pylons situated at either end of the roof, with one on each side of the stand too.

Opposite this, is the South Stand which is a covered terrace that runs the length of the pitch and is predominantly used by the home support. On the far side is the East Terrace, a slightly elevated, open terrace which is normally for the away following and has some industrial units over the back of it.

Directly facing this end is the West Terrace, which is slightly smaller meaning it has less capacity and is where you will find toilet facilities, along with the club shop. Behind this end of the ground is the main access route to Station Park. It looks like it could get pretty muddy in some choice weather conditions as a tractor plant is situated next to it.

The admission pricing at Forfar is reasonable, as is the food and service. The staff and local people we spoke with were friendly and went out of their way to help us, especially in trying to locate a match programme. We were treated to a decent game of football and overall, this was an enjoyable day out.

Forfar 2 (Templeman (12), I.Campbell (Pen 45))
Ayr United 1 (Bolochoweckyj og (36))
Referee: C.Charleston
Attendance: 622

Ding Dong In Dingwall

Ross County 1, Celtic 1
SPL - Sunday 5ᵗʰ May 2013

IT WAS AN EARLY RISE for this game, as we headed to Dingwall, for the Sunday ESPN live midday match between Ross County and Celtic. Both the AA route planner and the satnav informed us to go over the Erskine Bridge, past Loch Lomond, Crianlarich, Glencoe, Fort William and the likes. It was a stop, start, tedious journey along numerous country roads, but we still made it there, despite some appalling driving by some people, in just under four hours and a good thirty minutes before kick off.

We found a housing estate about ten minutes walk away from the stadium and parked the car there. It turned out to be an excellent spot for the journey home, as once you came out of the street, you turned right, taking you out of town and on the route south. I would rectify the earlier mistake of trusting the AA, by heading past Inverness instead, down to Perth, before heading for Glasgow!

In contrast to the weather yesterday, it was a lovely day for going to the football, though I never knew just how bad the pitch was until I saw the highlights later that night. There were a couple of sections that looked patchy, then there was the area near the tunnel which was completely devoid of any grass!

As this was a big game for the locals, it was busy on the approach to the stadium and there was a good atmosphere building outside. We walked round all four stands before heading to the East Stand area where we would be seated for this game.

The stand is close to the pitch and we had a good view, looking along the eighteen yard box at the home end. Ross County have had an exceptional season and are incredibly, still in the hunt for a Europa League place. They are possibly proof that if you speculate to accumulate and have sound investment and management, you will reap the benefits of this.

Ross County joined the Scottish leagues in 1994, along with Inverness Caledonian Thistle, when the leagues were expanded. It has been a slow process, but like their Highland counterparts, they are now experiencing life at the top end of the table.

Having been Scottish Cup Finalists in 2010, knocking Celtic out along the way, manager Derek Adams still has the nucleus of his Division One championship winning team, with players like Paul Lawson, Richard Brittain, Iain Vigurs, Martin Scott, Rocco Quinn, Scott Boyd and Stuart Kettlewell.

On top of that, he has brought in the SPL experience of Grant Munro, Sam Morrow, Mihal Kovacevic, Mark Brown, Evangelos Ikonomou and latterly, German striker Steffen Wohlfarth, goalkeeper Paul Gallacher and winger, Ivan Sproule.

Celtic continued to rest a few of their first team players, with Lukasz Zaluska in goal, Israeli centre half, Rami Gershon making a rare start. Dylan McGeoch played on the right of midfield with Anthony Stokes and Tony Watt up front, at the expense of Forster, Mulgrew, Samaras, Wanyama and Hooper.

The sun was out but it was still a bit cold in the shade. The atmosphere was good among the 5,873 crowd and it was Celtic who made the early breakthrough. A Commons corner on the far side was controlled by Stokes in the six yard box. He was surprisingly given the time and space to hook a shot high past Michael Fraser in the goal, to open the scoring.

Both teams had mixed spells of possession after the opener without threatening each other's goal. A McGeoch header and an effort from Watt failed to trouble Fraser, before Martin Scott tested Zaluska from distance just after the twenty minute mark, but his shot went wide.

I am unsure if it was due to the pitch not being conducive to a passing game, but both teams opted to play high balls up the park which was not the most entertaining. Worse still, both defences played high up the pitch meaning there were a lot of offside decisions and with all the play condensed in the centre of the pitch, there was a lot of petty fouling.

This continued through most of the first half and it was a clumsy foul on the left wing by Ambrose on Sproule, five minutes before the break, that led to the County equaliser.

The Celtic defence seemed to get caught cold as they expected a cross into the box from Brittain. Instead, the ball was squared to Vigurs who swept a first time drive goalwards and it curved over the despairing hand of Zaluska as it ended up in the top left hand corner. A truly wonderful strike that had the home fans on their feet!

Right on the stroke of half time Celtic could have taken the lead into the break, when, following a move down the right, Tony Watt turned the ball past Michael Fraser in goal. The away fans behind the goal saw their celebrations cut short, as the far side linesman had already flagged Stokes for offside, so the score remained level.

At the start of the second half it was Celtic who were the better side and managed to force County 'keeper, Fraser, into a couple of smart saves. First he turned away a Stokes shot from twenty yards out, then just before the hour mark, Fraser again saved well from an Ambrose header following a Commons corner.

Celtic seemed to have peaked after that spell of dominance and Ross County then got back into the game. A Sproule cross on the right wing with twenty five minutes left presented Wohlfarth with a free header in the six yard box. He had time to pick his spot, but he contrived to put his effort past the right hand post.

As Celtic replaced Commons with Tom Rogic, it was County who continued to assert themselves more. Martin Scott then held the ball up well in the penalty box, before turning to hit a snap shot which went wide. A couple of crosses by both Sproule and Vigurs were put into the visitors' box, but there was nobody on the end of them for the Dingwall side.

With just under ten minutes to go Paul Lawson tried his luck from fully thirty yards out, but his drive went just over the bar with Zaluska scrambling. Derek Adams made a double change in the last couple of minutes with Sproule and Kovacevic making way for Mark Fotheringham and Scott Boyd respectively.

Richard Brittain had a free kick blocked by Tony Watt, before Paul Lawson saw his close range shot saved by Zaluska with two minutes left. There were a further two minutes of injury time played and both teams played out the rest of the game as if they were content with a point apiece.

Given the condition of the pitch and the changes made among the Celtic personnel, this was still a decent game of football. As we left, I thought I heard one of the staff shout 'free pies'! I had already walked past, but stopped, doubled back and asked if she had just shouted what I thought she said! This must be a regular occurrence at home games, as other fans came over asking for specific makes of pies, but we were only too happy to indulge in a couple of gratis macaroni ones!

All the stands at The Global Energy Stadium are roughly the same height and it reminds me of a similar design at new St Mirren Park and at Livingston. The Main (West) Stand is probably the busiest, as home and away fans congregate outside it before kick off and similarly at full time. The away fans have to pass it to enter the North Stand behind the goal, which was previously an uncovered terrace, but was newly built in the last couple of years following promotion to the SPL.

Opposite this is the East Stand. It has seen a lot of work to it in the last eighteen months with extensions at either end of the original structure, which included the addition of new seating and Executive Boxes.

The Jail End (South) Stand is for the home fans, behind the opposite goal and again this has been refurbished in the last couple of years. In between this area and the East Stand are a couple of well stocked snack bars.

It is a long trek travelling up and down to Dingwall, but it was a decent day and an enjoyable experience overall. The match programme at £2 is a very good read and excellent value, although I felt the admission prices were surprisingly high.

I bought the tickets over the phone, a few weeks in advance of the game and including a £1 booking fee, it cost a total of £39 for a parent and child. It would put me off going up again, given the total outlay including fuel, but the local people are probably better placed to judge if this pricing policy is fair or not.

Ross County 1 (Vigurs (41))
Celtic 1 (Stokes (4))
Referee: S.McLean
Attendance: 5,873

QUEENS PAY THE PENALTY

Queens Park 0, Peterhead 1
Division 3 Play Off 1ˢᵗ Leg - Wednesday 8ᵗʰ May 2013

WE HAVE BEEN AT HAMPDEN PARK already this season for one of the League Cup Semi Finals, but similar to the situation with East Stirlingshire and Stenhousemuir ground sharing, I decided to cover all bases and watch Queens Park at home too! So off we went to the national stadium once again, to take in the Division 3 Play Off, first leg tie between Queens Park and Peterhead. Joining me is my youngest brother in law, Danny.

Getting here has been quite surreal. It took us twenty minutes and we got parked literally outside the front doors! How refreshing, I could certainly get used to this! There were only two entry gates open for both sets of supporters, which were to the left of the Main Stand.

We got a programme just as we got through the turnstiles, before going to get something to eat and a browse round the club shop. Both are situated in the main concourse, with the shop well stocked with the latest 'Spiders' memorabilia. We did contemplate trying to buy the current home kit in the sale, but the sizes available were quite limited.

There was still a good fifteen minutes to go before kick off, so we set about trying to get some decent seats. We eventually took up seats just to the left of the halfway line, with the Queens Park supporters.

Back in January we saw Queens win 3-2 at Stirling Albion, however, to date, Peterhead are one of the very few sides to have escaped us! Both clubs have had an excellent campaign and have been in the Play Off places throughout most of this season. The visitors have been on an incredible run of form, having won their last 8 fixtures, including a 3-0 win on the last day of the season, against Queens Park at Hampden, just four days go!

Queens Park are the only amateur club in Scotland and are managed by former St Mirren midfielder Gardner Speirs. They have Nick Parry in goal, with the main men at the back being young Andrew Robertson, Blair Spittal and James Brough. In midfield, they have David Anderson and Tony McParland, along with the skill and trickery of the diminutive winger, Aiden Connolly. The Spiders would be depending on their goals coming from Michael Keenan and Sean Burns.

In the opposite dugout, 'Blue Toon' manager, Jim McInally, has a bit more experience in his side and they have come good, so to speak, at the business end of the season. Graham Smith has been the number one choice in goal, with a defence which does not tend to concede, thanks to the likes of Steven Noble and Graeme Sharp. In midfield they have Dean Cowie and the industrious Brian Gilfillan, who was signed from Clyde in January. Up front, Rory McAllister is a decent target man and has contributed a lot to the team as well, with his 22 league goals to date.

There was a decent crowd in as the game got under way. Both teams looked nervous in the early exchanges, with passes going astray, niggling fouls and no real flow to the game at all. It took more than fifteen minutes to register a shot on target.

From a Queens' free kick some twenty yards out, following a foul by Gilfillan, McParland got a shot away, which went just over the bar. It did look like 'keeper Smith got a touch to it, but no corner was given, much to the chagrin of the home support!

Five minutes later some nice link up play down the right hand side by Peterhead saw McAllister get a shot in from close range, but it was expertly turned away by Parry, who also reacted well to block the follow up.

Ten minutes from the break Queens Park's David Anderson lost the ball in midfield and it was picked up by Ryan Strachan. His cross was met by the head of Gilfillan, but he failed to get a good connection and the ball drifted wide of Parry's right hand post.

The last couple of minutes of the half saw both teams create chances. First, Spittal fired a shot well wide for Queens Park, before McAllister was unlucky not to get a good touch on a lofted ball over the top of the Spiders defence. Right on the stroke of half time it was McAllister again who went close for the visitors. Gilfillan chipped a pass into the eighteen yard box and found the big striker who had time to hit a fine right foot volley, but it flashed just wide of Parry's left hand post.

At the start of the second period it was the home team who were quicker out the traps. Ten minutes in, a Burns shot for Queens Park from twenty yards out was saved by Smith, before they got another chance from a free kick just afterwards. McParland's kick was partially cleared and as it fell to Connolly, he put his shot wide of Smith's left hand post.

Just after the hour mark it was good news for Queens Park and despair for Peterhead and their fans, when Rory McAllister was substituted through injury. He had been a thorn in the home side's defence all evening and was replaced by Andy Rodgers. However, Rodgers did not take long to make an impact, as he cracked a shot from twenty five yards which came back off the crossbar, having only been on the park two minutes.

David Anderson created a good chance for Queens Park with twenty minutes left, when he cut inside two players at the edge of the penalty box, but his shot was saved by Smith. Both teams had made some decent forays up the pitch, but their crosses into the box were not met by any attackers.

Gardner Speirs then made two changes a couple of minutes apart, when he replaced both his forwards. Tony Quinn and Lawrence Shankland came on for Keenan and Burns. The visitors' 'keeper Graeme Smith, then had to look lively in the last five minutes, coming off his line well to collect a dangerous cross as the home team pressed for a winner.

As the game entered the fourth minute of stoppage time and with it looking like it would end goalless, it ended in some controversial circumstances. First of all, Peterhead were awarded a free kick some twenty yards from goal, after McParland was adjudged to have fouled David Cox.

The ball was crossed into the box and it looked as though the danger had been cleared. Blair Spittal controlled the ball and intended to run it out of the box, however, Andy Rodgers cleverly put his body in front of the youngster, so that the merest of contact would look like a penalty. There was a slight hesitation before referee McKendrick awarded the spot kick.

It was Rodgers himself who took the responsibility and he blasted his shot high into the right hand side of Parry's net to win the game. The young defender can justifiably feel aggrieved at the soft award, but he will hopefully benefit from such an unfortunate experience.

The Queens Park fans were extremely unhappy and let the officials know exactly how they felt as they left the field. This was possibly the worst abuse I had heard since the Clyde fans turned on their manager, Jim Duffy last November!

There is still the second leg to come in midweek, so it was not over yet for Queens Park, although due to this result, Peterhead may fancy their chances of finishing off the tie with them having home advantage. It would certainly make the journey home a lot easier for the couple of hundred travelling fans in the Hampden crowd of 651.

We got away from the stadium quite smartly, in amongst some very angry home fans as they discussed the penalty and we were home barely twenty minutes later. Happy days! Although we have gone to games and sat in the home end, there has been no preference on which team wins. However, in order to complete the mission of attending all forty two grounds in the one season, I effectively need Peterhead to get through to the Final. Sorry Spiders fans!

Hampden Park is a stadium I am very familiar with, having attended many games here over the last three decades. I've stood on the old terracing, sat in the old Grandstand and also sat in all four of the revamped stands following the refurbishments that took place throughout the 1990s.

I have always tended to approach it from the Shawlands/ Battlefield side of the ground, but over the last couple of years, when I have gone I have changed that to park closer to Govanhill/ Croftfoot at the other end.

Either way, it is a stadium I am not keen on and am at a loss to explain why, as I have attended some very memorable games over the years and equally been at some that I would like to erase from memory!

The BT (Main) South stand is the most impressive and is the more modern of the four. I have been fortunate enough to have seen a couple of games sitting there and also been at a wedding reception in the conference suites contained within it.

When the old terracing was replaced in the early 1990s it was an opportunity to do away with the big track behind both goals. Instead the stands are built pretty much round the shape of the way it was before and it really was an opportunity missed. If you are unfortunate enough to get tickets for rows A to F in the East or West stands (behind the goals) you will see very little of the game. The North and South stands are undoubtedly the best areas to view any games from, though again, if your seats are near the front, the view is not the best.

You could also argue that a 50,000 seated facility is too small for a Scottish National stadium, given there are two other grounds in Glasgow that hold the same capacity and more in the case of Celtic Park which holds 60,000. Indeed Murrayfield stadium in Edinburgh, although a rugby ground, holds just under 70,000. Hampden Park has however, had the prestige of hosting both Champions League and UEFA Cup Finals in the last decade.

With the Commonwealth games set to be staged in Glasgow during the summer of 2014, I am pleased to see that some money is being invested outside the ground too, with new parking areas and the transport links around it being enhanced. Normally, no matter what way you approach Hampden Park, all routes lead to congestion, street parking can be difficult and your best bet is to park at least a mile away if you want to avoid lengthy journey times to and from the ground.

I would also point out the problems you can face if you are in Section F or G in the East Stand, as the directions are misleading. You can only access one of these sections from the corner of the North Stand, even though both are next to each other!

I have had the misfortune on more than one occasion to have been informed by stewards based at the North Stand side that I would have to walk away round to the Main Stand side to access the other section which is nonsense, not to mention poor design and planning.

Hampden does look better now than it ever did, though the atmosphere is questionable a lot of the time and it remains an unpopular venue with a lot of people. The way the stands are built may be the reason for this but I am not sure how you can address this problem now.

Queens Park 0
Peterhead 1 (Rodgers (Pen 90+4))
Attendance: 651
Referee: J. McKendrick

Euro Dream Butchered

Inverness CT 1, Dundee United 2
SPL - Saturday 11ᵗʰ May 2013

THIS FIXTURE REQUIRED A LOT OF PLANNING! I had to collect the wife from a nightshift first thing, then get to a family commitment at 10am, before making the trek up to Inverness in time for kick off.

We actually passed the Tulloch Caledonian Stadium last weekend on the return from Dingwall. It was a reasonable journey north, though a bit on the breezy side. The ground is quite secluded, sitting on its own, just off a busy roundabout and almost underneath the very large Kessock Bridge.

The club was formed out of an amalgamation of Inverness Caledonian and Inverness Thistle in 1994. On promotion to the SPL in 2004, the club had to play their home games at Aberdeen's Pittodrie for the first half of the 2004/05 season, while the relevant work took place to bring the Tulloch stadium up to the required criteria.

We went for a wander round the ground before collecting tickets from the small office outside the Main Stand, which also doubles up as the club shop. After a quick conversation with the programme seller, we then headed into the ground.

Having endured the long journey here, I then had to prioritise getting the boys fed! I was surprised to establish that the only food outlet available is a local burger van selling very expensive fast food. I had some money on me, but forgot to lift more before setting off and left myself short, meaning the kids got but I went without. As I carry a few spare tyres, I was not likely to pass out and managed to tough it out!

Prior to kick off a pipe band were marching round the pitch, with what I can only imagine were some local people alongside them. In amongst the parade, was none other than the home manager, Terry Butcher! The club have had a tremendous season, almost punching above their weight. They have been in the top three league positions for most of the season, currently aiming for a Europa League place and they also reached the semi-finals of the League Cup, losing narrowly to Hearts on penalties.

Antonio Reguero has been the first choice goalkeeper, having deposed of Ryan Esson. The defence has been solid, thanks mainly to the likes of David Raven, Chris Hogg and Josh Meekings. The Shinnie brothers are very versatile, with Graeme the more defensive player of the two and Andrew the more creative. In the midfield there are Englishman Ross Draper and local lad Nick Ross. In the forward positions, Inverness have three Irishmen with a bit of everything! The height, strength and experience of Richie Foran, the skill and creativity of Aaron Doran, with the work rate and goals of Billy McKay.

United boss, Jackie McNamara was able to recall Johnny Russell up front, following a couple of months laid up with a broken leg. He partnered Jon Daly and they would likely get support from the creativity of youngsters Ryan Gauld and Gary Mackay-Steven. The centre halves for the Tangerines were John Soutar and Brian McLean.

It was clear from the start that Inverness were well up for this game and hungry to secure the three points. They forced a succession of early corners and the United defence had to block efforts from Shinnie and Foran. Having been under the cosh for the first twelve minutes, it was United who had a great chance to open the scoring on the counter attack. Caley struggled to cope with the pace of Gary Mackay-Steven and when he cut the ball back for Stuart Armstrong, his shot was goal bound, only for Josh Meekings to block on the line.

Six minutes later it was Caley's turn, as a McKay shot looked goal bound, only for McLean to get a touch on it, to divert the ball wide for a corner. United then broke again and following a nice run by Ryan Gauld, he played in Rankin, whose cross was headed well over by Russell. On the half hour Caley 'keeper Reguero saved well from a Russell shot, having been played in by Mackay-

Steven, however the Assistant had already flagged for offside.

A couple of minutes after this it was United goalkeeper Cierzniak who was called into action, turning a McKay shot from twenty yards out round the post. With just over ten minutes from the break Inverness had a great chance to open the scoring from the penalty spot. Aaron Doran was fouled in the box by Rankin, with the United midfielder picking up a booking for his trouble. Top scorer Billy McKay took responsibility, but his kick was saved by Cierzniak at his left hand post and the scores remained level.

Five minutes from half time Andrew Shinnie had two opportunities of his own to open the scoring. His first effort went wide of the left hand post, before he hit a twenty five yard effort that cleared the crossbar. Three minutes later, Inverness eventually broke the deadlock and over the balance of play, it was more than justified. Aaron Doran received the ball at the edge of the box and his turn and low shot beat Cierzniak at his right hand post.

United nearly equalised right on the stroke of half time, when Reguero saved Daly's powerful header, following a Ryan Dow corner. We then spent the fifteen minute interval trying to keep warm! It might be May and I was probably not appropriately dressed for a football match at this location, but good god this place is exceptionally cold! The pipe band that were out pre match were back out again, masquerading as entertainment!

Inverness came at United at the start of the second half and created two excellent chances. From a Graeme Shinnie free kick, Doran forced Cierzniak into a save, then Foran was unlucky with a shot from distance, that went just wide.

Just as you thought Inverness were going to build on their one goal advantage, United were level, five minutes after the restart. A Willo Flood free kick into the box was partially cleared by the Caley defence, but only as far as Ryan Dow, who almost ran into the ball to volley past Reguero for the equaliser. The band of vocal United fans behind that goal fair enjoyed the moment!

Inverness responded well, with two good opportunities before and after the hour mark. First, an Aaron Doran volley from twenty yards out dipped just over the bar, before McKay slid in at the back post following a cross from the right wing, but he was flagged for offside in any case.

A couple of minutes apart, United made two substitutions, with Mark Millar replacing Ryan Dow and Michael Gardyne on for Ryan Gauld. As the changes were announced over the tannoy system, the announcer said "coming on for United is Michael Gardyne.....I think!!!"

With less than twenty minutes left Gardyne and Stuart Armstrong both had good chances a couple of minutes apart, with shots from distance that went just over the bar. Daly then put a header over the bar from a Flood corner, as United pressed for a winner.

Some of Inverness's link up play was very impressive, sweeping through the midfield and always looking a threat on the counter. After some good play by Nick Ross, Aaron Doran put a shot so high over the bar, I actually think it cleared the roof! Just after that, Graeme Shinnie floated a dangerous cross into the United box, but there was nobody able to take advantage and the ball went out for a goal kick.

With just under five minutes left United forced two corners in quick succession, with Daly again heading just wide from Flood's second corner. I thought that would be one of the last chances of the game and decided to give in to the boys moaning to leave early! We headed to the corner of the North Stand to watch the last couple of minutes and I was glad that I did not actually leave!

A sweeping United move on the right, saw Armstrong pick out Gary Mackay-Steven at the back post. The young midfielder volleyed high into the net to pretty much seal the victory, with an absolutely superb finish, worthy of winning any game and with a technique that is difficult to perfect. United were able to see out two further minutes of injury time, despite a late effort from Andrew Shinnie, which Cierzniak was equal to. The result was a big blow for Terry Butcher's European dream, but they still have one more game left to rectify this set back.

We managed to get to the car and back on the road home quite quickly. It was a cold, but enjoyable day out overall. The people we spoke with were friendly and talkative. The ticket pricing for the North (Family) Stand was both reasonable and affordable at £16 for adults, £7 concessions. The official match programme is like an extended, glossy A4 sized team sheet, which is priced at only 50p, but comes with an option of also buying the club magazine at £2.50. Both together are very good value souvenirs.

The Main Stand runs the length of the pitch and has uncovered seating at either side of it. To the right of this and behind the goal is the North Stand, which houses the home support and is the designated Family area. Opposite this is the South Stand, which is for away fans only and both of these stands are pretty much identical.

Across from the Main Stand is the completely vacant west side of the ground. All this has on it is an elevated television gantry built on scaffolding and I am unsure if there has ever been temporary seating or standing in this area over the years.

Inverness have a decent team on the park to go with a modern, compact stadium. As it is quite low down, you are close to the action and provides a very good, unobscured view of the football.

Inverness C.T 1 (Doran (42))
Dundee United 2 (Dow (50), Mackay-Steven (90+1))
Referee: C.Allan
Attendance: 3,728

Capital Classic

Hearts 1, Hibernian 2
SPL - Sunday 12th May 2013

AFTER RUNNING LATE LAST MONTH when we visited Edinburgh, we were in the capital again and at Tynecastle, for our first ever Edinburgh derby. This is the featured live game on ESPN, in another Sunday midday kick off, in what is the penultimate weekend of the season.

We left the house just before 10am, to make sure we got there in plenty of time and got a good run through, until we hit the city bypass again! On the final hurdle to the stadium the traffic started to crawl, so I pretty much ditched the car next to what looked like a quiet housing estate, about fifteen minutes walk away.

As usual, as soon as we got out the car, down came the rain! We walked round as much of the ground as we possibly could, taking a few pictures along the way, looked into the club shop, bought a programme, then headed to the turnstiles. Once in, the crowd looked quite sparse, but come kick off it was near capacity and the atmosphere was excellent. I have only been here once before, for a cup game in the mid 1980s, suffice to say, Tynecastle has undergone massive changes since then.

Hearts have had a torrid season both on and off the park, while Hibernian have surprisingly had the upper hand in this fixture during this campaign and are preparing for a Scottish Cup Final at the end of the month. With confusion over what the future holds for all staff at the club, due to issues with the owner, Vladimir Romanov, in Lithuania and the team just escaping relegation, Hearts will be keen to end the season on a high, with victory over their rivals.

The home side welcomed Andy Webster back into the centre of the defence, following a suspension and he partnered Darren Barr, who confirmed recently that he will be leaving the club in the summer. Michael Ngoo started up front with John Sutton, even although he was not fully fit, but it is in the midfield area where these kind of games are won and lost. Ryan Stevenson and Mehdi Taouil were the older heads in the centre of the park, with promising youngsters Jason Holt and Jamie Walker alongside them.

Hibernian had their own injury concerns, most notably the absence of James McPake in defence. In a bold move, manager Pat Fenlon gave a debut to nineteen year old Jordon Forster at centre half, along with an opportunity to Ross Caldwell up front, with another prospect in the making, Alex Harris in midfield.

Fenlon would be looking for the likes of Alan Maybury and Kevin Thomson to use their experience in this fixture and lead by example to the other players. This was also likely to be Leigh Griffiths last appearance in the green shirt of Hibernian, before returning to his parent club, Wolverhampton Wanderers.

The pitch was in great condition and the ball moved quickly across the wet surface. Hibs had a lot of the early possession and did well to keep hold of the ball, yet it was Hearts who had the best chance to score with just ten minutes played. Hibernian goalkeeper Ben Williams failed to take a McHattie corner cleanly, Darren Barr headed goalwards and it was cleared by Lewis Stevenson. It fell only as far as Ngoo, who headed it back and this time Maybury cleared it to safety.

With twenty minutes played the visitors had their first real shot at goal, when Harris forced 'keeper Jamie MacDonald into a save from twenty five yards. At the other end a couple of minutes later Walker put a shot over the bar from the edge of the eighteen yard box for Hearts.

Kevin Thomson then irked the home support, when he appeared to go down in the box a bit theatrically, but referee Steven McLean was not buying it and waved play on. Just after the half hour mark Leigh Griffiths hit an ambitious free kick at goal, some thirty yards out, after Taouil had fouled the Hibs talisman, but it was deflected off the wall for a corner.

Five minutes before the break an excellent run by Jamie Walker for Hearts saw him cut in from the left wing, before getting a shot away that went just over the bar. Right on half time though, Hearts made the break through, despite Hibs players' protests that there had been a foul committed in the build up.

Having failed to learn their lesson from a couple of previous inswinging corners by Kevin McHattie, Hibs paid the ultimate price. The kick was met by Ngoo, whose downward header seemed to hang in the air and landed at the feet of Darren Barr. He swept the ball into the net from a couple of yards out to open the scoring, as three sides of the ground erupted!

From the restart following the goal Hibs were straight up the park and had Jamie MacDonald worried, when his cross come shot from the left side, went narrowly past the post and this proved to be the last action of the half.

Barely two minutes had been played of the second half, when Hibs drew level and again, it was following a free kick awarded for another Taouil challenge, this time on Harris. It was a considerable distance from goal, but Griffiths has made this type of situation his specialty.

As the Hearts players lined up the wall, in anticipation for a strike at goal, the home fans were going off their head, shouting for Ngoo to stand at the other side of the wall. If only the players had listened! The big striker's height may have prevented Griffiths getting the ball up and over the wall and into the top right hand corner of the net, had he been positioned on the left side of the Hearts wall. This is maybe proof that sometimes the fans are right!

Right after the goal Hibs were on the attack again, when Harris's low cross to the back post from the right hand side had to be turned away for a corner by Jamie Hamill. Hearts then had two similar chances a couple of minutes later, when first Hamill then Walker put crosses to the back post which Sutton failed to properly connect with.

A long ball played into the Hearts half saw Hamill misjudge the bounce of the ball and it was collected by Harris. He fed Griffiths, who then laid it on for Caldwell, but his cut back was poor, Hearts cleared the danger and left several Hibs players well out of position.

Hearts then had a period of dominance in the game. Just before the hour mark Ngoo was fouled by Forster and from the resultant free kick, Jamie Hamill's effort forced Ben Williams to tip the ball over the bar for a corner.

Walker then fired a shot just wide of Williams' right hand post, following a neat knock down from Ngoo. A sweeping move again from Hearts nearly gave them the lead, when Holt and Hamill combined to play in Stevenson. His cutback into the six yard box was decent, but it was cleared by Hanlon for a corner.

With ten minutes left both teams made changes, with Hearts replacing Taouil with David Smith and Hibs' Kevin Thomson making way for Scott Robertson. If anyone looked likely to score it was Hearts. They were very unfortunate with five minutes left, when Jamie Walker was booked for simulation. He had made a good run from the left into the penalty box and from our position, it looked as though there was contact and that a penalty should have been awarded.

Hibs' Maybury then fouled Stevenson, out on the left flank and from the resultant free kick, McHattie floated a ball in for Sutton, but he glanced his header just past the post.

In a rare foray up field, Hibs forced a corner in the last minute, but MacDonald collected Harris' effort. As we entered the last minute, the home team suffered the ultimate sting in the tail, when Hibs, having been outplayed for large parts of the second half, scored the winner. Griffiths found himself breaking down the left, but as he was closed down by Hamill, the ball fell into the path of Scott Robertson. He burst into the box and was robustly challenged, with a good shout for a penalty, but Ross Caldwell picked up the loose ball and curled a fine shot into MacDonald's top left hand corner. Three stands remained silent, with one coming alive, as a handful of Hibs fans also spilled onto the pitch in celebration!

A number of Hearts fans decided to leave and it could have been even worse for them, when two minutes into stoppage time, Hibs nearly scored again. Caldwell outpaced Andy Webster and as he bore down on goal he hit a tame shot into the body of Jamie MacDonald, when he should have buried it.

This was pretty much the last action of the game as referee McLean blew for full time. It was a fast paced, entertaining game, with both teams having great chances to score. A draw may have been a fairer result, given that Hearts had dominated most of the second half.

Hearts players intended doing a lap of honour round the pitch once the Hibs fans and players had left the field at full time. We hung about for maybe five minutes after the final whistle and there were not many fans who had stayed behind. As we got out onto the concourse, next to the exits, there was a young family in front of us, with about four kids under the age of ten. With people naturally disappointed losing to your local rival and a lot of glum faces in among those leaving the Gorgie Road end, one of the kids says "so did we win that match then?" If looks could kill, as a number of people turned to see who posed this bizarre question!

After the walk back to the car, we were soaked through and the traffic was tediously slow for the first mile or so, but then made good progress on the road home.

Due to the early kick off, we didn't buy any food, so I cannot comment on this, but with tickets priced at £30 for parent and child in the Gorgie Stand, I felt it was decent value for a big derby game like this. The programme is made of high quality paper and maybe explains why the cover price is £3.50, however, it is does not alter the fact that it is a good read. Although we were in the home end and it was not the result the fans would have desired, this was still an excellent stadium visit all round.

Tynecastle saw major redevelopment work take place in the mid 1990s, with three sides of the ground completely rebuilt. The Main Stand has had the roof repaired and replaced in recent years, but is a bit dated looking in appearance and is the smallest of all four stands. It will provide a decent view of the pitch and the rest of the stadium, however there are a number of supporting pillars which may obstruct your view in certain parts.

Across from this is the biggest of the new structures, the large Wheatfield Stand, which holds a majority of the Hearts support. The Gorgie Stand which is behind the left goal is dedicated as the club's Family Stand. Opposite this is the Roseburn Stand which is for the away support.

All three of the newer stands are single tiered and with them being situated close to the pitch, the atmosphere generated for high profile games or when it is near capacity is excellent.

For the sake of the game in Scotland, I hope Hearts and all their creditors can amicably resolve their differences in the coming weeks and months.

Hearts 1 (Barr (45))
Hibernian 2 (Griffiths (48), Caldwell (90))
Referee: S.McLean
Attendance: 15,994

GRANITE CITY STALEMATE

Aberdeen 1, Hearts 1
SPL - Saturday 18ᵗʰ May 2013

IT IS THE LAST WEEKEND of the SPL season, as we embark on visiting ground forty one, which is Aberdeen's Pittodrie Stadium. Today's opposition are Hearts, who we have now seen so many times in the last few weeks, I feel like a diehard Jambo! I was last here for a game in March 1998, long before the kids were born and recall it for the most obscure of reasons! I had been out drinking the night before, I was extremely rough in every way, having had only one hour's sleep and nothing to eat for hours. During the game, I made a shameful three visits to the food kiosk and amassed a ridiculous four pies, having hit 'the munchies'! They were the days!

As we have neared the end of our 'Grounds Tour', one thing I was looking forward to, as we headed into summer, was better weather! Someone up there was having a laugh, as we endured possibly the wettest day of the year in the Granite City! Despite the conditions, we still made good progress up north, avoiding the vast amount of speed cameras, before hitting the city centre traffic, which was at an absolute standstill.

I had intended to meet an old friend who now lives in Aberdeen before the game, but due to the latter hold ups, we had to end up parking the car and walked briskly to the ticket office. As it was the last game of the season, the Dons had announced through the week that the admission prices for this game would be £5 for adults and £1 concessions.

As we approached the ticket office, I got a programme which looked to be as drenched as the guy selling it! It is as thick as a government report, but great value and must be made with an incredible quality of paper, as it had no tide marks or signs of being wet! The tickets we had were for the Richard Donald Stand, behind the goal. For the first half we sat upstairs and went to the lower tier for the second.

There has been some talk in recent years about Aberdeen relocating to a new stadium in a different area, but there has been no recent update to this. The club claim to have had the first all seated stadium in Scotland, a feat challenged by the now defunct Clydebank FC who put benches on their terraces to achieve this.

The Dons have had a mixed start to life under new manager, Derek McInnes. For this game, he gave an opportunity to a handful of young fringe players. The team were also wearing their new home kit, which is reminiscent of the old Liverpool, Adidas kit of the mid 1990s, with the big v-neck collar.

Jamie Langfield was in goal, with Clark Robertson and Joe Shaughnessy being given a start in defence. Nicky Low was deployed in the centre of midfield, with Cammy Smith playing further forward. They were ably assisted by the more senior players Mark Reynolds, Johnny Hayes, Niall McGinn and Gavin Rae, who was making his last appearance in a red shirt.

For Hearts, their manager, Gary Locke stuck with a familiar looking side, which included Jamie MacDonald in goal, Kevin McHattie, Jamie Hamill, Ryan Stevenson, Jason Holt and Michael Ngoo. It was likely to be the last game in a Hearts jersey for Andy Webster and substitutes John Sutton and Marius Zaliukas, who both came on for late cameos.

By the time we got in and seated, the game had already kicked off. The weather clearly had a detrimental effect on the attendance and although there was nothing to play for, Hearts brought a good travelling support, who were vocal throughout.

The game started at a pretty frantic pace, with Aberdeen having a bulk of the early possession. They had the first reasonable efforts on goal, when McGinn put a shot wide of the left hand post, before MacDonald easily claimed an effort from Rae.

Hearts themselves forced a couple of corners and youngster Dale Carrick called Jamie Langfield into action, with a shot from the edge of the box. The first clear cut chance of the game fell to Aberdeen and the conditions helped play a part. A long ball from Reynolds in the Dons half, was played up to Josh Magennis, who outmuscled Webster, before lifting the ball over the advancing MacDonald in goal. The big striker looked favourite to tap the ball into the net from six yards, but Dylan McGowan managed to slide in and clear the ball to safety.

Cammy Smith was putting in a shift for the Dons in attack and came close, when his flicked header from a Shaughnessy cross on the right, looped just over the bar. Then, from a Hearts counter attack, Taouil threaded a pass through the left channel for Holt. He crossed into the box, but it deflected off Isaac Osborne and was goal bound, had Langfield not managed to parry for a corner.

Just after a quarter of an hour a lovely sweeping move which started from an Osborne clearance, was flicked on by Smith in the centre circle for Hayes, wide on the right. His low cross was met by McGinn on the penalty spot and his first time effort was instinctively put over the bar by MacDonald, for what was a tremendous save. On twenty minutes a Smith shot was parried by MacDonald, only as far as Hayes and his shot was blocked by Webster for a corner. The game then got a bit scrappy, with play halted for petty fouling, although again, this was partly down to the wet conditions.

Ten minutes from the break Aberdeen created another great chance to score. A superb whipped cross from Clark Robertson on the left, was impressively taken first time by Magennis, but once again, he found MacDonald in the way, with a similar save to the one that had kept out McGinn earlier. This was the last real chance of the half, despite some late pressure being applied by the visitors in the last few minutes of the game.

We then spent the interval trying to find vacant seats in the lower tier of the stand for the second forty five, as the seagulls swooped in around the stands, which can be a bit freaky if you are not used to it!

The second half was ten minutes old when MacDonald pulled off another great save for Hearts, following an impressive Aberdeen move on the left. McGinn rolled the ball down the line for Low, who crossed for the onrushing Cammy Smith, whose first time volley was palmed over the bar for a corner by the Hearts stopper.

The Dons kept up the pressure, but could not find the net and succumbed to a Hearts sucker punch, just after the hour mark. A corner from the right saw Ryan Stevenson rise almost unchallenged in the box and his header flew high past Langfield into the net for the opener.

Aberdeen reacted by replacing Smith with another young forward, Declan McManus. McGinn and Hayes then linked up on the left hand side and from Hayes' cross, the ball deflected off Stevenson and spun into the air, before being touched onto the bar by MacDonald, as McHattie cleared.

With twenty minutes left Aberdeen replaced Magennis with Scott Vernon as they continued to pursue an equaliser. A Hayes cross, this time from the right, was met by the head of McManus, but his header dropped just over the bar. With Hearts winning, 'keeper Jamie MacDonald was in no hurry to take the goal kick, but he saw the funny side of a big Aberdeen fan, who yelled "move yer ar$e ya wee baldy b@stard!!"

There were less than fifteen minutes left, when Hearts gave the ball away on the half way line and it was collected by McGinn on the left wing. His cross evaded everyone and was picked up by Hayes on the opposite side. He cut into the box, evading the challenge by McHattie and two other covering Hearts defenders, to square the ball low across the six yard box. McManus and Hamill both slid in for the ball and it squirmed into the net, past the despairing MacDonald, who had been the scourge of the Dons all afternoon! It was almost comical and the equaliser was given as a Hamill own goal.

The Hearts full back nearly made up for his faux pas just a couple of minutes later, when, after a couple of intricate passes on the right, he struck a shot from twenty five yards out that must have stung the palms of Langfield, as Shaughnessy hooked the loose ball clear.

Hearts then gave Sutton and Zaliukas a run out for the last couple of minutes, replacing Ryan Stevenson and the anonymous Michael Ngoo. One minute into stoppage time, Johnny Hayes cut into the box and flashed a shot across the left hand post, but it went out for a goal kick. This proved to be pretty much the last action of the game, as both teams ended the game and the season with honours even.

We took our time leaving the stadium and walked round to see the other side of the ground, as we never got the opportunity before kick off. It took us a while to get our bearings and initially could not remember where we had parked the car! The traffic out of the city was horrendous and it was a good hour after full time before we made any real progress on the road home. It was still a good all round trip, with the only real downside being the weather.

The Main Stand at Pittodrie is quite distinguished, with its two tone roof and floodlights on the lip of the roof front. The dugouts are situated in the centre of it and there is a high wall of advertising boards that run along the front, meaning anyone on the bench almost has to look up to the supporters.

It has two tiers and eight supporting pillars, which again may obscure part of your view and is very similar to Hearts' Tynecastle. To the left of this is the very large and impressive Richard Donald Stand. It was officially opened in 1993 and towers above the other three stands. It is also a two tiered structure and replaced the famous 'Beach End' terrace.

We watched the first half in the upper deck, but moved down to the lower tier in the second half, mainly as there were a number of leaks in the roof that were soaking us! Either way, both areas provide a very good view of the pitch. The players' tunnel is situated between the Richard Donald and Main Stands.

The South Stand is opposite the Main. It runs the length of the pitch, is all seated and caters for both home and away supporters, with some uncovered seats either side of it, almost in the corners. There are two dividing fences in this section, which I am assuming is to segregate the away fans, while maintaining order within the home support.

Behind the other goal is the Merkland Family Stand. This is the smallest of the four stands and looks like it was an old terrace area that has had modern seats built into it. There are four supporting pillars in it, but would not imagine it would interfere much with your view of the pitch. After the game we walked past this stand and it has an intriguing monument type wall, which states that it is the Merkland Stand.

As much as the weather was atrocious, I still think Pittodrie is an impressive venue and definitely one of Scotland's most prestigious football stadiums.

Aberdeen 1 (Hamill og (78))

Hearts 1 (Stevenson (62))

Referee: C.Allan

Attendance: 10,465

Survival Sunday For Fifers

Peterhead 0, East Fife 1
Division 3 Play Off Final 2nd Leg - Sunday 19th May 2013

SO WE HAVE FINALLY MADE IT, ground forty-two is Peterhead's Balmoor stadium, meaning we have visited the home of every professional club in Scotland in the space of eight months.

This weekend has seen us clock up a lot of miles, having been down the road at Aberdeen yesterday, we return north hours later, to take in the Division 2 and 3 Play Off Final second leg tie, between Peterhead and East Fife.

I have had to make my apologies to the family, as this visit coincides with my niece's Christening. With one game left to complete the mission, rightly or wrongly, the football has taken precedence! Unlike the weather the day before, it was thankfully quite a bright morning and it was a decent drive up. The latter part of the journey is a bit stop-start, with a lot of roundabouts that break your momentum.

You travel up a steep hill and the ground is on the left hand side. Greeting us on arrival was a piper, who contentedly played away until kick off. I am unsure if this is a regular match day occurrence or just for the big occasion. We parked the car on a side street, just a couple of minutes walk from the Main Stand and went for a brief wander round the perimeter of the ground, then went through the home turnstiles.

Like quite a few football venues in Scotland, once you have paid to get in, all the facilities are in front of you. The toilets are to the right, there are staff facing you, selling the match programme and half time draw tickets, with a snack bar situated on the left.

The first leg of this Final, played in Methil earlier in the week, ended goalless and the outcome of who goes up and who stays down, will be decided by the end of this game. We have seen both sides play in recent weeks and there were no surprises to either line ups. Peterhead boss Jim McInally had his regular 'keeper Graeme Smith in goal, with Steven Noble and Graeme Sharp, two of his key players in defence. Dean Cowie and Bryan Gilfillan would have the main roles in the midfield. Up front, there was a combination of pace and goals through Rory McAllister and Andy Rodgers.

For the Fifers, the only notable omission was Bobby Barr, who was on the bench. Manager, Billy Brown went for Calum Antell in goal, Scott Durie and David White being important starters in defence, with Paul Willis and Darren Smith, two key men in the East Fife midfield. Up top, they had the hard working Paul McManus and the physical presence of Collin Samuel.

The game got under way and I watched the game from the congested corner, to the left of the Main Stand, while my lad went to get himself some lunch. We then walked behind the goal, over to the opposite corner. The wee man then said to me, "do ye want these chips, they're stinkin'". After a look over them, I realised why he thought this. Instead of putting salt on them, he had drowned them with sugar! I still ate them all the same!

In between this, Rory McAllister was unlucky for the Blue Toon, when after two minutes, he got a shot in that went just past Antell's left hand post. Paul Willis replied for East Fife, when he fired a shot high over the bar, before Smith in the home goal managed to gather a through ball intended for McManus.

Just after twenty minutes, East Fife nearly fell behind when Antell saved well from a Rodgers shot. There was then a Peterhead claim for a penalty, when McAllister felt he was challenged unfairly in the box, but the referee showed no interest. The visitors replied five minutes later, when McManus neatly controlled the ball on his chest, before hooking a shot across goal. Smith in goal did not appear to get a touch, but the corner was awarded in any case. From the resultant kick, David White put a header just over the bar.

Outwith a shot from Willis on the half hour, that Smith comfortably saved, East Fife spent the rest of the first half on the back foot. McAllister nearly opened the scoring again for Peterhead, when he hit a direct free kick from twenty five yards out, which went just past the left hand post. The visitor's goal was under siege, when the Blue Toon forced three corners in quick succession. They rode their luck out though, with Antell saving from a McAllister shot, before Ross Smith put a header narrowly past the left hand post.

McAllister then hit a woeful free kick into the ground after which East Fife managed to get up the pitch and got a corner, which failed to trouble the Peterhead defence. That brought an end to a fast paced first forty five, with both teams having good opportunities to score.

During the interval we walked round to the other side of the ground, where the away fans were congregated. The intention was to stand on the terrace again, but we ended up sitting in a section of the stand, in with the East Fife fans. I am not sure what inspirational speech Billy Brown gave his players at half time, but with their Division 2 status at risk, the players responded to the challenge.

Just three minutes after the restart East Fife surprisingly took the lead. A corner on the far side was swung in by Craig Johnstone, the Peterhead defence failed to react, David Muir reacted quickest and he turned the ball into the net, from only a couple of yards out. We stood and applauded as a courtesy, while several hundred Fifers jumped about deliriously! Only five minutes later it could have been two, when Collin Samuel took the ball for a run, before cracking a shot from twenty five yards out, which went just wide of the right hand post.

Just before the hour Samuel again found himself in a similar position and like a carbon copy of his last attempt on goal, his effort flashed just wide of the right hand post. It took Peterhead some time to respond but they struck back, with a McAllister shot that Antell had to turn away for a corner and a Rodgers strike from eight yards, which went just wide of the right post.

With fifteen minutes left to play, East Fife then made the first substitution of the game, when Bobby Barr replaced Paul McManus. There then followed a fracas, after the referee had stopped play to allow treatment to an East Fife player, following a clash of heads, while Peterhead were in possession. East Fife wouldn't return the ball and played on, resulting in Scott Ross chopping down Collin Samuel. Several players got involved in some shoving and both Assistants came onto the pitch to help restore order. When things calmed down, Rodgers and Ross of Peterhead, along with David Muir for East Fife, found themselves cautioned.

From the best part of thirty yards out, Paul Willis' direct free kick for East Fife went inches past Smith's left hand post. The Blue Toon then added another forward, when they introduced Martin Bavidge for Bryan Gilfillan. The home side tried to press up the pitch, but found the East Fife defence equal to the task. Darren Smith blocked a McAllister effort with five minutes to go and with barely two minutes left, McAllister made space in the penalty box, but put a shot wide of the left post.

East Fife then broke up the park and Smith was forced to turn a Willis shot away for a corner. As Samuel attempted to run the clock down, he was caught offside, giving Peterhead the chance to get the ball up to the other end of the pitch. Two minutes into stoppage time, they did get the ball into the box but Scott Durie blocked a Ross Smith shot from six yards, as the ball went out for a corner. Blue Toon 'keeper Smith came up for it and as David Cox crossed the ball over, it was cleared, before referee Clancy blew for full time.

After an unbeaten run stretching back to March, Peterhead fell short and would stay in Division 3 next season, while East Fife retained their Division 2 status. With about five minutes of the game to go, we had made our way round to the home end again and watched the last action from the corner. Some of the home fans stayed behind to applaud the players, others could not face hanging around. We left with the latter and got away without any hitches, to commence the long road home.

Balmoor is set at the top of a hill and has two stands opposite each other, that are practically identical. The Main Stand has hospitality available, with entry being outside it, next to a small portakabin, which serves as the club shop and ticket office. Food bar facilities are available next to both of these stands and everything on sale is reasonably priced.

Behind both goals and all four corners, there are standing areas to watch the game. There is an interesting look about the terracing, situated directly behind both goals. It is made up of thick wooden planks on what looks like scaffolding and is a couple of feet raised off the ground. The home end was very busy, so although it is a bit rough looking on the eye, it did not put the locals off turning up, with a crowd of nearly two thousand present for this game!

This was a long, tedious journey and the way the fixtures fell, we found ourselves in this part of the world, twice in twenty four hours, but it had to be done! The end of the Scottish football season coincided with the end of our Grounds Tour and we took great satisfaction in seeing it through to the end.

I had planned a couple of beers when I got home, to celebrate the achievement, but it turned out to be a bit of an anti climax, as on our return, there was nobody in the house! I think in my head I had a vision of it being like the finishing line of a big race, yet reality was something very different! Still, the notes, experience, stories, photographs and the memories are all mine!

Peterhead 0
East Fife 1 (Muir (48))
Referee: K. Clancy
Attendance: 1,855

CONCLUSION

End of the Tour

The Grounds Tour is now complete. All forty two Scottish football grounds and stadiums visited during the 2012/13 season over an eight month period. A few thousands miles were covered, not to mention a few thousand pounds taken off the value of my car! Every speed camera caught, no fines or tickets received, several wrong turns made, many a delicacy eaten, a lot of swear words uttered and no wildlife harmed while on the road!

We travelled to and watched games, in every type of weather imaginable. From the forty two games, there were only three that ended goalless, but despite that, they were not the worst games I had ever seen. There was a feature on our 'Tour' in the Dundee United programme for their match against Aberdeen in April, our Grounds Tour website got coverage on the Berwick Rangers and East Fife official websites, along with a mention on the Ayr United Twitter feed.

With regards the total outlay to finance this venture, I will take the Fifth Amendment, as my wife may read this!

Education and Dedication

As well as travelling round the country to watch the football, it has also been an education along the way. It has altered my opinion somewhat on certain aspects of our game and Scottish culture. We saw famous landmarks in passing hills, rivers and lochs, in places I had barely heard of, let alone knew where they were.

On top of improving our geography, we met some great, friendly people along the way. It was also heartening to see some the sheer dedication of some club officials, who take on so many roles to make a match day happen. They don their club tie and blazer and are normally the first ones at the ground and one of the last to leave.

All of this effort to cater for, in some cases, a mere few hundred spectators. It is reassuring to the supporters of provincial clubs that they will always survive with such people at the helm.

Contacting the Clubs

A lot of Scottish clubs know their limitations as community clubs who depend on these few hundred hardy followers who turn up and pay their gate money every fortnight. I would not suggest that some clubs radically change their match day practices, but having observed a number of things at various grounds, there are a couple of basic improvements I would recommend.

On deciding what venue to visit, apart from checking out the weather forecast in advance, I always had a look at the particular club's website for news on the up coming fixture and their admission prices. A lot of club sites are very informative, some less so.

On contacting some of the clubs in advance of a game by e-mail, a couple of the responses were very poor, with no greeting or formality, which I thought showed a distinct lack of courtesy and professionalism.

Looking more positively on this, I contacted Montrose FC about their prices in advance of their home game with Annan Athletic, in February but did not receive a reply. On the Monday after the game, I received a reply back saying that kids under twelve years old were admitted for free. I replied back saying that I paid my two boys in at £6 each on Saturday and that the club had not advertised this on either their website or at the turnstiles.

It may be a complete coincidence, but days after exchanging these e-mails, the official Montrose website had been updated with a new tab on the home page displaying their admission prices.

Local Communities

Back in the day, the majority of football clubs up and down the country depended on local people, who were also fans, to come and work at the ground on a match day. The stewards, turnstile operators, programme sellers, staff in the club shop and food bars, were all part of the local community.

As the game itself has become more commercialised and business like over the last couple of decades, a lot of clubs have lost their community togetherness. The game has become a luxury that a lot of working class families have been priced out of and therefore cannot attend with any regularity, or at all.

Over the course of the season, I found on a few occasions that some stewards had a look of bewilderment and were unhelpful, when being asked the most basic of questions, like where the ticket office was located or where you could buy a programme. On the flipside of this, there were other stewards only too willing to go out their way to assist with any queries.

One explanation for this could be the fact that clubs tend to use external agencies to provide the stewarding at games. As such, some of the staff working on a match day are not locals and therefore have little knowledge or co-ordination about what goes on, in and around any given venue.

Advertising and Marketing

Some clubs have aspects of their match day services well signposted. It is clear where to park, where you can find the social club, match programme, half time draw tickets, where the club shop is located and what area is designated for each set of supporters.

Again, in complete contrast, there are clubs who do not have clear signs on where you can find any of the above. I found myself wandering about a couple of times, pre and post match looking for a programme for example. There were some clubs who had young people selling the match programme, but as they were not wearing the likes of a hi-viz vest, holding one in the air and shouting "programme!" you had to almost second guess if this was what they were selling!

I am not suggesting that the rest of Scottish clubs follow those in the top league, in terms of marketing. However, if you depend on a dedicated hardcore support of between say 300-600 people every home game, they must be encouraged to part with their cash, by enticing them with good, affordable offers. The club shops we visited at Ayr United's Somerset Park and Dens Park, Dundee were doing a roaring trade, as they were doing a well publicised 'Buy 1 get 1 Free' and '50% off' respectively.

Partick Thistle, through Greaves Sports, have been selling the previous two seasons shirts, in all sizes, for £5 each. As they were riding high at the top of the First Division table, there is a likelihood that there will be a lot more yellow and red on display in parts of Glasgow!

Similarly, Berwick Rangers were selling off old shirts for £10 and this would be reduced to £5 at the end of the season. Incentives like this set the foundations for young fans, who will ask to wear their shirt out playing and maybe want to attend games with their parents, breaking the trend of wanting to go and watch a more higher profile club. A good example of this was when we travelled to Elgin, where a lot of the young kids at the game were wearing the club colours.

To emphasise my point further, I bought both my boys the Partick Thistle long sleeved home shirt and my eldest the Berwick Rangers away!

Admission Costs

The issue of admission costs, I feel, is a fundamental one just now in the Scottish game. Towards the end of the season we were fortunate enough to benefit from some clubs reducing their match day prices. Games at Dundee, Hibernian, Forfar Athletic and Aberdeen were all reduced, with the latter two only charging £5 entry for adults.

Some clubs have it spot on with family tickets and discounts. The likes of St Mirren, Motherwell, St Johnstone and newly promoted Partick Thistle lead the way in the new Premiership. In the rest of the Scottish leagues, Morton, Cowdenbeath, East Fife, Stranraer, Annan Athletic and Queens Park offer excellent value and incentives to bring one or more child to their grounds.

Some clubs will argue that they need so much income to break even and this is understandable. I do feel however that, in some cases, clubs have a very short term way of thinking that could potentially back fire on them.

For example you are a club who charge £14 for an adult and £7 for a concession. What happens when that club hits a poor run of form, or worse still, a run of poor form that sees them rooted to the foot of their respective league? The average local fan will not go along with their family, paying between £20-30 a time to watch their team face an inevitable defeat. Maybe if the pricing is right, they may be inclined to tough it out and continue to lend their support to the team and the club.

Regardless of league position and form, I have taken my two boys along to both Cappielow and Firhill over the last few years. I like both venues, they are relatively local, the football is decent and both their admission charges are competitively priced.

With the current financial plight within the U.K in general, the public are more prudent with how they spend their money. Over the last few years I think people have adopted an attitude of, if they cannot afford to go to the football, or feel they are not getting value for money, they won't go. I know friends and family who have felt this way and the attendances in Scotland pretty much reflect this.

All Change In Scottish Football

The game in Scotland has found itself at a particular point of crisis. With no sponsor for the top league, following the end of the Clydesdale Bank contract and, up until recently, four leagues governed by three separate bodies, the Scottish Football Association (SFA), the Scottish Football League (SFL), and the Scottish Premier League (SPL), change is required and fresh investment is drastically needed.

Following constructive talks during the summer, on how to improve the Scottish game during 2013, progress has at last been made on an amalgamation of the three decision makers and also league reconstruction. There is now a replica model of the English leagues, with the formation of a Premiership, Championship,

League One and League Two, replacing the SPL and Divisions One, Two and Three.

A name change is fine, but I sincerely hope that new sponsorship and investment is high up among the list of priorities for the senior figures of the Scottish Professional Football League (SPFL).

I am personally pleased with the re-introduction of the play off system. This represents a massive step in the right direction to improving the game. It will assist in preventing too many meaningless games in all divisions, especially towards the end of the season. It will hopefully add a competitive edge at both ends of the tables, while providing excitement for the fans too.

While the initial league reconstruction talks had started taking place, Dunfermline Athletic went into administration at the end of March. They were then followed by Hearts only weeks after the season had ended. Only twelve months previously, we endured the almost farcical events at Rangers, going from administration in the February of 2012, to liquidation in June. The media had originally peddled the line that the Scottish game of football would face "Armageddon" following the re-launch of the new look Rangers in Division 3, instead of allowing them back into the old SPL or Division One.

To be honest, our game had been in rapid decline long before the problems surfaced at Rangers. While the English Premiership has continued to be funded with a vast amount of cash, which has seen them continue to attract the biggest names in world football, the Scottish game has suffered greatly in comparison. Reduced amounts of income from television, a lack of investment and sponsorship at a lot of clubs, along with dwindling attendances over recent years, have all contributed to the downturn in our game.

I would also suggest that the highly public demise of the national team in the last decade and the failure to qualify for a major tournament since 1998, has also had a negative effect on the game north of the border.

Positive Outlook!

For all the doom and gloom, there remains a staunch pride among fans of all clubs in the country. Whether you play in front of 500 or 50,000, the passion remains the same.

The humour on the terraces, from the heckling of players and officials to impulsive chanting is second to none. For us, some of the best moments this season came at places like East Stirlingshire, Stranraer, Montrose, Berwick and Brechin. I believe it is this spirit and attitude that draws people's interest in Scottish football. There are so many elements that frustrate you, but ultimately you return for more. You watch the highlights on television, or online and you just cannot stay out of a debate in your work place or in the pub!

For me though, there remains an ignorance among some Scottish football fans who are quick to dismiss the lower league clubs. I think if you asked some people who plays at Balmoor, who the Brechin goalkeeper is and the name of Arbroath's ground, you may receive a blank look!

The overall quality of football was of a higher standard than I expected and it was great to have the opportunity to see a lot of young players in action, who could quite evidently play at a higher level. Some of the goals witnessed as well were superb and would suggest you would need to go along to some of these grounds to really appreciate the full experience.

Match Officials

You cannot discuss any aspect of football without passing opinion on the match officials. Having seen games at all levels in Scotland this season, the standard of the officials, like that of the football, can be variable.

With the bigger grounds and crowds in the top league, the officials are relatively sheltered from hearing any of the obscenities aimed in their direction! In the lower leagues, with fewer people and tighter pitches closer to the terraces, this means that, unless they are exceptionally hard of hearing, they will catch just about every word said to them!

The humour in the lower leagues is unparalleled in my opinion and a few games into the season, I heard the first reference to some guy "Lino" a small number of fans spoke of! It was of course in reference to the Referee's Assistant, or Linesman as some people still call them. I think the first ground I heard it at was the Excelsior Stadium, Airdrie, as an animated Morton support vented their spleen at the stand side Assistant! The first time I heard it mentioned, there was that initial pause, when you think to yourself, surely his name is not Lionel?!

A few weeks later, there was another reference to "Lino" at Clyde's Broadwood Stadium. The comments aimed in their direction were rarely complimentary and it was usually because a player was flagged for offside, or play was allowed to continue when there should have been a flag. There are times they cannot win!

The officials are often known for their serious demeanour, but there were a couple of occasions when the Assistants acknowledged or smiled when something was shouted at them, about them being unfit, partially sighted, follically challenged or sometimes all three! Games at Forthbank, Stirling and Stair Park, Stranraer were two such times I can recall.

Something I found of interest was some of the Assistants talking to the players as they contested for a ball in the corner for example. At Somerset Park, Ayr and Station Park, Forfar, I heard advice like 'keep it clean' and 'nothing stupid lads' being given out by the Assistants.

The aspects of officiating that get fans worked up is indecisiveness. For example, the ball goes out of play, the referee is maybe unsure what decision to make and looks to his Assistant for guidance. The Assistant has not raised his flag to indicate what side should be awarded the advantage and both officials appear as flummoxed as each other! They then seem to hazard a guess as to what side should be awarded the advantage, before maybe being persuaded by the reaction of the players or the crowd! Can they not just call it as they see it? It would make their lives so much easier!

Over the course of the season, there were a number of decisions made, for fouls and penalties that clearly only the referee saw, while the mystified crowd fell into a stunned, confused silence! One such award at Arbroath's Gayfield was just laughable. On the other side of the coin, there was some fine, sensible officiating, with play being allowed to flow and good advantage played. A lot of fans acknowledged this and the officials were given recognition for it. Football fans from all over would like to see more examples of consistency when it comes to the officials making decisions!

Planning Fixtures

We were fortunate to see fixtures in all divisions, along with games in the Champions League, League Cup, Scottish Cup, Play Offs and even the Ramsdens Cup. There were no games postponed or abandoned, so I am taking the credit for some sound judgement and decision making! The closest we came to a disaster was going to Berwick after the Brechin game had been called off, only to discover that it was a 2pm kick off due to a speedway meeting!

I had originally included covering Hampden Park in January for one of the League Cup Semi Final matches, however, having agreed to go to all forty two grounds, it was only right that Queens Park should be the feature team of any club playing at Hampden.

Trying to maintain some variety with the teams we watched proved difficult and we sometimes saw the same teams a lot more than we intended! There was a spell when we saw Montrose, Ayr United and Hearts play, it felt like we were becoming part of their regular diehards! Having got talking to an older Montrose fan at Links Park, I then bumped into him again when they were playing up in Elgin!

As we approached the final hurdle, planning the last few fixtures proved to be difficult. A decision had to be made on whether we should go to see Peterhead or Forfar Athletic. It looked as though Peterhead were guaranteed to make the Division 3 Play Offs, so we went along to see Forfar Athletic on the last day of the season instead. The opposition for this game, you guessed it… none other than Ayr United!

Had Peterhead not beaten Queens Park over the two legs, there would have been no visit to Balmoor, leaving us one ground shy of completing all forty two. As it goes, the Blue Toon won both games, setting them up for the Final against East Fife. Due to other commitments it meant I could not stay over night for the penultimate venue, which meant a visit to Aberdeen's Pittodrie Stadium on the Saturday and then back up to Peterhead less than twenty four hours later!

In hindsight, it would have been ideal to space out some of the fixtures, making it slightly less hectic, rather than cramming all the games into a short space of time like we did.

Decisions had to be made in haste on some occasions and due to work and family commitments, it meant that we were on a tight timescale for just about every ground visit. There were a couple of times however when we arrived at our destination well in advance, like at Elgin, Inverness, Dingwall and Brechin.

For me, personally, I am delighted to have visited every ground in Scotland and all within the one season. It was a gruelling schedule, but an enjoyable and worthwhile venture overall. Would I do it again in the future? Yes I would like to. Would I recommend it to others? Most definitely, but I would recommend they save some money up first!

STATS

SCOTTISH FOOTBALL GROUNDS TOUR

GROUND	DATE	FIXTURE	COMP.
1. Central Park	Sat 15 Sep 2012	Cowdenbeath v Morton	Div 1
2. New Broomfield	Sat 29 Sep 2012	Airdrie Utd v Morton	Div 1
3. Falkirk Stadium	Sat 6 Oct 2012	Falkirk v Dunfermline	Div 1
4. Palmerston Park	Sun 14 Oct 2012	Q.of the South v Arbroath	Ram. Cup S/F
5. New Douglas Park	Sat 20 Oct 2012	Hamilton Acc.V Livingston	Div 1
6. Cliftonhill	Sat 3 Nov 2012	Albion Rovers v Morton	Cup 3rd Rd
7. Parkhead	Wed 7 Nov 2012	Celtic v Barcelona	CL Group G
8. Broadwood	Sat 10 Nov 2012	Clyde v Montrose	Div 3
9. The Bet Butler St.	Sat 17 Nov 2012	Dumbarton v Morton	Div 1
10. Ochilview	Sun 25 Nov 2012	East Stirling v Berwick R.	Div 3
11. Almondvale	Sat 8 Dec 2012	Livingston v Dunfermline	Div 1
12. Forthbank	Sat 5 Jan 2013	Stirling Albion v Queens Park	Div 3
13. New Bayview	Sat 12 Jan 2013	East Fife v Brechin City	Div 2
14. Cappielow Park	Sat 26 Jan 2013	Morton v Raith Rovers	Div 1
15. Stair Park	Sat 2 Feb 2013	Stranraer v East Fife	Div 2
16. Recreation Park	Sat 9 Feb 2013	Alloa Ath v Ayr United	Div 2
17. Links Park	Sat 23 Feb 2013	Montrose v Annan Ath	Div 3
18. Gayfield	Sat 2 Mar 2013	Arbroath v Ayr United	Div 2
19. Shielfield	Sat 9 Mar 2013	Berwick R v Montrose	Div 3
20. Tannadice	Sun 17 Mar 2013	Dundee United v Dundee	SPL
21. Ibrox	Sat 23 Mar 2013	Rangers v Stirling Albion	Div 3
22. Firhill	Sat 23 Mar 2013	Partick Thistle v Livingston	Div 1
23. East End Park	Wed 27 Mar 2013	Dunfermline v Falkirk	Div 1
24. Somerset Park	Sat 30 Mar 2013	Ayr United v East Fife	Div 2
25. St. Mirren Park	Sun 31 Mar 2013	St.Mirren v Celtic	SPL
26. McDiarmid Park	Mon 1 Apr 2013	St.Johnstone v Dundee Utd	SPL
27. Starks Park	Tue 2 Apr 2013	Raith Rovers v Partick Th.	Div 1
28. Rugby Park	Wed 3 Apr 2013	Kilmarnock v St.Mirren	SPL
29. Borough Briggs	Sat 13 Apr 2013	Elgin City v Montrose	SPL
30. Ochilview	Tue 16 Apr 2013	Stenhousemuir v Q.of the S.	Div 2
31. Galabank	Sat 20 Apr 2013	Annan Ath v Stirling Albion	Div 3
32. Easter Road	Mon 22 Apr 2013	Hibernian v Aberdeen	SPL
33. Glebe Park	Tue 23 Apr 2013	Brechin City v Stranraer	Div 2
34. Dens Park	Sat 27 Apr 2013	Dundee v Hearts	SPL
35. Fir Park	Sun 28 Apr 2013	Motherwell v Celtic	SPL
36. Station Park	Sat 4 May 2013	Forfar Ath v Ayr United	Div 2
37. Victoria Park	Sun 5 May 2013	Ross County v Celtic	SPL
38. Hampden Park	Wed 8 May 2013	Queens Park v Peterhead	Div.3 Play Off 1st Leg
39. Caledonian Stad.	Sat 11 May 2013	Inverness CT v Dundee Utd	SPL
40. Tynecastle	Sun 12 May 2013	Hearts v Hibernian	SPL
41. Pittodrie	Sat 18 May 2013	Aberdeen v Hearts	SPL
42. Balmoor	Sun 19 May 2013	Peterhead v East Fife	Div 3 Play Off Final 2nd Leg

BEST 10 MATCHES (NOT IN ORDER)

Cowdenbeath 3 v Morton 4
East Fife 2 v Brechin City 2
Dundee United 1 v Dundee 1
Partick Thistle 6 v Livingston 1
Elgin City 3 v Montrose 2
Hearts 1 v Hibernian 2
Celtic 2 v Barcelona 1
Alloa Athletic 2 v Ayr United 2
Stranraer 3 v East Fife 1
Stirling Albion 2 v Queens Park 3

BEST 10 GROUNDS (NOT IN ORDER)

Albion Rovers – Cliftonhill
Cowdenbeath – Central Park
East Fife – Bayview
Stranraer – Stair Park
Arbroath – Gayfield
Berwick Rangers – Shielfield
Dundee United – Tannadice
Dundee – Dens Park
Elgin City – Borough Briggs
Brechin City – Glebe Park

BEST MATCH PROGRAMME (IN ORDER)

*Aberdeen; Dundee United; Motherwell; Kilmarnock; Dundee;
Dunfermline Athletic; Stirling Albion; Albion Rovers; Ross County
Cowdenbeath*

FRIENDLIEST VENUE (IN ORDER)

*Brechin City; Annan Athletic; Dundee United; Dundee; Forfar
Athletic; Arbroath; Dumbarton; Ross County; Elgin City; Queen
of the South*

TOUR STATISTICS

APPROXIMATE DISTANCE TRAVELLED: 5,862 MILES (about the distance from my house to New Delhi.)

TOTAL TICKET COST: £745.

ESTIMATED TOTAL FUEL COST: £850.

Club Directory

Aberdeen

Pittodrie Stadium
Capacity: 22,199 (all seated)
Address: Pittodrie Street, Aberdeen, AB24 5QH
Telephone No: 01224 650 400
Pitch Size: 110 x 72 yards
Club Nickname: The Dons
Year Ground Opened: 1899
Home Kit Colours: Red & White
Official Web Site:
www.afc.co.uk

Airdrieonians

Excelsior Stadium
Capacity: 10,171 (all seated)
Address: Craigneuk Avenue, Airdrie, ML6 8QZ
Telephone No: 07710 230775
Pitch Size: 115 x 75 yards
Year Ground Opened: 1998
Club Nickname: Diamonds
Home Kit Colours: White, Red & Black
Official Web Sites:
www.airdriefc.com

Albion Rovers

Cliftonhill Stadium
Capacity: 2,496 (Seated 489)
Address: Main St, Coatbridge,
Lanarkshire. ML5 3RB
Telephone No: 01236 606 334

Pitch Size: 110 x 72 yards
Year Ground Opened: 1919
Club Nickname: Wee Rovers
Home Kit Colours: Yellow & Red
Official Web Site:
www.albionroversfc.com

Alloa Athletic

Recreation Park
Capacity: 3,100 (919 seated)
Address: Clackmannan Road, Alloa, FK10 1RY
Telephone No: 01259 722 695
Pitch Size: 110 x 75 yards
Year Ground Opened: 1895
Club Nickname: Wasps
Home Kit Colours: Gold & Black
Official Web Site:
www.alloaathletic.co.uk

Annan Athletic

Galabank
Capacity: 2,500 (500 seated)
Address: North Street, Annan,
Dumfries & Galloway DG12 5DQ
Telephone No: 01461 204108
Pitch Size: 110 x 71 yards
Club Nickname: Black and Golds, or Galabankies
Year Ground Opened: 1953
Home Kit Colours:
Black & Gold stripes
Official Web Site: www.annanathleticfc.com

Arbroath

Gayfield Park
Capacity: 4,153 (seated 814)
Address: Arbroath, Angus, DD11 1QB

Telephone No: 01241 872 157
Pitch Size: 115 x 71 yards
Year Ground Opened: 1925
Club Nickname: Red Lichties
Home Kit Colours: Maroon & White
Official Web Site:
www.arbroathfc.co.uk

AYR UNITED

Somerset Park
Capacity: 10,243 (seated 1,549)
Address: Tryfield Place, Ayr, KA8 9NB
Telephone No: 01292 263 435
Pitch Size: 110 x 72 yards
Club Nickname: The Honest Men
Year Ground Opened: 1888
Home Kit Colours: All White
Official Web Site:
www.ayrunitedfc.co.uk

BERWICK RANGERS

Shielfield Park
Capacity: 4,131 (Seated 1,366)
Address: Tweedmouth, Berwick-upon-Tweed,
TD15 2EF
Telephone No: 01289 307 424
Pitch Size: 110 x 70 yards
Club Nickname: The Borderers
Year Ground Opened: 1954
Home Kit Colours: Gold & Black
Official Web Site: www.berwickrangers.net

BRECHIN CITY

Glebe Park
Capacity: 3,960 (Seated 1,519)
Address: Trinity Rd, Brechin, Angus, DD9 6BJ

Telephone No: 01356-622-856
Pitch Size: 110 x 67 yards
Club Nickname: The City
Year Ground Opened: 1919
Home Kit Colours: Red & White
Official Web Site:
www.brechincity.com

CELTIC

Celtic Park
Capacity: 60,832 (all seated)
Address: 18 Kerrydale St, Glasgow, G40 3RE
Telephone No: 0871 226 1888
Pitch Size: 105m x 68m
Club Nickname: The Bhoys
Year Ground Opened: 1892
Home Kit Colours: Green & White Hoops
Official Web Site:
www.celticfc.net

CLYDE

Broadwood Stadium
Capacity: 8,029 (all seated)
Address: Ardgoil Drive Cumbernauld, G68 9NE
Telephone No: 01236 451 511
Pitch Size: 112 x 76 yards
Club Nickname: Bully Wee
Year Ground Opened: 1995
Home Kit Colours: White, Red & Black
Official Web Site:
www.clydefc.co.uk

COWDENBEATH

Central Park
Capacity: 5,268 (Seated 1,622)
Address: Cowdenbeath, Fife, KY4 9QQ

Telephone No: 01383 610 166
Pitch Size: 107 x 66 yards
Club Nickname:
Cowden or Blue Brazil
Year Ground Opened: 1917
Home Kit Colours:
Royal Blue & White
Official Web Site: www.cowdenbeathfc.com

DUMBARTON

The Bet Butler Stadium
Capacity: 2,050 (all seated)
Address: Castle Road, Dumbarton, G82 1JJ
Telephone No: 01389 762 569
Pitch Size: 105m x 68m
Club Nickname: The Sons
Year Ground Opened: 2000
Home Kit Colours: Yellow & Black
Official Web Site: www.dumbartonfootballclub.com

DUNDEE

Dens Park
Capacity: 12,085 (all seated)
Address: Sandeman St, Dundee, DD3 7JY
Telephone No: 01382 889 966
Club Nickname: Dark Blues or The Dees
Pitch Size: 101m x 66m
Year Ground Opened: 1899
Home Kit Colours: Dark Blue, Red & White
Official Web Site:
www.dundeefc.co.uk

DUNDEE UNITED

Tannadice Park
Capacity: 14,209 (all seated)
Address: Tannadice Street, Dundee, DD3 7JW

Telephone No: 01382 833 166
Pitch Size: 110 x 72 yards
Club Nickname:
The Terrors or The Arabs
Year Ground Opened: 1909
Home Kit Colours: Tangerine & Black
Official Web Site: www.dundeeunitedfc.co.uk

DUNFERMLINE

East End Park
Capacity: 12,500 (all seated)
Address: Halbeath Rd, Dunfermline,
Fife. KY12 7RB
Telephone No: 01383 724 295
Pitch Size: 115 x 71 Yards
Club Nickname: The Pars
Year Ground Opened: 1885
Home Kit Colours: White With Black Stripes
Official Web Site:
www.dafc.co.uk

EAST FIFE

Bayview Stadium
Capacity: 2,000 (all seated)
Address: Harbour View, Methil, Fife, KY8 3RW
Telephone No: 01333 426 323
Pitch Size: 115 x 75 yards
Club Nickname: Fifers
Year Ground Opened: 1998
Home Kit Colours: Black & Gold
Official Web Site:
www.eastfife.info

EAST STIRLINGSHIRE

Ochilview Park
(Ground share with Stenhousemuir)
Capacity: 5,267 (2,117 Seated)
Club Contact Address: Gladstone Rd,
Stenhousemuir, FK5 4QL
Telephone No: 01324 629 942
Pitch Size: 110 x 72 yards
Club Nickname: The Shire
Year Ground Opened: 1890
Home Kit Colours:
Black & White Hoops
Official Web Site:
www.eaststirlingshirefc.co.uk

ELGIN CITY

Borough Briggs
Capacity: 3,927 (478 Seated)
Address: Borough Briggs Road, Elgin, IV30 1AP
Telephone No: 01343 551 114
Pitch Size: 110 x 75 yards
Club Nickname: Black & Whites
Year Ground Opened: 1921
Home Kit Colours: Black & White Stripes
Official Web Site:
www.elgincity.com

FALKIRK

Falkirk Stadium
Capacity: 9,200
Address: Westfield, Falkirk, FK2 9DX
Telephone No: 01324 624 121
Pitch Size: 110 x 72 yards
Club Nickname: Bairns
Year Ground Opened: 2004

Home Kit Colours: Navy Blue, White & Red
Official Web Site: www.falkirkfc.co.uk

FORFAR ATHLETIC

Station Park
Capacity: 4,602 (Seated 739)
Address: Carseview Road,
Forfar, Angus, DD8 3BT
Telephone No: 01307 463 576
Pitch Size: 115 x 69 yards
Club Nickname: Loons
Year Ground Opened: 1888
Home Kit Colours: Navy & Sky Blue
Official Web Site:
www.forfarathletic.co.uk

GREENOCK MORTON

Cappielow Park
Capacity: 11,100 (Seated 5,741)
Address: Sinclair Street, Greenock, PA15 2TY
Telephone No: 01475 723 571
Pitch Size: 110 x 71 yards
Club Nickname: Ton
Year Ground Opened: 1879
Home Kit Colours:
Royal Blue & White
Official Web Site:
www.gmfc.net

HAMILTON ACADEMICAL

New Douglas Park
Capacity: 6,000 (all seated)
Address: Cadzow Avenue, Hamilton,
Lanarkshire ML3 0FT
Telephone No: 01698 368 652
Pitch Size: 115 x 75 yards

Club Nickname: The Accies
Year Ground Opened: 2001
Home Kit Colours: Red & White
Official Web Site:
www.acciesfc.co.uk

HEART OF MIDLOTHIAN

Tynecastle Stadium
Capacity: 18,008 (all seated)
Address: Gorgie Road, Edinburgh, EH11 2NL
Telephone No: 0871 663 1874
Pitch Size: 107 x 74 yards
Club Nickname: Hearts or Jam Tarts
Year Ground Opened: 1886
Home Kit Colours: Maroon & White
Official Web Site:
www.heartsfc.co.uk

HIBERNIAN

Easter Road
Capacity: 20,451 (all seated)
Address: 12 Albion Place, Edinburgh, EH7 5QG
Telephone No: 0131 661 2159
Pitch Size: 112 x 74 yards
Club Nickname: The Hibees
Year Ground Opened: 1893
Home Kit Colours: Green & White
Official Web Site:
www.hibs.org.uk

INVERNESS CALEDONIAN THISTLE

Ground Name: Tulloch Caledonian Stadium
Capacity: 7,512 (all seated)
Address: East Longman, Inverness, IV1 1FF
Telephone No: 01463 222 880
Pitch Size: 115 x 75 yards

Club Nickname: Caley Thistle
Year Ground Opened: 1996
Home Kit Colours: Royal Blue & Red
Official Web Site: www.ictfc.co.uk

KILMARNOCK

Rugby Park
Capacity: 18,128 (all seated)
Address: Rugby Park, Kilmarnock, KA1 2DP
Telephone No: 01563 545 300
Pitch Size: 115 x 74 yards
Club Nickname: Killie
Year Ground Opened: 1899
Home Kit Colours: Blue, White & Red
Official Web Site:
www.kilmarnockfc.co.uk

LIVINGSTON

The Energy Assets Arena
(commonly known as Almondvale Stadium)
Capacity: 10,000 (all seated)
Address: Livingston, West Lothian, EH54 7DN
Telephone No: 01506 417 000
Fax No: 01506 418 888
Pitch Size: 110 x 76 yards
Club Nickname: Livi Lions
Year Ground Opened: 1995
Undersoil Heating: Yes
Home Kit Colours: Amber & Black
Official Web Site:
www.livingstonfc.co.uk

MONTROSE

Links Park
Ground Name: Links Park
Capacity: 3,292 (1,338 seated)
Address: Wellington St, Montrose, DD10 8QD
Telephone No: 01674 673 200
Pitch Size: 113 x 70 yards
Club Nickname: The Gable Endies
Year Ground Opened: 1887
Home Kit Colours:
Royal Blue & White
Official Web Site:
www.montrosefc.co.uk

MOTHERWELL

Fir Park
Capacity: 13,742 (all seated)
Address: Fir Park, Motherwell, ML1 2QN
Telephone No: 01698 333 333
Pitch Size: 110 x 75 yards
Club Nickname: The Well or The Steelmen
Year Ground Opened: 1895
Home Kit Colours: Amber & Claret
Official Web Site:
www.motherwellfc.co.uk

PARTICK THISTLE

Firhill Stadium
Capacity: 13,079 (10,887 seated)
Address: 80 Firhill Road, Glasgow, G20 7AL
Telephone No: 0141 579 1971
Pitch Size: 114 x 75 yards
Club Nickname: The Jags
Year Ground Opened: 1909
Home Kit Colours: Red, Yellow & Black

Official Web Site:
www.ptfc.co.uk

PETERHEAD

Balmoor Stadium
Capacity: 4,000 (seated 998)
Address: Lord Catto Park, Peterhead, AB42 1EU
Telephone No: 01779 478 256
Pitch Size: 105 x 70 yards
Year Ground Opened: 1997
Club Nickname: The Blue Toon
Home Kit Colours: Blue & White
Official Web Site:
www.peterheadfc.co.uk

QUEEN OF THE SOUTH

Palmerston Park
Capacity: 6,412 (3,509 seated)
Address: Dumfries, DG2 9BA
Telephone No: 01387 254 853
Pitch Size: 112 x 73 yards
Club Nickname: Doonhamers
Year Ground Opened: 1919
Home Kit Colours: Royal Blue & White
Official Web Site:
www.qosfc.com

QUEENS PARK

Hampden Park
Capacity: 52,500 (all seated)
Address: Mount Florida, Glasgow, G42 9BA
Telephone No: 0141 632 1275
Pitch Size: 115 x 75 yards
Club Nickname: Spiders
Year Ground Opened: 1903
Home Kit Colours: Black & White

Official Web Site:
www.queensparkfc.co.uk

RAITH ROVERS

Starks Park
Capacity: 10,104 (all seated)
Address: Pratt Street, Kirkcaldy, KY1 1SA
Telephone No: 01592 263 514
Pitch Size: 113 x 70 yards
Club Nickname: Rovers
Year Ground Opened: 1891
Home Kit Colours:
Navy Blue, White & Red
Official Web Site: www.raithrovers.net

RANGERS

Ibrox Stadium
Capacity: 50,411 (all seated)
Address: 150 Edmiston Drive,
Glasgow, G51 2XD
Telephone No: 0871 702 1972
Pitch Size: 115 x 78 yards
Club Nickname: The Gers or Teddy Bears
Year Ground Opened: 1899
Home Kit Colours: Blue, Red & White
Official Web Site:
www.rangers.co.uk

ROSS COUNTY

Global Energy Stadium
(commonly known as Victoria Park)
Capacity: 6,300 (All seated)
Address: Jubilee Road, Dingwall, IV15 9QZ
Telephone No: 01349 860 860
Pitch Size: 100 x 75 yards
Club Nickname: Staggies & The County

Year Ground Opened: 1929
Home Kit Colours: Navy Blue & White
Official Web Site:
www.rosscountyfootballclub.co.uk

St Johnstone

McDiarmid Park
Capacity: 10,673 (all seated)
Address: Crieff Road, Perth, PH1 2SJ
Telephone No: 01738 459 090
Pitch Size: 115 x 75 yards
Club Nickname: The Saints
Year Ground Opened: 1989
Home Kit Colours: Blue & White
Official Web Site: www.perthstjohnstonefc.co.uk

St Mirren

St Mirren Park
Capacity: 8,006 (all seated)
Address: Greenhill Road, Paisley,
Renfrewshire, PA3 1RU
Telephone No: 0141 889 2558
Pitch Size: 110 x 70 yards
Club Nickname: The Buddies
Year Ground Opened: 2009
Home Kit Colours: Black & White
Official Web Site: www.saintmirren.net

Stenhousemuir

Ochilview Park
Capacity: 5,267 (2,117 Seated)
Address: Gladstone Rd,
Stenhousemuir, FK5 4QL
Telephone No: 01324 562 992
Pitch Size: 110 x 72 yards
Year Ground Opened: 1890

Club Nickname: Warriors
Home Kit Colours: Maroon & White
Official Web Site:
www.stenhousemuirfc.com

STIRLING ALBION

Forthbank Stadium
Capacity: 3,808 (Seated 2,508)
Address: Springkerse, Stirling, FK7 7UJ
Telephone No: 01786 450 399
Pitch Size: 110 x 74 yards
Club Nickname: Albion or Binos/Beanos
Year Ground Opened: 1993
Home Kit Colours: Red & White
Official Web Site:
www.stirlingalbionfc.co.uk

STRANRAER

Stair Park
Capacity: 5,600 (1,830 Seated)
Address: London Road, Stranraer, DG9 8BS
Telephone No: 01776 889 514
Pitch Size: 110 x 70 yards
Club Nickname: The Blues
Year Ground Opened: 1907
Home Kit Colours: Royal Blue & White
Official Web Site:
www.stranraerfc.org

TEENAGE KICKS

THE STORY OF MANCHESTER CITY'S
1986 FA YOUTH CUP TEAM

BY PHILL GATENBY & ANDREW WALDON

THERE WASN'T MUCH TO CHEER about for Manchester City fans during the mid-1980s. With the club's coffers empty following a disastrous series of signings at the start of the decade, City seemed in decline as attendances dwindled and interest waned.

The only relief from the gloom came in the form of a talented crop of youngsters that arrived at the club from 1983 onwards. Fourteen teenagers who would go on to acomplish something supporters had waited 33 years to achieve.

Producing one's own players has always been an emblem of pride for football supporters. Established in 1953, the FA Youth Cup has always been the litmus test of a club's youth policy. Until 1986 Manchester City had reached the final twice but actually winning the trophy had proved to be a step too far.

Teenage Kicks is the story of how 'The Class of 1986' won the prestigious trophy for the first time in the club's history and using both exclusive and archive interviews, it describes how the team came together and details what became of each of the fourteen teenagers from that point onwards.

ORDER DIRECT FROM THE PUBLISHER FOR JUST £8

CALL 0161 872 3319